ANCHORED & REACHING

The Visionary Life & Ministry of
KEVIN MANNOIA

BARRY L. CALLEN
Foreword by **GEORGE BARNA**

ALDERSGATE
PRESS

ANCHORED & REACHING

THE VISIONARY LIFE & MINISTRY OF

KEVIN MANNOIA

By Barry L. Callen

PUBLISHED BY:
ALDERSGATE **PRESS**

The publications arm of
WESLEYAN
HOLINESS
CONNECTION

HOLINESSANDUNITY.ORG

Publication Design & Management: LAMP POST *publishers*
lamppostpublishers.com

Printed in the United States of America

Soft Cover ISBN 13: 978-1-60039-314-3
ebook ISBN-13: 978-1-60039-986-2

Dedication

These pages are dedicated to the parade of visionary saints of God who have cherished the past and positioned themselves and others to face forward with God on behalf of a better future. To them, now including Kevin W. Mannoia, yesterday was foundational. Tomorrow is today's mission and challenge. God is the maker of all things new, and God's servants must be alert and inventive, conscious instruments of the God of *ongoing* creation.

This biographical work is dedicated to the new patterns, blurred lines, integrated thinking, and dynamic nature of the church that Kevin Mannoia has embraced and enhanced so well. He chafes at anything that limits the church's effectiveness in the contemporary world. Kevin's lifetime of embracing the dynamic of God's contemporary Spirit is what's recounted and celebrated in these pages.

Dr. Barry L. Callen

Personal Tributes

Kevin Mannoia has ventured into the murky environs of the "messy middle," eschewing the safety of the known or expected in favor of mining ambiguity or uncertainty in the quest for clarity, breakthroughs, and improvements. That has produced brilliant victories—and bruising defeats. Such is the life of a true leader. So, settle in and prepare to read about one of the most accomplished spiritual leaders in America.

George Barna, research specialist, intersection of Christian faith and American culture

---

A storied ministry is skillfully highlighted here. Kevin Mannoia is a visionary leader with a heart for relationships that better reflect unity in the body of Christ. When he was President and I Board Chair of the National Association of Evangelicals, I watched with pride his multiple efforts for the churches to truly fulfill Christian mandates. He coupled the historical past with a passion for present and future generations. Here's a gifted servant leader with integrity, an authentic representative of Jesus Christ in our time.

Rev. Dr. Edward L. Foggs, General Secretary Emeritus, Church of God Ministries

---

I have known Kevin Mannoia from the time he was the gifted child next door. Years later, as professionals in Christian higher education, Kevin and I found common passion for the integration of faith and learning at the core of our Wesleyan heritage. Now, in our retirement years, the vision has come into its sharpest focus. I prize Kevin as an esteemed colleague, a beloved brother in the faith, and a major contributor to the health and unity of contemporary Christianity worldwide. Readers of this carefully researched and warmly written biography will be inspired by Kevin's life and ministry.

Dr. David L. McKenna, President Emeritus of
Spring Arbor University, Seattle Pacific University,
and Asbury Theological Seminary

Honored here is a remarkable Christian leader dedicated to church ministry, ecumenical leadership, and denominational cooperation. Accomplished especially among Wesleyan, Holiness, and Pentecostal churches and institutions of higher education worldwide, his ministry has been through powerful sermons, inspiring pastoral care, remarkable books, a passion for inclusiveness and church unity, and tireless Christian networking, particularly through the National Association of Evangelicals and the Wesleyan Holiness Connection. He's a living testament to the transformative power of Christian love.

Dr. Don Thorsen, Professor of Theology,
Azusa Pacific University

Dr. Callen skillfully weaves the threads of Kevin Mannoia's life, creating a tapestry of Kingdom impact on individuals, organizations, and the world. The manuscript chronicles his story and serves as a compelling testament to the transformative power of a life lived with passion and purpose for Christ. Kevin's journey has been a source of inspiration and guidance shaping my own life. This endorsement is a heartfelt acknowledgment of that profound influence.

Dr. Deana L. Porterfield, President,
Seattle Pacific University

Contents

Acknowledgments

The people of God are amazing in their individualities. My first biography, *She Came Preaching*, was written more than thirty years ago. A woman in the pulpit? If God calls, dare we interfere because of gender prejudice? My more recent biography, *John S. Pistole*, makes obvious that the divine call includes roles far beyond the local church. Another of my biographies was the dramatic life story of Canadian theologian Clark H. Pinnock. The Introduction to follow below reveals Clark's link to this present work.

Researching and writing a biography is a community enterprise. The biographer may be at the wheel, but without a quality crew the task goes nowhere. Since Kevin W. Mannoia is a gregarious person, an active encourager of the promising young, there was no limit to the availability of knowledgeable persons anxious to assist with this project. What a blessing!

The complex process behind this work began with the initiative of Bishop John Mark Richardson, current Executive Director of the Wesleyan Holiness Connection. Since Kevin was a mentor and great friend, John was anxious to have this life story told. He also announced that the teller of the story should be someone "with the stature who could command the respect of the Pan-Wesleyan family." I am humbled that he thought of me in such elevated terms.

This biography has been enriched by the assistance of Cathy Robling who directs the Free Methodist archives in Indianapolis, Indiana, and Grace Yoder, longtime archivist at Asbury Theological Seminary in Wilmore, Kentucky. The artistic and layout skills of Brett Burner are obvious. Dozens of individuals have invested time in Zoom interviews, including all members of Kevin's immediate family and Kevin himself on numerous occasions. There have been countless emails, phone calls, and document reviews. Kevin opened to me his extensive personal and unedited journal. I am humbled by such trust.

Kevin responded frankly to all kinds of probing questions, showing no defensiveness, although some insecurity at the potentially risky process of opening his life wide to the world. He said to me, "What's out there that I don't know about? If it's there, you'll likely find it. I rest in the identity of being anchored in Christ, a servant of God doing all I can for Kingdom purposes."

When statements by Kevin appear in this biography and are quoted without a source citation, they come either from one of my many recorded video interviews or from the pages of his personal journal. When published works are the sources, they are noted in footnotes, with the publishing detail available in the final pages.

Kevin himself is responsible for nothing written here. I shared a draft with him, but not for him to control the manuscript in any way. The purposes were alerting me to any bad information I may have had or to suggest any critical information new to me that might allow a fuller and fairer perspective for the reader. I am in debt to Kevin for the considerable time invested. I also am grateful for the assistance of his wife, brother, sister, children, and many colleagues.

To know Kevin well is to know his Lord just a little more. That's been a gift to me and now to all readers. Kevin and I join in gratitude to George Barna who graciously took valuable time to prepare the Foreword for this book. If now there is good in these pages, all glory belongs to God who gives life, calls to service, and enables whatever success there has been or yet will be.

Foreword

Being a close friend and ministry colleague of Kevin Mannoia for over two decades, I was truly honored when Dr. Barry Callen invited me to write this Foreword for this biography. Kevin is an effective leader in both the Christian church and American culture. Being handed a chance to toot his horn is a blessing. Too often, we take such leaders for granted, and we do so to our own detriment.

Based on my many years of relationship with Kevin, I hope you will exploit the opportunity to learn more about one of God's stealth weapons in this age of self-proclamation and attention-seizing. Most Christians today are unaware of Kingdom jewels like Kevin. Following his life trail and the attendant adventures with God provides a deeper understanding of how God works.

Like most of the strong leaders about whom biographies are written, Kevin is a man of great vision, deep and sincere passion for that vision, and an unflagging commitment to converting that mental portrait of a preferable future into a transformative reality. He has labored more than four decades to move that vision forward. Unlike most of the strong leaders in our nation and even in the church, the vision that compels Kevin is a gift received directly from God. This is vitally important in explaining his influence.

Kevin is not driven by a self-constructed ideal designed to provide him with pleasure, power, authority, fame, or riches. Quite the contrary. His pursuit of God's vision has produced pain, hardship, frustration, confusion, and material loss. But that's part of the process of being surrendered to God. Leading for him does not come with a guarantee of comfort and security. It comes with challenges and complexities we cannot foresee and often do not expect.

That, I suspect, is part of God's leadership test. Will the leader abandon the quest to serve God in favor of an easier, more rewarding leadership path? Only those who are devoted to following God's Spirit through thick and thin will experience the joy of nurturing the vision toward fruition. Kevin is one of the few so devoted.

Hanging out with Kevin has always been a treat for me. He is a unique leader, exhibiting contrasts I have rarely experienced in the hundreds of leaders with whom I have worked over the years. He is a rare combination of head and heart, a brilliant, deep thinker who consistently demonstrates the tender love of Christ toward those whom he influences. Unlike the many faith leaders who talk a good game and wait for their followers to perform prescribed acts of service, Kevin proves his faith by his works, a wonderful demonstration of the James 1 principle.

Further, Kevin is well-schooled in and truly an aficionado of church tradition, yet he has worked hard to blend the past and future in ways that do not compromise God's truths while making them fresh, accessible, and valuable to all.

In the course of my worldview research, I coined the term "integrated disciple" to describe people whose lives are animated by their faith in and relationship with Christ, tangibly exhibited by driving and infusing every dimension of their lives with those faith perspectives. Kevin is a stellar example of an integrated disciple. His decisions are preceded by prayer. His choices are informed and shaped by biblical principles. His self-assessments are based on his determination to obey God's will and affirm biblical teachings. He doesn't just know what the Bible teaches; *he lives it*. In fact, his life, as you will discover in this book, is a consistent study in living the Christ-like life.

Don't get me wrong; he's not perfect. Kevin sins like all of us, but his imperfections really bother him. I've listened to him agonize over some of his choices that may not have turned out to glorify God. (An obvious proof of his imperfection is his relative disinterest in baseball, but I digress . . .)

He often has ventured into the murky environs of what he calls the "messy middle," eschewing the safety of the known or expected in favor of mining ambiguity or uncertainty in the quest for clarity, breakthroughs, and improvements. That has sometimes produced brilliant victories—and bruising defeats. But such is the life of a true leader. Controversy and stalled progress are what make the journey interesting, and heighten the rewards when success is secured.

My appreciation for the invitation to compose this Foreword is not simply because I am proud to call Kevin a friend and colleague. It also is because of my debt for all he has taught me personally. Having grown up in a Catholic family, attended a Jesuit college, and been married within the Catholic Church, then naively winding my way through various Protestant churches in hot pursuit of Jesus and an authentic Christian life, Kevin entered my life at a very opportune moment in my spiritual journey.

For instance, I was wrestling with the distinctions between the Reformed and Wesleyan views of Christianity. Discovering that such a schism in viewpoints exists was both perplexing and troubling to me. After reading various volumes regarding these different interpretations of Scripture, I remained baffled.

Who would be better to explain the differences than Dr. Mannoia, the articulate and balanced expositor of holiness doctrines? Over the years we have spent hours discussing what holiness looks like in contemporary America, and why it matters. His patience with me has been exceeded only by his knowledge of the subject and his creative and practical explanations of the holy life.

As you read Dr. Callen's well-researched profile of Kevin, you will marvel at the breadth of professional and ministry challenges that the restless and indefatigable mind of Kevin Mannoia has accepted. He has championed critical themes, such as fostering unity amid diversity and experiencing and expressing God's grace. He has advanced these themes in his numerous leadership roles: pastor, church planter, missionary, chaplain, denominational bishop, professor, academic dean, president of a high-profile Christian socio-political ministry, radio host, author, conference speaker, ministry catalyst, and consummate networker. Add to that his no-less-important duties as a father and grandfather that he takes so seriously and you can imagine the wealth of stories required to narrate his life.

In those varied roles Kevin has artfully applied his wealth of gifts and skills. They include collaborator, communicator, creator, grace-giver, networker, prayer warrior, problem-solver, servant-leader, visionary, and more. The applications have been in ways that have crafted a unique and fascinating life, and have positively impacted the world and advanced God's kingdom on earth.

I don't know about you, but that's the kind of mark I'd like to leave on this planet, not for my legacy but for God's glory. Kevin has somehow figured out how to do that. And that's what this book describes. So, settle in and prepare to read about one of the most accomplished spiritual leaders in America. If you ever have the chance to interact personally with Kevin, take advantage of the opportunity. You will be blessed by this man of God in ways you never expected. He is one of God's great servants and the church's treasured resources.

George Barna
Ventura, California

Introduction

Where does one begin when trying to tell the whole life story of a prominent religious leader who also is a complex human being and a Christian still in process? This challenge is compounded even more when the person has been engaged creatively within numerous cultures of today's diverse world. Some thoughts from one of my previous biographical works are helpful.

Journey Toward Renewal is my biography of prominent evangelical theologian Clark H. Pinnock. It's a life story of yesterday that attracted my renewed attention as I approached this present biographical task. Clark was a Christian pilgrim during the final decades of the twentieth century. He courageously blazed some new trails, some of which now are being followed rather closely by many, including Kevin W. Mannoia.

Being Divinely Bipolar

Clark Pinnock once said, "I see the task of evangelical theology being to assist the church in its renewal through faithfulness to God's Word on behalf of a timely witness to today's world." He searched for "a wiser and more generous Christian orthodoxy." He said the Christian theological enterprise is "bipolar," that is, simultaneously reaffirming the foundational truths of classic Christianity while restating these truths in fresh ways sensitive to contemporary language and culture.[1]

---

1   See Barry L. Callen, *Journey Toward Renewal, the Intellectual Biography of Clark H. Pinnock*, pp. 5-7, 9-10, 270, 272.

Such dual tasks, if both pursued together with creative courage, can join to become a prophetic voice and catalyst for relevance and renewal in the Christian community of any time. They also will attract negative attention and resistance because they tend to challenge the church's status quo. Kevin Mannoia has been bipolar in Pinnock's sense, foundational yet relevant, sometimes creatively and painfully.

What's necessary for success of the Christian mission? In large part it's finding the right balance of *text* and *context*, yesterday's Bible and today's culture, the timeless and contemporary, the ancient foundations and the fresh frontiers. Continuity with yesterday keeps one properly anchored; communication with today requires one to keep thinking, translating, journeying, experimenting with new mediums and applications.

Rare indeed is the person who can honor both the Christian text, with its eternal truths, and the current context, with its differing styles, languages, and sensitivities. One of Kevin's favorite slogans is "Anchored *and* Reaching." He is one of the rare ones.

Such a bipolar person will dare to initiate, risk, experiment, dialogue, refuse to abandon yesterday or ignore today. She or he will be open to the new and willing to take criticism from some beloved brothers and sisters in the faith too anchored in the old. Why criticism? Because those too comfortable with the status quo are trapped in tradition and suspicious of almost anything new and unfamiliar. They quickly grow defensive in the face of unwelcome diversity.

Kevin W. Mannoia's life passion can be captured by this thought. There must be no defensiveness in the face of today's growing diversity. In fact, embracing diversity is the first step toward achieving the Christian unity so essential to engaging in faithful contemporary witness to the Kingdom of God on earth. Believers must "let go and jump. The faith leap is a wonderful moment in the life of God's people!"[2]

---

2   Kevin Mannoia, *Church 2K: Leading Forward*, ix-x.

These pages tell the story of how Kevin has sought to live with integrity the true Christian life in multiple contemporary contexts. By nature, he has been a bridge person, by heritage and instinct a world citizen, by activity a constant catalyst open to dialoguing patiently with diversity. He has walked through today's troubled world in hope and with vision.

Admittedly something of an aggressive idealist, Kevin has offered no apology for experimenting and venturing on behalf of his beloved Lord. He has welcomed frontiers and dared to cross them as the Spirit of Jesus has directed. He's been what his friend Larry Walkemeyer calls an "irenic force" sometimes standing in "the messy middle."

Kevin has been much like the famous holiness missionary E. Stanley Jones, called by *Time* magazine in 1938 "the world's greatest missionary evangelist." Why this generous assessment of Jones? While in India he experienced a major reorientation of his Christian theological stance. The change freed him for his unusually productive ministry to follow. At first the Christian theology of Jones had been defensive and judgmental of Indian religious extremes.

Soon, however, Jones placed the securities of his faith on the altar and was freed to explore and appropriate any good or truth found anywhere. This fresh freedom stance allowed him to *love* rather than *pity* India. He now could treat all people encountered with justice and mercy, their religious deviance from Christian beliefs notwithstanding. This was a "messy middle" that released him to be an "irenic force" in the world of Christian evangelism.

A woman once said about Jones: "Apart from the Holy Spirit, Brother Stanley would be a mess." Jones humbly reports his response: "But with the Holy Spirit I am not a mess but *a message*."[3] What a difference! Jones became a living "Yes!" to the world because God

---

3   E. Stanley Jones, *Song of Ascents* (Abingdon Press, 1968).

had first said a redeeming "Yes!" to him. Christian holiness had become a manner of being and speaking, a way of life rather than so many biblical prooftexts or clever spiritual cliches and demands. It was love's acted-out substance, God's provision and intention for all his children.

Here's a quick sample of Kevin Mannoia's own "Yes!" language, often acted on and well spoken in our present time:

> I am committed to surrendering to the nudges of the Holy Spirit in guiding me to live more fully in my call as a child of God, a servant of God, and a leader. It is exhilarating to partner with God, watching as Kingdom values continually manifest in relevant and impactful ways all over the world, bringing unity and wholeness to Kingdom people. Growing clarity allows me to give myself with greater passion and focus to lifting and empowering others in becoming all God has called them to be.[4]

Kevin has quite a bold style and yet quite a humble heart. He maintains a clear theological orthodoxy while insisting on exhibiting it in a truly generous and open manner. His orthodoxy features more love than pity and as much listening and modeling as preaching. He has waited for the anointing of the Spirit as Jesus instructed all disciples to do. The Spirit has directed him into all the world with good news that leads with love and not immediate judgment of others.

Kevin has done this for decades, reflecting the broad perspective of what Pinnock called the evangelical "Big Tent." It's the whole community of sincere Christians, a community enriched particularly for Kevin by the Wesleyan-Holiness tradition of the faith. He says:

---

4   Appears at the end of Kevin Mannoia's professional Vita.

Picture in your mind's eye a vast expanse of desert. Then notice a river, a grand river that runs through it. This is the holy river of God's restorative mission in the world, principally represented by the work of the church. Amidst the dryness and human struggle for meaning, value, and wholeness, this river runs in stark contrast. Just like every river, this one is always moving; it is always changing; it is always life-giving.[5]

Kevin is a river man. He's a life-giving agent of the restorative God. He recognizes the many streams that flow into the one river of God and he loves them all.

A Literary Diversion

Allow a literary diversion that hopefully serves as an insightful parallel. *Don Quixote* by Miguel de Cervantes is a classic novel about a middle-aged landowner from a village in La Mancha who stays awake at night. Doing what? Reading books about chivalry, concentrating so hard that he rarely eats or sleeps, finally insanely believing that the tales he reads are true. He sets off on a skinny nag in a heroic quest to resurrect old-fashioned chivalry and heroism in the modern world. A picture of Kevin's journey? To a degree. All parallels falter a bit.

By contrast, so far as I know, Kevin has slept quite well over the years and cared reasonably well for his health. He loves cars and doesn't own a skinny nag. He certainly has read many books, especially the Bible where he finds none other than God alive and moving in this world for the purpose of redeeming it in love. Fantasy? Imagination? Groundless even if noble faith? We'll try to let the facts speak for themselves.

---

5   Kevin W. Mannoia, in Barry L. Callen, ed., *The Holy River of God* (Aldersgate Press, 2016).

Kevin has set out on a heroic quest on many airplanes, his modern nag, wandering the world representing the Jesus he gratefully serves. He's been determined to stimulate a recovery of old-fashioned Christian holiness and activate its special relevance for contemporary life and cultures. His many adventures along the way tell quite a tale of excitement and frustration. He's a heroic character in the modern world, tolerated by some and applauded by many others.

Learning about the life journey of Kevin is to encounter a man guided by a divine vision and love that pulsates in his very being. They shine with a "Yes!" to God's presence. They are driven by a determination to bring God's Kingdom very near. Coming to know this man will be worth the effort because it can enrich your own search for life's meaning and even destiny in our time. It may even cause you to join Kevin's quest as a valiant Christian knight seeking to know God and make God known in many foreign territories.

Unlike Don Quixote who wearied of the frustrations faced on the road and one day announced that he had regained his sanity and now scorned his knighthood, no such give-up day has yet come for Kevin, and likely never will. He still rides on in hope and joy. Come, follow his trails and maybe even join his journey. It's lighted by God's Spirit and showing the way to a better world. Kevin's story begins long ago and far away with the Mannoia family struggling in Sicily.

ANCHORED & REACHING

The Visionary Life & Ministry of
KEVIN MANNOIA

CHAPTER ONE

THE STRANGE "M" FACTOR

The story of Kevin Mannoia has distant beginnings that soon would have impact in the "new world." Maria was Kevin's beloved grandmother. She set a fast pace of courage and even confrontation on behalf of Christ in very challenging circumstances. A series of "Ms" emerged to mark this family legacy. They include Maria, Misilmeri, Mannoia, Melrose, Mafia, Murder, Methodism, Mission, Migration . . . and More. It's a stunning story well told in a little book published in Maria's honor and cherished in her family to this day.[6]

Maria Mannoia was fortunate indeed. She was a little girl living in a stone house in Sicily that clung to the side of a hill not far from the Mediterranean Sea. One way was the vast expanse of sparkling water or the other the lovely hills that surrounded her little village of Misilmeri. Maria couldn't help but be filled with pride when gazing at the vineyards of olives and grapes tended so carefully by her extended family. They were proud and successful people by local standards. Surely there was no more beautiful place on God's earth, the general poverty notwithstanding.

Fortunate indeed was Maria despite the many challenges of life always on the edge. Twelve children blessed this family, but not without considerable suffering. Six had died in infancy. She, however, was a survivor and her dear Papa took her each week for two years to the nearby city of Palermo. They went by burro

---

6   Arleta Richardson, *Maria* (1998).

and cart for her to attend a private school. There she was trained as a professional seamstress and became really good at this highly desired skill.

Meanwhile, she matured as a devout Roman Catholic. Everyone she knew was Catholic. One way to show her deep dedication to God's one holy church was to become something of an irate athlete for Christ. She stepped forward as a leader in protesting against the local Salvation Army. On Saturday nights these strange non-Catholic Christian people would gather in the village square, play their odd songs, and push on to anyone foolish enough to listen some off-beat Protestant brand of heretical Christianity. Maria would throw rocks and tomatoes at these misguided religious people, little knowing that years later in a far-off land she would be the oddity and target of others.

Maria Mannoia

Maria Mannoia couldn't yet imagine that as a young adult she would take two of her own children and sail away from her beautiful home forever, part of a mass migration in the early years of the twentieth century. Hard indeed would be the day when her son Jimmy would leave her new home in the United States to be a Protestant missionary in Brazil—a Protestant! Beyond imagination was the future fact that Jimmy's son Kevin one day would be the President of the National Association of Evangelicals, Protestants by the tens of thousands, including the Salvation Army. How could such things ever be? God has mysterious ways and Maria did believe deeply in God.

Murder and Migration

Suddenly spoiling the lovely local scenery around Misilmeri was a harsh and very unwanted fact. The area Mafia had become powerful even in Maria's little town. They began demanding protection money from landowners. One day Maria's Uncle Niccolo was instructed to bring ruin on one of his non-cooperating neighbors, cutting his plants and thus his livelihood. He refused but was told that refusal was not an option. One evening soon after, as Niccolo stood in his own doorway, Mafioso men came by and shot him to death!

That's where the strange elements of the "M" factor come in. It's a volatile mix indeed. Murder by the Mafia in Misilmeri brought eventual migration to Maria and other of the Mannoias.

Somewhere in this "M" mixture, Maria was sure, lay the Mystery of divine providence. One day her grandson Kevin would experience the grace of such providence and bask in the joys of its enablement. He would dare to mimic the courage and faithfulness of his beloved Grandmother Maria.

In the first fifteen years of the twentieth century, more than one million Sicilians emigrated, most choosing the United States as their preferred destination. It would be the Chicago area for the Mannoias, location of a "Little Italy." These newcomers would bring music and movies, and unfortunately the Mafia. Director Frank Capra is best known for his nostalgic and optimistic movies such as *You Can't Take It With You*, *Mr. Smith Goes to Washington*, and *It's A Wonderful Life*. Al Pacino would win much acclaim for his portrayal of the stereotypical Mafia role in *The Godfather*. Frank

Sinatra recorded some 800 songs, like "I've Got the World on a String" and "Witchcraft." Among the arriving Italian crowd was Lucky Luciano, considered the father of the American Mafia.

After Niccolo's murder, Vincenzo had been the first of the Mannoia family to flee Sicily for the United States. Maria feared she would never see him again. But he did return as promised and after a courtship of six months he and Maria married. Soon they had five children born to them in Sicily, although only Rosalina and Dominic would live to come to America 1913. Vincenzo would go first to find the family somewhere to live when they followed. It would be in the Chicago area.

Many years later, grandson Kevin Mannoia would respond to a kindness of his sister Sharla. While he was suffering through a difficult assignment in the awful poverty of Haiti, he wrote this in his personal journal: "Sharla sent pictures of Ellis Island and the station where Grandpa Mannoia entered the U. S. She saw his name on the passenger list. I found myself looking at those pictures with deep gratitude. Thank you, Grandpa! I thank you for your faith-venturing, courageous sacrifice for me!"

Maria, age thirty-one, finally was able to follow her husband from Sicily with their two surviving children. After eighteen days on a ship, they landed in Massachusetts and had to take a long train ride to Chicago. They were hardly destined to bring with them more of what the famous Italians would bring to the American world of popular entertainment, but significant nonetheless they would be!

Immigrants naturally formed "ghettos" of people with like language and culture. Little Italy in Chicago was typical, and this was the community into which the Mannoia family moved. Being staunchly Roman Catholic, Italian immigrants typically faced intense negative feelings if any were ever to convert to a Protestant church. Maria was a zealous Roman Catholic, but not for long. Once settled in the Chicago, Illinois, area, many things really changed for her. At first she couldn't have imagined what all would happen.

The Lord is My Shepherd!

Additional children soon arrived in the Mannoia home and one small baby died of a fever. They moved to Melrose Park, a small village some miles northwest of Chicago's sprawling city center where there was a dominant Italian presence. It was there in Melrose Park that a Seventh-Day Adventist couple visited their home and gave Maria her own Bible to read, an unusual possession for an Italian lay Catholic of the time. There would be no long relationship for Maria and that church body. Still, she read that Bible intently and soon tried to find some "evangelical" church in Melrose Park. She had come to long for a community of believers that taught and lived the Bible's teachings that she was discovering and valuing.

There was a small Presbyterian mission nearby. The minister was Italian and a positive relationship developed during 1920. The longer Maria attended this little mission the more she learned about God and the Bible and the less she was satisfied with her own Catholic heritage. When this news got to the Mannoia landlord, they were forced out of their rented house. Leaving God's one holy church was an intolerable act in this community. Son Jimmy, born in 1922, recalls that Maria "became our priestess. Father was a tender man despite his bursts of anger. He came to the faith more slowly."

There soon came a heated exchange between Maria and the two local priests of the Roman Catholic Church. Thrown at her was this. "Are you prepared to defy the shepherd priests whom God has set before you?" Her response was straightforward and courageous indeed. "According to the Bible, *the Lord is my Shepherd*." Now supposedly being separated from God's one church, Maria continued to visit neighbors throughout the community, spreading the good news of her love for her dear Shepherd, Jesus himself.

Such public exposure of this deviant behavior may have been the reason Maria's husband soon was targeted. The Mafia killing of a Mannoia family member back in Sicily years before had brought this family to the United States. Now some well-dressed young Mafia gentlemen began to visit Vincenzo and put on some extortion pressure. He tried to explain to Maria that paying them was something he had no choice but to do. This explanation was rejected and sent Maria into countering action.

Unbelievable for anyone except Maria, she now intended to go straight to the top of this extortion racket in Chicago. She learned where the headquarters of the "Capo" was located and took the long streetcar and train ride from Melrose Park. She marched into the office and insisted on an immediate audience with the head of the organization. Perhaps it was the unusual site of such a determined little lady demanding the impossible. Whatever the reason, she actually got ushered into the inner sanctum and found herself standing face-to-face with Al Capone.

Here is what apparently Capone heard in no uncertain terms from this little nobody woman who believed that she had been sent by Jesus Christ himself on behalf of justice. She told Capone that her family had come from Sicily as had his. She had fled persecution and sought the freedom of a new life in a new land. "If you don't stop bothering my husband, I'm going to report you to the police!"

Finally, the strong man rose from his big desk and spoke, with his glaring bodyguard poised to handle any trouble. This is all it's believed that Capone said to Maria. "You have my word, Mrs. Mannoia. Now, good day to you!" She was promptly ushered out. There was no more extortion of the Mannoia family![7]

---

7   An alternate memory in the family is that it was Maria's daughter Rose who was being harassed by the Mafia because she was so beautiful. But, as Kevin's sister Sharla comments, "Maybe that was just Aunt Rose's version!"

There now is that little book titled *Maria* that recounts her numerous exploits as a self-appointed biblical evangelist. She was a strong woman of prayer who became known for having the gift of healing and the daring to be outspoken for Jesus. She worked in a factory among many Roman Catholic Italian immigrants and Jews. To virtually anyone she encountered, she would announce the good news of Jesus. "I want to reach the people of every nation for the Lord."

Maria and Vincenzo Mannoia

One way Maria found to do that was to witness to the public entering the grounds of the World's Fair staged in Chicago in 1933. She held high a large sign attached to a poll that said, "PREPARE TO MEET YOUR GOD!" (Amos 4:12). She positioned herself at the most prominent place she could find. A billboard with a similar message was placed by her at the Melrose Park train depot.

Maria's husband, Vincenzo, was not an equally enthusiastic Christian evangelist, but he defended his wife and became increasingly supportive of her ministry over the years. He knew her as a good wife who did not neglect her family or home whatever she did in public. "This God business has clearly made her a better person. I see the love of God in her."

Maria eventually led her husband and their six children to saving faith in Jesus Christ. The fruit of her work spread to many other families and through them on to the future. Today there are scholarship funds at Greenville University and Asbury Theological Seminary in her honor. They are intended to perpetuate her witness through young ministers of new generations.

Maria's led a small Italian church mission which became associated with the Free Methodist Church in Melrose Park, in part through the generosity of this denomination helping her purchase property. The Free Methodist pastor, A. G. Previte, said this in April, 1928, about what he now called the Italian Free Methodist Mission in Melrose Park. "There are over two thousand Italian people here persuaded that there is no salvation outside the Roman Catholic Church. Many, however, are dissatisfied with their priest's example and do come to the Mission but want only the loaves and fishes and can't withstand the persecution if they dared convert."

He continued on a more hopeful note, however. "Things are now stirred up in Melrose Park among the Italians. Sinners are throwing away their cigarettes, bootleggers are quitting their moonshine jobs, and thieves are going to honest work. Twelve of these have recently been received into our church on probation. Thank God for salvation!" A recently successful three-week revival had been assisted by Frances Di Catania from New Brighton, Pennsylvania. Maria Mannoia, of course, was a prime person steering the community toward Christ. She now had association with the Free Methodist Church in which one day her son Jimmy would be a leader and her grandson Kevin a bishop.

A New Future Emerges

Inspired by the ministry of this Italian Free Methodist Mission in Melrose Park, several Italian families began sending their children to Christian colleges, especially Free Methodist campuses like Spring Arbor in Michigan, Greenville in Illinois, and even as far away as Seattle Pacific in Washington state and Roberts Wesleyan in New York state. A day would come when grandson Jim would be president of one of these and grandson Kevin a member of the governing board of two of the others.

One such college-going child of a local Italian family would be Robert Traina, born in Chicago to Angelo and Argia Giovanonni Traina. Robert would become a prominent Christian scholar and seminary teacher. Another of future prominence would be Jimmy Mannoia, born in Melrose Park in November, 1922, to Vincenzo and Maria. Eventually Jimmy's three children would themselves be prominent Christian educators and ministers. Jim, Jr., Sharla, and Kevin would be exceptionally intelligent, well educated, and highly motivated to carry on the ministry of their Grandma Maria in their own particular times and ways.

In 1940 it was learned that all men age 21 to 36 would be required to register for military service since war was raging in Europe. "That includes me, Mama," Joe told Maria. "I don't have a reason to be deferred like Dominic and Jimmy. They are both in college and preparing for the ministry." Joe would wind up in the heat of battle during World War II. After the American troops landed on Normandy Beach in France, Joe's battalion pushed into Germany. One day, Joe was on top of a tank that was hit and he was severely injured.

Even so, by God's grace, Joe appeared at his brother Jimmy's graduation from Greenville University. Walking on crutches after his awful ordeal, Joe didn't hesitate to credit the prayers of his mother Maria and the grace of God for his safe return home. Jimmy had been converted and received his ministry call at age nine. It had been one stormy night at the campground west of Chicago where the Mannoias attended in summers. He was now well on his way in the Christian journey. Much later his children, Jim, Sharla, and Kevin, would join a parade of emerging Christian leaders.

On April 28, 1964, in Jackson, Michigan, only ten days after her 82nd birthday, Maria Mannoia went home to be with her Lord. Her grandson Kevin, born in Jackson in 1955, had met his beloved grandmother only a few times and remembers especially that she was a loved woman who gave him wet kisses and spoke in broken English. He was impressed by her stalwart stance for Jesus in the most difficult of circumstances.

One day Kevin would vow to do much as had his Grandma Maria, "Know God and Make God Known." She had stood up to threatening priests, faced down Al Capone, and challenged the arriving people at the 1933 Chicago World's Fair to repent and believe in Jesus. How might grandson Kevin one day mimic this daring Christian evangelism and also the dreams of Disneyland that opened in California in 1955, the year of his birth? Only time would tell, and only the grace of God would enable. Meanwhile, in Kevin's family DNA was Sicilian strength, Mannoia pride, a migration mentality, and a legacy of Christian ministry in ever-changing circumstances.

There was a day back on Harmony Road in Spring Arbor, Michigan, when little Kevin's strength had been absent and his very future in question. A coach at the local Free Methodist college was building a home next to the Mannoia's when community harmony took a disruptive turn. There was a large pile of dirt next to the Mannoia home caused by the construction in progress.

Jim, Kevin's older brother, began his later physics studies very early at this time. It was with a little but risky gravity experiment. Somehow, maybe with the usual candy bribe, shy little Kevin was gotten into an old baby buggy that the kids placed on top of the pile. The goal? To see how fast it would roll down to the bottom. Instead, it tumbled down, over and over. The flipping passenger apparently survived or there would be no biography of Kevin to write today!

CHAPTER TWO

PROMISING VISIONARY PARALLELS

To all who come to this happy place, welcome. Disneyland is your land. Here age relives fond memories of the past and youth savors the challenge and promise of the future. Disneyland is dedicated to the ideals, dreams, and hard facts that have created America, with the hope that it will be a source of joy and inspiration to all the world.

Walt Disney, 1955

The Free Methodist denomination dates back to 1860. The "free" came from opposition to slavery, the freeing of God's Spirit in worship, the willingness to ordain women, and the refusal to continue the practice of renting church pews that discriminated against the poor.

A visionary is an idea person who loves to think big, brainstorm, dream, and be daringly creative. Such a person is a risk-taker not patient with institutions that obstruct needed change. He or she provides creative solutions that open new futures. Such enabling of fresh tomorrows is possible because of people with deep convictions and novel ideas who can achieve key objectives. They can unite a team around a cause, casting a vision and getting others excited about it.

John Wesley and then B. T. Roberts were such persons for the Free Methodist Church. Walt Disney's was that in a very different environment. His development department was known as "Walt Disney Imagineering." It functioned long after his death. All visionaries hope for the same longevity, even religious pioneers like Kevin W. Mannoia.

The scene of the Walt Disney dedication remarks above was the initial opening of Disneyland in Anaheim, California. Walt had been born in Chicago and moved to California when the Mannoia family was just becoming prominent in Melrose Park. Walt had worked as a commercial artist before setting up a small studio in Los Angeles to produce animated cartoons. In 1928 his short film *Steamboat Willie,* starring the new character "Mickey Mouse," soon was a national sensation. It was the first animated film to use sound.

In 1955 this and related entertainment sensations appeared in the visionary form of a magnificent new fun world. Walt had created a fantasy land of his own, Disneyland. That same year, back in Michigan, Kevin Mannoia was born. Hardly a sensation at the time, eventually he would carry his own visions and pioneering spirit onto the American religious landscape and beyond.

Walt and Kevin form an interesting parallel. One created fascinating new characters; the other would champion one particular "character" from long ago, Jesus. One character was the product of a man's imagination; the other had been sent by God to fill the imaginations of all humanity with new hope. Kevin would enjoy Mickey and come to worship and represent Jesus.

Frontier Adventures

The Disneyland opening in 1955 coincided with the birth of Kevin, son of Jimmy, grandson of Maria Mannoia. Soon there would be teasing among the Mannoias about the possible parallel between the two events. Disneyland became a family favorite. It was a place for fun and fantasy, and maybe some dreaming about a better world one day.[8]

---

8   By 2023 Kevin Mannoia, now with grandchildren, admits that Legoland may have overtaken Disneyland as the family favorite. In such places, he is something of a big kid himself!

Kevin would himself be a dreamer. The substance of his dreams, however, is where the similarity ends. The land he had in mind would not be "Mannoialand" but the greater nearing of the Kingdom of God in the gracious presence of the Spirit of Jesus Christ. Entering it wouldn't require the purchasing of tickets. It would be only by divine grace and would require personal sacrifice, not just days of entertainment. As opposed to Disneyland, relatively few have been anxious to pass through its gates.

Frontier adventures rarely happen without some pain, and Kevin's coming life eventually would cross many frontiers and face a range of difficult challenges, as Grandma Maria's certainly had decades before him. Even the opening day of Disneyland didn't come off without unwanted incident. Special invitations had been sent out for the opening on July 17, 1955. Unfortunately, the pass was counterfeited. Thousands of uninvited people were admitted. The park wasn't ready for this. Food and drink ran out, a woman's high-heeled shoe got stuck in the wet asphalt of Main Street USA, and the Mark Twain Steamboat nearly capsized from too many passengers aboard. No matter. Success soon would overcome struggle for Walt's imaginative place.

This present world, now long removed from 1955, remains quite a distance from being a truly happy place. Many manage to survive by reliving fond memories of the past. Some of today's youth are able to savor the challenge and promise of the future. Unfortunately, so many others despair of there even being a future and turn to various forms of addictive self-destruction. There certainly are hard facts now to be faced and a great longing for some fresh source of joy and inspiration. Could the relatively unknown Kevin Mannoia bring any? Certainly not on his own.

This biography of Kevin seeks to trace the story of his life-long attempt at being a fountain of new hope amid pools of church stagnancy and cultural despair. In the summer of 1955 Walt Disney spoke to many his dedication words about the new land of fun.

Only a few rejoiced that Kevin, son of James and Florence Mannoia, had been born on October 6, 1955, in Jackson, Michigan.

These two events are unrelated, of course, although not entirely. Some of the Mannoias would enjoy the dream and entertainment investment of Walt on family vacations. Of what benefit to the world would be the parallel birth of Kevin? Only the grace of God and a considerable amount of time would manage to tell. In fact, the full telling is yet to be complete.

James, son of Vincenzo and Maria Mannoia, had become a student at Spring Arbor College in southern Michigan, a small Free Methodist campus at first only a high school and junior college. Eventually Jim met there the lovely Florence Gilroy who attended this small campus for two years. Her father, Arthur Gilroy, was a Canadian immigrant and then Superintendent of the Marble, Lime, and Stone Company in upper Michigan. Arthur had married Stella Maude Cutler and to them Florence was born in 1924, the youngest of seven children. During her childhood she and her mother were the only Christians in the family that was living in the tiny town of her birthplace, Manistique in the Upper Peninsula of Michigan.

Spring Arbor College featured a special table in its dining hall for those with birthdays in given months. Jim and Florence may have first met at such a table, both with birthdays in November. The *Re-Dit* was born during the 1943-1944 school year through the efforts of Florence Gilroy (later Mrs. V. James Mannoia) and other students and soon became established as Spring Arbor's student newspaper, renamed the *Crusader* in the mid-1960s.[9]

Soon dating Jim, Florence developed a real interest and had to deal somehow with a prevailing prejudice against Italian immigrants. She addressed this problem by seeking the advice of the wife of the school's president, a compassionate but forthright

---

9   Howard A. Snyder, *Concept & Commitment: A History of Spring Arbor University*, 66.

woman. She asked the older lady, "Is it OK to become serious with this attractive young man?" The remembered response went something like this.

James and Florence (Gilroy) Mannoia

"Well Florence," admitting awkwardness between a Canadian-Americans and an Italian-Americans, "you know that we don't believe here in interracial marriage!" That shocking piece of caution may have slowed but clearly didn't stop the growing relationship. Who's to define "race"? Is a diversity of national backgrounds to be considered a wall that God has built? How should one deal with such deep social prejudice? Florence chose to live by her own judgments. Jim was more than willing to do the same.[10]

Jim Mannoia and Florence Gilroy were married in 1945 as he was completing his undergraduate degree at Greenville College, another Free Methodist campus. She would become an elementary school teacher and Christian speaker and writer. Jim would remain

---

10   Kevin's sister Sharla recalls their mother reporting that the concern included what the children of such a union would look like. "Mama said she wished she had been able to bring her beautiful kids to show her counselor!"

in school, attending Northern Baptist Theological Seminary for two years before completing his Bachelor of Divinity degree at Asbury Theological Seminary in 1948. They were a great match of Christian servants with decades of prominent service ahead, service always to be done together.

Initially their service reflected in some ways that of Jim's mother, Maria Mannoia. The new couple moved back to the Chicago area and served as assistants at a Chicago church focusing on children's mission work in an impoverished area of the city. Their calling to be pastors and educators soon surfaced.

Florence and Jim served two Free Methodist pastorates, Beloit, Wisconsin, and East Peoria, Illinois. James then went back to the Spring Arbor campus and taught for seven years while Florence completed her B. S. degree at Eastern Michigan University and taught for several years at the public school in Spring Arbor. Their home on Harmony Road still stands proudly not far from the campus of what now has become Spring Arbor University.

Mother Maria and now son Jim were on parallel tracks, both being thoroughly committed to the ministry of Jesus Christ through the ministries of the Free Methodist Church. In each case, their own children would grow up and call their parents blessed. Born to Jim and Florence were Vincent James in August, 1949, and Sharla Joy, in March, 1952, both in Beloit, Wisconsin. Finally there arrived Kevin Wayne, born in Jackson, Michigan, in October, 1955. Biographies of all three could easily be justified. We will discipline ourselves to only the large story of Kevin, the youngest of the three.

Is Roberts Alive Again?

B. T. Roberts was born in 1823 in the state of New York and became central to the founding and early formation of the Free Methodist Church. In several ways he and the much later Kevin Mannoia would travel parallel tracks, although in very different times and places. In fact, it's reported that Kevin almost carried the historic Roberts name. Born in the hospital in Jackson, the family story is that, while father Jim was looking at this newborn through the glass, he was joined by another new father who inquired, "Which one is yours?" Jim pointed at Kevin.

"And what are you going to call him?" asked the man. "We think 'Robert Wesley Mannoia,' about as sturdy a connection with our family's Free Methodist tradition as you can get." Trouble came with this stranger's quick response. "Too bad. Anyone can call their kid 'Bob'." That comment led to more conversation between Jim and Florence and somehow plans changed to "Kevin Wayne." What didn't change were the strong parallels that years later would emerge between the gifting and accomplishments of this newborn and the elite leader of his family's denominational tradition.

Benjamin T. Roberts had been a sophisticated and politically active religious leader in the American holiness movement of the nineteenth century. He was key to the founding of the Free Methodist Church and Roberts Wesleyan University.[11] This present biography of Kevin was begun in 2023 on the 200th anniversary of the birth of B. T. Roberts. In Kevin, the legacy of the elder Roberts would continue.

Like Roberts, Kevin has featured "the Bible standard of Christianity," the free and abundant life in the Spirit of Jesus, the equality of all people, including the freedom of women to preach and lead, and the end of the evils of slavery and oppression as they are appearing again in our day. Roberts was, and Kevin would be . . .

- A gifted speaker, writer, and church pastor
- A nurturer of young believers, dedicated to education and the liberal arts

---

11   Yours truly was privileged to nominate Howard A. Snyder's 2006 biography of B. T. and Ellen Roberts to receive the 2007 Smith/Wynkoop Book Award of the Wesleyan Theological Society.

- A leader of church reform and outspoken opponent of the oppression of others
- A dedicated elder of the Free Methodist Church with a vision of the wider church
- A loyal graduate and former trustee of Roberts Wesleyan University founded by Roberts

There are other parallels that will emerge as Kevin's story is told. A few occurred to Kevin himself recently as he read Dan Runyon's abridged version of the large biography of B. T. and Ellen Roberts.

This reading helped Kevin realize how much the Roberts/Mannoia lives and journeys of faith have paralleled. As a loyal Free Methodist, Kevin feels "intensely connected" in part because of his contemporary role of influencing a range of church-related institutions of higher education, some associated with Free Methodism and many not. This influence usually has two primary thrusts, for the institutions to be increasingly enriched by their Wesleyan traditions and engaged constructively with the cultural issues of today. Kevin has found great encouragement in recalling that the Roberts couple were not so much innovators as reformers, people wanting to stay true to "Old Methodism" in the face of encroaching "New Methodism." They were holding steady to the tradition and Scriptural hermeneutic that had served Methodism and the Wesleys so well for so long. Holding on to yesterday, however, would not exclude innovations needed by tomorrow.

Kevin would come to understand himself to be a catalyst for change, "a traditionalist calling the church to a new and grace-filled posture of engagement, one without compromise of the historic and traditional hermeneutic that has guided us heretofore." Kevin would see many parallels as he read the Roberts' history, including a strong commitment to higher education and ecumenism, a priority on the unfettered role of women in church leadership, and a balanced holiness that refuses to endorse extremism but rather enables an integrated and holistic and fulfilled way of life, a way not heavily dogmatic or propositional in nature. He admits that "there are so many similarities that it is almost uncanny."

Biographer Howard A. Snyder refers to B. T. and Ellen Roberts as "populist saints." He is not claiming, of course, that these very human persons were spiritually spotless or populists in an ideological sense. Rather, they sought to live lives of freedom, holiness, and justice that was for *all the people,* and especially for the poor. Why live that way? Because that's what they saw in Jesus Christ. In this sense they were prime representatives of a holy populism. Kevin would be very much in their debt. He actively calls on today's Christians, all Christians, to engage contemporary culture with the transforming potential of Christian holiness.

Kevin: Old jacket, always a new mission.

When a student at Roberts Wesleyan College in the 1970s, Kevin bought a jacket featuring the campus name and logo. Loyalty layered with sentimentality led him to wearing it well into the second decade of the twenty-first century, despite grease and paint stains covering the one sleeve. Taking a group of young educators to Brazil and getting his deserved share of teasing about the old thing, his travel companions bought him a new jacket once home. Kevin was willing to shift to the new without in any way showing disrespect for the old. This was an apt symbol of his stance toward the church and its tradition, doctrine, and mission in today's world. Old foundations? Yes. Needed changes today? Absolutely.

Key Parental Traits

A humorous cartoon shows smiling parents with their newborn. The adults are heavily tattooed, although the baby has clear skin and is said to have "come out blank." In fact, none of us is born blank in many respects. We pass along much to our children, even if not acquired characteristics like body art. Still, in Kevin Mannoia's case, we will see that he seems to have inherited so much from his parents, DNA based and otherwise. Much of it is extremely good.

There are no obvious tattoos decorating Kevin today, at least as far as I've seen, and now he is approaching seventy years old. There is, however, the obvious transference of native intelligence, the tendency to strong Christian faith, a flair for energetic activism, and a clear passion for growing young leaders and stimulating the cross-cultural impact of Christian faith. In these cases at a minimum, like Father and Mother Mannoia, like Son Kevin.

To be more specific, according to his older brother Jim, "Kevin and I tended to come at things from different directions. At first he was essentially a pastor and I studied and taught physics. He was more like Father and I like Mother. She was more the scientist, the analytic person. He was more the pastor, even when he taught philosophy. When in college I had lots of questions. It was Mother who stayed up with me exploring the questions and issues. Kevin always has had more of the pastoral spirit, focusing on people and relationships." Later the analytic and communication skills of mother Florence would be acquired with need and practice.

Much of worth exists and has moved generationally in the Mannoia lineage. This is true whether in the United States or abroad, in the local parish or seminary classroom, while counseling students or coaching institutions, putting words on paper or eloquently unleashing them from a pulpit or lecture stand. Although this biography focuses on Kevin, similar things could be detailed about his brother Jim and sister Sharla. Telling those stories, worthy as they are, is left to others.

Mannoia siblings, Kevin, Sharla, and James.

The personality and Christian commitment of Jim, Kevin's father, would be very much paralleled by his three children in their later and very prominent Christian ministries. They all have been change agents, wanting to push the good toward the best, not fearing to act on behalf of an envisioned tomorrow. Such leaders often are misunderstood, even thought egotistical, resisted by those committed to the status quo. Father Jim set the pace and Mother Florence was right there with him.

How should one respond to injustice to one's very person? What about when people misread your heart, take unfair advantage of circumstances, claim that something, even if very good, was done too much, too fast, not in exactly the right way, and maybe for one's own benefit? Fight back? No! Rarely did the Mannoias strike back, justified or not.

Son Jim says his parents were some of the most humble people he has ever met. "When mistreated, Father just sucked it up and endured things for righteousness sake. If handled the right way, such an approach can build solid Christian character. If just absorbed and unprocessed, it can destroy one." Jim then adds this. "Kevin and I are both extroverts, although he was very shy as a kid. Time has brought us closer together. He has grown into this outgoingness while I always was that way. At twenty-five I was the president of the collegiate club at Park Street Church in Boston and of InterVarsity at the Massachusetts Institute of Technology."

Jim and certainly his kid brother Kevin later would parallel more closely with an aggressive and inspired pattern of leadership in a range of Christian institutions. On occasion they would pay personal prices for this. They both are visionaries and agents of change, and this has brought more than their shares of pain. Kevin in particular would struggle on occasion with the internal results of misunderstanding and even rejection from persons around him who were resisting change. Such was seen in action by Jim, Sharla, and Kevin early in their lives. Their parents broke old missionary molds in Brazil while their kids were young and very impressionable. The lessons would be well learned by the younger generation.

Sister Sharla, the "rose between two thorns" she teasingly reports, says this. "I've seen this over and over in Kevin's life. An organization needs and wants to change and calls Kevin because he has excellent skills at shifting the culture and direction of an organization. He moves, maybe too much and too fast, who knows, and elements of the organization begin to resist, turning against him. He avoids striking back, like Daddy, and struggles inside to grow through it and move on."

Later, Kevin would have a close friend, Larry Walkemeyer, who would put the situation this way. "There have been times when Kevin has gotten a little too far ahead of his troops and a few of them started shooting him in the back! Others, however, followed gladly." Having now read closely Kevin's personal journal, I have seen the several holes in his back. A few may have been deserved; so many have not.

The Story Now Begins

With caution and awareness of the historic connections to outstanding reformers of an earlier time, and knowing the exceptional parenting received, our life story of Kevin begins. He always would be energetic, visionary, anxious to act. Some would say he had the intelligence but lacked the warmth of his father. Others would quickly disagree, insisting that he has been very much like his beloved father.

Perceptions are fragile and undependable things. Kevin would make at least this much clear. Human sin takes different forms in different times, although its core remains the same—*selfishness*. The *integrity* (holiness) and *unity* of Christian believers are critical characteristics if the church expects to effectively spread the good news of Jesus Christ. High on Kevin's personal agenda, then, would always be spreading the good news, and thus necessarily doing all possible to enhance integrity and unity in the fellowship of the Jesus people of our time.[12]

Church life must Spirit-infused, empowered, and engaging the issues of the day with wisdom and courage. B. T. and Ellen Roberts in the nineteenth century and Kevin Mannoia in the twentieth and twenty-first centuries, are different people with quite similar instincts, in the same religious tradition and serving the same God who is over all and in all and always lover of all.

---

12   One of Kevin's most popular books would be *The Integrity Factor* (1996, 2006).

B. T. Roberts once was traveling alone by train in the 1870s. At one stop a group of about ten well-dressed young African Americans entered his first-class car. One passenger was incensed and insisted that the conductor put them where they belonged as Black men, in a second-class car. "But they have first-class tickets," the conductor explained. This passenger wouldn't back off, convinced that he shouldn't have to ride with "niggers."

Roberts heard enough and intervened, defending the young men. The youth were permitted to take their seats where their tickets said they belonged and the train went on to its destination. Before getting off, the youth gathered around Roberts and began singing a most beautiful private concert. They turned out to be the "Jubilee Singers" from Fisk University, internationally acclaimed for introducing white audiences to Negro spirituals like "Steal Away" and "Swing Low, Sweet Chariot."

Roberts had acted in a way of courageous holiness engagement, to be mimicked often by Kevin Mannoia in more recent decades. For him it would be on behalf of at least real respect for Pentecostals, African-Americans, women, Hispanics, and the LGBTQ community when such was unpopular at best among many evangelical Christians. Truth standards are to be honored, but never unjustly in ways that demean any people of God's own creation. Roberts and Kevin's own parents had shown him the way. Actually, it was Jesus of Nazareth who first had put his life on the line for all of us in just such redeeming ways.

For Kevin, the roots of his future ministry began to be planted in a place far away from where he was born in southern Michigan. God was calling his parents southward as Free Methodist missionaries.

CHAPTER THREE

SOJOURN SOUTHWARD

In 1973 Florence Mannoia recalled a communion service in a Brazilian village a few years before. She and her husband Jim were Free Methodist missionaries. He was officiating, she was playing a small pump organ, and their teenage daughter Sharla was kneeling next to a new Christian coughing profusely. This convert had walked eight kilometers in the cold night air to be there.

The younger son Kevin was kneeling next to a man with a badly infected arm caused by a neglected burn. This man also had walked barefoot for several kilometers to be at this sacred Table of the Lord. As Florence played, she noticed the national pastor offering bread and grape juice to her children. Her family was worshiping humbly with the people of Brazil and being graciously served by them. It had been the family's privilege to be living in Brazil and sharing Christ with the people. The Mannoia children would never forget or ever be the same.

Rev. Dr. James Mannoia had been born to Vincenzo and Maria Mannoia in 1922. He had grown up in Melrose Park near Chicago and at age nine given his life to Christ at the Downers Grove, Illinois, Free Methodist Campground. Later when about to complete his initial pastorates as a young Free Methodist minister, a retired preacher told him that he saw "*SA*" coming next in Jim's future. Jim thought of **S**outh **A**merica, and indeed it would be that one day, except not until years at **S**pring **A**rbor University in southern Michigan. It would be a double "*SA*" for this ministering family.

There came seven years of Jim's teaching at Spring Arbor, at the time only a high school and junior college located on a small campus of the Free Methodist Church. Very committed to education, Jim had graduated from Greenville College (B. A., 1945), attended Northern Baptist Seminary (1945-47), and then Asbury Theological Seminary (1947-48). He would graduate twice from Michigan State University (M. A., 1957, and Ph. D., 1962) and hold honorary society memberships in Phi Delta Kappa and Theta Phi. His teaching expertise ranged from philosophy and Christian doctrine to pastoral counseling, ethics, preaching, and New Testament Greek.

All three of the children of Jim and Florence would earn multiple academic degrees and later be active professionally in higher education. Father Jim wrote this in a 1968 issue of *Youth in Action*: "Talent and money are essential to God's work, but a commitment to His calling and faith in His providential leadership are indispensable." Jim and Florence had limited money but seemingly unlimited talent, commitment, and faith.

After the years teaching at Spring Arbor, the Mannoia eyes finally turned toward their next "*SA.*" At first Jim had considered a seminary presidency offered to him by OMS in Ecuador, but instead leaned toward Brazil, presumably because of loyalty to his own denomination. The Free Methodist Church there had begun through pastors and laypersons migrating from Japan in the 1930s. Understandably, the period during and after World War II had been difficult for the Brazilian Japanese community in Brazil. Public meetings in Japanese or even speaking Japanese in the streets was prohibited. Japanese pastors were threatened with imprisonment for just being Japanese.[13]

---

13 A very special day in Kevin's later life would involve a commencement ceremony at Azusa Pacific University in California where he presided. He conferred a series of degrees on Japanese Americans whose educations had been interrupted by WWII. It was an emotional and highly publicized event. Kevin noted in his remarks that he was wearing his father's regalia, himself a second-generation immigrant who had started the first Japanese Nissei church in Brazil.

After the war there came financial support and the first Free Methodist missionaries. A course of study for new pastors was recommended by the missionaries and approval was given, but only with the understanding that there be "no taint of higher criticism" in the teaching. Such "liberalism" was perceived to be a threat to the faith's integrity. When Jim Mannoia became president of the tiny Brazilian seminary, such defensive narrowness would be largely abandoned. Jim had broad academic experience and respect for its open processes and potential benefits.

Ending also would be many of the "old school" missionary procedures that Jim and Florence weren't prepared to honor. Such freedom to alter and innovate soon would become natural for the three children. Several deep-set attitudes of young Kevin were formed here even if he were largely unaware of it until later in life.

The enrichment to be experienced by the Mannoia family in Brazil would be considerable, although Jim, Jr., would recall later that he and his sister Sharla and their young brother Kevin "had been pulled away from the tiny rural town of Spring Arbor, Michigan, away from the only friends we'd ever known, and plunked down in a city of seven million people where everyone spoke Portuguese."

They had lived on Harmony Road among a set of neighbor kids of Free Methodist families and within walking distance of school and college campus. São Paulo was a different world and growing up there certainly would be a stretching, demanding, and life-changing missionary experience.

Leaving Spring Arbor, Michigan, was full of unknowns. Jim and Florence Mannoia were both Christian visionaries with faith. They also were practical people with good sense. For instance, they rented their Spring Arbor home on Harmony Road rather than selling, though they surely could have used the money. That way the property paid for itself over time and eventually became the equity enabling the purchase of their final home at 100 Johnson Court in Wilmore, Kentucky, long after their years of missionary service in Brazil.

Changing Missionary Strategies

A divine call had come to Jim and Florence Mannoia for missionary service abroad. The call probably had its roots back to 1951 when they were part of a Youth for Christ preaching mission to central Italy. For a decade beginning in 1945, Jim already had served the family's church affiliation in the United States, the Free Methodist Church, filling pastoral roles in Illinois and Wisconsin before the years of teaching religion at Spring Arbor in Michigan. Then in 1962, with their children Jim, Jr., Sharla, and Kevin, Jim and Florence felt the divine call to be involved in the evangelism and seminary education of their denomination overseas. It would be *SA* number two.

Denominational officials had come to recognize the pioneering spirits and educational background and skills of Jim and Florence. The opportunity therefore came for their family of five to sojourn southward to the nation of Brazil. Such, however, would have to be done on their own terms. They judged that some of the "old school" missionary strategies needed to be changed, at least in their case. They set acceptable guidelines for their going and these were approved by the denomination and then lived out.

To begin, the family would not spend the usual weeks on a ship to reach their field assignment. They instead flew to Florida, spent a week of family vacation as needed transition, and then flew on to their new home in Brazil. Kevin was only six years old and had never flown before. He recalls vividly looking out the little window during their Detroit take-off and seeing the cherry-red heat from the back of one the four engines. It was making the air wavy and the earth below blurry. That engine exhaust was fascinating and scary. Kevin cried in fear and was allowed to shift seats to snuggle with his parents. More discomfort was just ahead.

They spent a restful week in Florida prior to the long journey on to Brazil. Not used to the hot sun on a tropical beach, Kevin and his two older siblings had gotten significant sunburns. Brother Jim admits that scars still remain in the form of freckled Mannoia backs. Soon, soreness and all, they were in the air again, on to South America and eventually stopping briefly in the middle of the night so the plane could refuel. Kevin was sound asleep in a bulkhead seat when other Mannoias slipped off the plane for a quick stretch and restroom relief. While kindly being left to sleep undisturbed, these moments remain burned in Kevin's memory. "I awoke and they were gone. Boy was I afraid! Thankfully, the stewardess was so kind to comfort me and soon they were back." Missionary life was bringing unexpected challenges even before the family landed in the new world of Brazil.

Once safely on the ground, it was made plain to denominational officials that the family would not live in the isolated countryside with the other missionaries (where the tiny seminary was) but in the city where the future of Christian ministry surely lay. Nor would they begin with an extensive time in language school, typical of the other missionaries of the time. Within weeks of being immersed in this new Portuguese culture, James was managing to preach in the local Portuguese language, his native Italian being a great learning help.

Both missionary parents were clear about something else. They intended, partly at their own expense if necessary, to break another typical missionary pattern. Usually the children of missionaries were placed in a boarding school, sometimes a considerable distance from the parents. It would not be so for the three Mannoia children. The younger two would attend a new school, the Pan American Christian Academy located not far from a home found for the family in the city of São Paulo. The instruction there would be half in English and half in Portuguese. Kevin would be in first grade at this school and his sister Sharla in fifth. Several of the teachers were from other missionary families stationed in the area.

What about Jim, the oldest? The parents were willing to spend their own savings if necessary to be sure that Jim, then thirteen, could go to one of the finest schools in the city of São Paulo, while still continuing to live at home. Their modest salaries were only $1,000 per year each but they would do whatever it took. These were educated missionaries with high standards expected for their children.

They found the American Graded School operated by the U. S. Chamber of Commerce. It was designed for children of expatriates and wealthy Brazilians. It had a reputation for top academics and would prepare young Jim well in the sciences, the foundation for what would be an elite education ahead of him later back in the United States. The problem was that this fine school, apart from the expense, was its location a considerable distance from the family home in a huge city.

In a recent book of his, Jim, Jr., describes to a Greenville University chapel audience his initially getting to this school. His parents escorted him the first day, but beginning with the second he was on his own. That was "the longest trip I ever took." The school was two bus rides away from the Mannoia home, each ride some forty-five minutes long. The "handoff" downtown was nightmarish for a sheltered rural Michigan boy. Other aspects of the long and lonely rides made things even worse.

"The people were different colors, the noise was terrific, and the diesel fumes made me a little sick. The odd body odors of people jammed together so closely meant I could hardly breathe. They almost made me not want to breathe. Because of the crush, I had to stand. The consequences of becoming lost in a city that size, not speaking a word of Portuguese, with no cell phones, and not even a phone at home, were unthinkable. The school bus driver was a surly chain-smoking non-English-speaking Japanese man, one I later speculated had been a survivor at Hiroshima and hated little American boys."[14]

Kevin (youngest) and family, called to Brazil.

There in São Paulo the Mannoia family would live for eight years, serving extensively both of the two existing Free Methodist conferences, the Brazilian and Nikkei Japanese. Father Jim would preach extensively, serve on various committees, and chair the seminary commission. During these years he would be president of the Free Methodist Theological Seminary, at first consisting of fewer than ten students and located in very rural Mairipora where he had chosen for the family not to live. Soon he would arrange for the seminary to cease living there.

---

14 V. James Mannoia, Jr., *Paradox and Virtue: Talks to My Students.* Dr. Mannoia, older brother of Kevin was serving as president of this fine Free Methodist campus and cared about quality education as had his father before him.

The purchase of this rural land had been enabled by funds coming from Spring Arbor College in Michigan where the Mannoias had lived and Jim had taught. Buildings had gone up on the new Brazilian campus beginning in 1954. Over a period of about five years, more than $60,000 was raised for the Brazil seminary school through the combined efforts of students, faculty, and the local church in Spring Arbor.[15] Regardless, Jim insisted that the seminary he now was seeking to lead be moved into the big and bustling city of São Paulo.

It would happen as he hoped. In the early 1960s the original rural campus was sold and the seminary moved into the heart of São Paulo. Under the direction of President V. James Mannoia, a Spring Arbor alumnus and former faculty member, the seminary took on a new and expanding life. There was increased focus on quality academics being an essential part of proper ministerial preparation. Opportunity for enrollment by extension was established, quickly enabling a growing student body.

The chapel of a lovely new building would be built late in the Mannoia missionary years, with it being named in honor of mother Maria Mannoia. Years later, with Jim Mannoia, Sr., then completing his teaching career at Asbury Theological Seminary, there would be a Maria Mannoia Scholarship Fund established there to assist individuals preparing to serve Christ sacrificially and boldly in their days the way Maria had served in hers.[16]

As already noted, in the Brazilian Free Methodist Seminary there had been an earlier restriction of the curriculum. It had to

---

15   Howard A. Snyder, *Concept and Commitment.*

16   Dr. James Mannoia, Sr., had returned in 1978 to teach at Asbury after having completed a B. D. there in 1948 (later called Master of Divinity). The scholarship fund was established by the family in 1990 "to perpetuate the continuing witness of persons who are called to prepare themselves as ministers of the gospel of Jesus Christ. Free Methodist students preparing for pastoral ministry or missions will be given first preference." There also is now a Mannoia lectureship at Greenville University in honor of Jim and Florence Mannoia, one of the lectures delivered by Maria's grandson Kevin. In addition, Greenville has a scholarship honoring Grandma Maria and a Mannoia Residence Hall named for Ellen Mannoia, wife of Kevin's brother Jim, president of the university for some years.

have "no taint of higher criticism." This had to be rethought, insisted President Mannoia. Quality seminary education for future ministers must be considerably more open and thoughtful than that. Personally, he had been trained in Northern Baptist and Asbury Theological seminaries and held two graduate degrees from Michigan State University. Serious academics was hardly foreign to him, nor was it now to be considered an enemy to serious Christian faith and ministry on the field where he served.

Brazilian chapel dedicated to the beloved Maria Mannoia.

To increase the service reach of the little seminary, President Mannoia introduced the concept of theological education by extension. By 1967 there were some fifty students active in the seminary, sometimes referred to by some as "Little Spring Arbor." By 1968 there were about 130 students studying in a network of local churches. In was in that year that Dr. Mannoia oversaw the purchase of property and the construction of a lovely three-story building on the very busy street in São Paulo, Domingo de Moraes, only blocks from the house in which the seminary had first operated once moved to the city. That new building would serve the seminary into the twenty-first century.

Dr. Mannoia was added to the Board of the Pan American Christian Academy, serving for only a brief time. One accomplishment was his helping to find a chicken farm that became the school's first owned property. His time was brief in that governing role, presumably because he was perceived to be too "liberal." This was the first time that young Kevin realized there were theological differences in the Christian church. He would learn plenty more about that in the years to come!

When sister Sharla was ready for high school, there being none at the Academy, she also went to the Graded School attended by her brother Jim. As had Jim in the sciences, there she received a strong background in languages, key to her professional future.

In the Brazilian missionary years, Florence Mannoia expressed "new school" thinking in ways similar to her progressive husband. "Our nationals must be trained to fill competently the role of leadership which eventually will fall to them, and we must not fail them. Along with quality academic training, we want to share the genius of our heritage as a holiness church around the world." The Mannoias loved their home denomination even while seeking to update some of its standards and processes. Young Kevin would absorb and later duplicate the same loving and seeking.

Later Florence would gather and publish in the little book *Amigos* a series of the family's experiences in Brazil. It would be in Portuguese and for the Children's Youth Crusaders of the Free Methodist Church. Much later she and her husband Jim would co-teach a class at Asbury Theological Seminary called "The Parsonage Couple." In 1989 she would conduct a national survey of the perceived training needs of the wives of Free Methodist pastors. What were their frustrations, concerns, and dreams? Here's what was learned, hardly surprising to Florence.

Many wives didn't buy into their husband's ministerial calling, coming to resent its intrusion into their homes and families. Not so with Florence Mannoia. Jim's calling was readily accepted as her own. Their son Kevin later would marry Kathy who would follow the good lead of Florence in truly owning her husband's calling. Their daughter Sharla would not marry a minister but would herself write pastoral prayers and lead Bible studies and Sunday school classes for her local church in Texas. Her husband would be fully supportive of her ministries.

Sharla recalls her mother Florence writing an Advent guide for a congregation pastored by her husband Jim in New York state years after their return from Brazil. It would be a guide later adopted for use by Sharla's brother Kevin in his first pastorate in Texas after seminary graduation. For some years Sharla would be an active layperson in that Dallas congregation and most recently heads an effort in the greater Dallas area to prepare apartments for incoming refugees. Such ministries are examples of mother Florence always hoping to give her children "roots and wings!" All three have flown quite high, and without losing their solid family, faith, and church roots.

Stressful but Successful

The three children of Jim and Florence, Jim, Jr., Sharla, and Kevin, all would receive quality educations in Brazil, both at home and in the two local institutions. They became multi-lingual and well prepared for their continuing educations once back in the United States. For instance, Jim recalls having had high-quality teachers at the American Graded School. "I had a math teacher for two years on leave from his professorship at Princeton University. My biology teacher was a medical doctor from Italy. My drama coach was the voice of Tonto on the original Lone Ranger radio program. In my junior year in English, we had to read and write reports on at least twenty novels. I still have mine."

Students were held to high standards. Nearly all of Jim's classmates went on to college in the United States, one to Stanford, another to Princeton, etc. The Mannoia children also were being prepared at home to be strong Christians. They also would mature into skilled educational professionals who are all-world in their outlooks. Jim, the oldest son, finished high school in Brazil. With his family back in the U. S. briefly on deputation work, he was enrolled at a top-flight New England university on a generous scholarship.

When having to say goodbye to son Jim at the airport as the family headed back to Brazil, having to leave him behind, mother Florence was both conflicted and proud. Later she wrote, "He was a man! He was on his own. Would he make it? Would temptation break him down where he was weak? Would he fall? Or would the roots of family love, discipline, family worship, and sharing support adequately his uncharted flight? We waved and committed him to God's keeping."

In only a few years Jim, Jr., would hold a B. S. degree from Massachusetts Institute of Technology and soon be a professor of physics at Grove City College in Pennsylvania, with other degrees and prominent roles in higher education to follow. Sharla (Martin) would complete high school in Brazil and then teach French and work on a master's degree at the University of Texas in Arlington.

Youngest son Kevin eventually would earn academic degrees in New York, Illinois, and Texas and be Superintendent of the Southern California Conference of the Free Methodist Church after serving a similar role in Texas. For each of them, so much yet lay ahead. Family love and support had been strong and successful in supporting them as mother and father had so hoped. Of course, they also had been committed to God's keeping, and God always has been faithful.

And the parents? They returned to the United States after eight eventful years of service in Brazil. At first Jim, Sr., studied at the Overseas Ministries Study Center in New Jersey, enabling a time of study at Temple University and part-time teaching at Trinity Evangelical Divinity School in Illinois (surprisingly important for the future seminary education of his son Kevin).

Then the family moved from New Jersey to the denomination's headquarters in Indiana, with Jim serving there as Executive Secretary of the Free Methodist World Fellowship and Latin America Area Secretary. This role took him on trips to Haiti, the Dominican Republic, and the Asia Area Fellowship Conference convened in Taiwan. Such international ministry soon would be a model for so much that eventually would be characteristic of the extensive ministry of son Kevin.

While a trusted administrator, educator, and world Christian leader, it should not be forgotten that Dr. James Mannoia, Sr., also was a sensitive spiritual guide. From 1972 to 1978 he would serve as the Lead Pastor of Pearce Memorial Church in North Chili, New York, the historic Free Methodist campus congregation of Roberts Wesleyan University. Still in his future beyond that would be years of faculty service at Asbury Theological Seminary where Jim would retire in 1994 prior to his death in 2001.[17] At Asbury he would serve as Director of Supervised Ministries, doing things like placing ministerial interns in "teaching churches."

As part of the celebration of the retirement of Dr. James Mannoia, Sr., close friend Laurence Wood observed that Jim had been an outstanding advocate of the Wesleyan-Holiness tradition of Christianity. Colleague William Faupel added:

> I think Jim shares in common with Will Rogers the fact that he has never met a person he didn't like or, more to the point, who did not feel an instant rapport with him. He had those qualities so desirable in a pastor, teacher, missionary, evangelist, counselor, and denominational leader—all roles fulfilled so ably through the course of his life.

Meanwhile, Florence served as a beloved "First Lady" of the New York congregation when pastored by her husband. She also was a skilled writer and totally supportive of Jim's ministry, partly by herself being an eloquent speaker to student and faculty groups. The joint lives and ministries of Jim and Florence had prepared

---

17   Husband James and wife Florence Mannoia are buried in the cemetery adjacent to the campus of Spring Arbor University in Michigan, his death in 2001 and hers in 2012.

a sturdy Christian foundation on which all three of their children would build. Like his father, son Kevin would have a likable personality and be a natural networker and reconciler of people and movements within the church and society.

One day Kevin also would travel the world in ministry to an extent far exceeding his beloved father. He also would cross denominational lines and challenge some "old school" thoughts and practices no longer adequate for contemporary times. In his personal journal in 2006 Kevin reports that he just visited the Brazilian seminary served so well by his father years before. His judgment? "It was so impressive what he did!"

Then in 2010 Kevin was back in Brazil, this time showing his wife Kathy around. He admits, "I found myself deeply missing my father. I hope I can somehow tell my own children these lessons. Amid all the pressures of missionary work, Father maintained a healthy balance, often against the opposition of the mission board and other missionaries. He represented grace and breadth of thinking that served as a foundation for my own future and health."

CHAPTER FOUR

A HIGHER HIGHER EDUCATION

The Methodist tradition originating in England migrated and grew rapidly in the young United States. Pastors often had two or three preaching posts and traveled among them. The Free Methodist Church, begun in 1860, continued the pioneer pattern of "stationing" preachers where judged most needed. Such mobility often forced minister's children to attend multiple schools, occasionally with resistance and negative results.

The Mannoias certainly were on the move as a Free Methodist family. Even so, the quality education of their children was a high priority, eventually one "that goes beyond" (son Jim's phrase in a book title). It would come to include a *higher* higher education, one "expressing life" (son Kevin's phrase in a book title). While Kevin, youngest of the three Mannoia children, would have to attend four different high schools in two countries and three states, it would be a rich experience overall, one that prepared him well for the future.

The educational journey of Kevin Mannoia started out awkwardly. The family moved to Brazil as new Free Methodist missionaries when he was in the first grade. Children in this new land were taught cursive writing very early. Kevin was still working with block letters and had to learn cursive quickly—which his sister Sharla says is why his handwriting is still terrible.

He was hardly a scholar in his early schooling years, in some contrast to his academically inclined brother Jim who would excel academically. Sister Sharla also would proceed well in the academic world and have children who would earn a range of scholarships, one being a national merit scholar. A daughter would become a senior pastor in the United States.

The educational experience of Kevin, despite the mobility of cultures and diversity of institutions, would turn out to be graciously God-directed. The Mannoias certainly were on the move, causing son Kevin to attend four different high schools located in two countries and three U. S. states. When he finally graduated, ahead for him would be college, seminary, and doctoral degrees granted by three different institutions in widely separated parts of the United States. Although all this was stressful at points, the net result was quite positive. Kevin came to understand the rich dimensions included in a truly Christian *higher* higher education. He eventually would do more than understand. He would dedicate much of his later life to furthering this critical cause, particularly in relation to institutions worldwide with a Wesleyan heritage.

The cause in question would be the delicate but very enriching relationship between Christian faith and higher learning. B. T. Roberts had pioneered this rich relationship in the Free Methodist tradition and Kevin later would write insightfully about it in *The Integrity Factor* and then in *Expressing Life*. Worth noting he would be anxious to add are related books by Kevin's good friend Jonathan Raymond, *Higher Higher Education,* the one by his own brother Jim, *Christian Liberal Arts: An Education that Goes Beyond*, and the one he considers a classic in the field, *The Idea of a Christian College* by Arthur F. Holmes.

Eventually Kevin would be traveling the world explaining and supporting institutions seeking to implement such Christian higher education. He was inspired by the earlier international work and educational commitment of his father, James Mannoia, Sr., who surely would be proud of the worldwide scope and substance of the eventual Christian service of all three of his children.[18]

The High School Maze

The freshman year of high school for Kevin Mannoia was spent at the Graded School in São Paulo, Brazil, where his sister Sharla was a senior. His brother Jim already had graduated from there and was back in the United States doing well academically. Kevin encountered high academic standards and his parents made his going there possible, whatever the cost. One day was particularly frightening for Kevin, the new freshman.

The bus driver suddenly took a new route home and the older kids started yelling with concern. Kevin didn't know why. Many of the others were children of senior corporate executives who could be asked to pay a substantial ransom to get their kids back. Such kidnapping was hardly unknown in that land of much poverty. That possibility hadn't crossed Kevin's mind. Who would want to kidnap a missionary's kid? Kevin smiles as he now remembers this day. "There's no money and you'd be making God mad!" Safely home without the feared incident happening, the family completed its Brazilian missionary assignment in 1970 and returned to the United States. The move, of course, put Kevin's education in motion again.

His sophomore year was spent at Atlantic City High School while his parents were doing missionary deputation work and living for a year at the Overseas Ministries Study Center in Ventnor, New Jersey. The family had a beautiful, fully-furnished apartment on Atlantic Avenue right across from the beach, a great blessing.

---

18 This biography is of Kevin Mannoia only. Given the extensive education and range of Christian service of his sister Sharla and older brother Jim, their stories would be exceedingly worth telling as well.

The facility had been built to provide easy re-entry of missionaries back into American culture.

Kevin was without his brother and sister, Jim in Boston and Sharla now in college in Illinois. He vacuum soon was replaced by his loving the fellowship of the other missionary kids and the fun of hanging out on the beach for the summer. In the winter he worked for a Jewish deli owner delivering groceries on a bicycle. Young Kevin even had some private theological stimulation. It was the first time he had met someone who believed in strong "predestination," one parent even saying he wasn't sure his own children were predestined!

Meanwhile, Kevin's father often traveled, including commuting weekly to teach a class at Trinity Evangelical Divinity School in Illinois where Kevin eventually would attend seminary. While his father studied and traveled, Kevin generally enjoyed himself, learning to surf and singing in one of the school choirs. His memory of school classrooms is vague. He was more of a people person. "My MO was to remain off the radar. The redeeming part of it was the Men's Glee Club."

After this generally delightful sophomore year of Kevin's, the family moved again, this time to cramped quarters on the second floor of an old hotel in Winona Lake, Indiana. It had been renamed "The International Friendship House" when purchased by the Free Methodist Church for its headquarters. Kevin was enrolled as a junior at nearby Warsaw High School and the family attended the Free Methodist congregation across the street from their new home. Once Kevin managed to get his driver's license, he loved driving the hotel pickup to the dump to get rid of trash. He also drove himself to school when his mother didn't need the family car. Otherwise, he car-pooled. No more threats of being kidnapped on a South American bus.

Cars would become something of a trademark of Kevin in later years. It began when he bought his first car during his senior in high school in North Chili, New York. It was with his own money, paying $75 to a neighbor for a 1967 VW Beetle. The running boards were rusted off but he worked on the problem with pride, painted the car a bright yellow, and it became an icon in the church youth group where his father was pastoring.

Kevin was frugal and seemed more than willing to take initiatives, if not in academics, then at least otherwise. In Warsaw High School he was something of an athlete and an especially excellent singer, active as a member of the school choir and tennis team. Like back in the New Jersey school, his focus still was not particularly on the classes and books. Although quite capable, they just weren't his main thing. He admits to being fine with "C" and "B" grades, valuing his musical, athletic, and social lives more than striving for top grades. He was more of a people person.

Warsaw was a typical Midwest town in northern Indiana, so much quieter and less crowded than the sprawling São Paulo, Brazil, that he had known and endured as a freshman. Kevin enjoyed this more relaxed atmosphere and, although not there long, was selected by Miss Voirol (choir director) as a member of the *European Sounds of Hope* choir that went to Scandinavia in the summer after his junior year. It was a great experience.

He had a crew cut when young, typical of the time, but with a related issue. "My cowlick presented no problem at first, but that changed when my hair was allowed to get longer." Then the scalp issue took regular attention, "tubes of hair crème, bobby pins, and even a nylon stocking each night to get that stubborn hair to bow to my will." Can anyone around the world now imagine the "polished" Kevin Mannoia with bobby pins in his hair and a night stocking on his head? Probably not!

While the junior year in Warsaw a really good one overall, there still was no chance for Kevin to settle down. His senior high school year would be spent in North Chili, New York, where his father was called as the Senior Pastor of the prominent Pearce Memorial

Free Methodist Church. Kevin now would drive each weekday to the Churchville-Chili High School while living in the parsonage of Pearce Memorial. Many youth from his father's church were attending this school, clearly easing the transition for Kevin.

Music again was a highlight. Kevin got heavily involved in the school's choir, and especially in a small octet known as the "Singing Saints," Miss Karen Babbes director. He even did a few solo "gigs" for women's clubs, although mostly with a group often called on for public concerts in the area. Kevin's high school commencement ceremony was held in the sanctuary Pearce Memorial Free Methodist Church, something of pride for the Mannoia graduate. The combination of school and church seemed a natural, as it always would for him.

Evaluating the years of his high school education generally, Kevin says this. "I remained a little reserved, although always finding a group to hang with. I didn't do much dating—always the new kid. I was just a plain guy in big schools." Older brother Jim says Kevin was quite shy when young. The socially saving factors after the freshman year in Brazil were music, athletics, and the church youth groups in which he always was active. Fortunate indeed is Kevin's general attitude about it all. "I was accustomed to moving and held no grudge for the work my parents were in. I treated it as an adventure."

Speaking for himself and his brother Jim and sister Sharla, Kevin says, "The education we received in Brazil was stellar and prepared us well for our American educations. It got my brother a scholarship to MIT and my sister honors at Greenville in French. When I was an incoming sophomore at Atlantic City High School, I knew I was coming from one of the more prominent private American schools in the world." Even so, strong academics was never his personal preoccupation when young. One might say he was more "well-rounded," a bright kid getting along rather well and generally having a good time.

The Brazilian background was an advantage, also an "adventure" to use Kevin's word. Being bi-lingual, English and Portuguese, was one result and a clear asset to Kevin's schooling and later ministries. He smiles when recalling that he could talk about people in front of them without them realizing it—he claims never nastily, of course! In years soon to come, his Portuguese would allow him to test out of a required language in college, with more advantages still to come.

He would make a required trip from North Chili to the State University of New York in Buffalo to test with a Portuguese professor there. "In ten minutes the prof told me I passed, that I spoke Portuguese better than he did." This language skill also would qualify as Kevin's research language for his later Ph.D. program at the University of North Texas. It allowed him to immediately start preaching in Spanish ("Spantuguese") in the churches he later would superintend in Texas and Southern California. People would graciously forgive his Portuguese accent when speaking Spanish.

Parents Jim and Florence, educators themselves, had insisted on quality education as a priority for their children, missionary and pastoral movements notwithstanding. For this, and the benefits of multi-culturalism in general, their children now all rise up and call them blessed.

Roberts Wesleyan a Default Choice

When time came for Kevin's senior year of high school, the Mannoias had relocated again, this time from Indiana to New York state in the home area of the beginnings of the Free Methodist Church. There sits the flagship college of that denomination, Roberts Wesleyan University, with Kevin's father called to be pastor of the adjacent college church, Pearce Memorial, perhaps the most influential church of the denomination.

Kevin soon graduated from nearby Churchville-Chili High School and was ready for his collegiate experience. The choice of where to go should have been almost automatic one would think. Roberts Wesleyan was right there, but it wasn't Kevin's first choice. He envisioned the future rather differently. While many of his high school friends were choosing to do the obvious, become freshmen at Roberts, Kevin had other ideas. The active military draft was still a concern as the Vietnam War was winding down and he considered joining the Air Force ROTC. He also was captivated by a big idea, being a United States ambassador to some country, maybe in Latin America (Brazil?).

This tantalizing thought likely was a lingering reflection of his having grown up overseas and already having experienced considerable mobility. He considered going to the American University in Washington, D.C., maybe focusing his study in political science. He actually managed to arrange an internship in a New York congressman's office in Washington, the usual way to launch a career in foreign service. After the senior year of high school, however, he went on a VISA trip to Brazil (Volunteers in Service Abroad) through the Free Methodist Church. This altered his path.

The trip was directed by a Mannoia family friend, Don Bowen, with its preparation staged on the campus of Roberts Wesleyan College where Kevin was living. Bowen thought Kevin, despite being young, would be a valuable team member given his previous experience in Brazil and his language skill in Portuguese. Kevin raised the money needed to go and it was a wonderful experience, although after the trip he had very little money left to start college. There would have to be a back-up plan.

The new plan was going to Roberts Wesleyan for the first year to take general education courses and then transfer to the American University for the political science specialization. He lived at home, just a block from the campus, and was awarded a nice discount of the tuition cost as a minister's son. By his sophomore year at

Roberts, however, he had developed a cluster of new friends and had gotten into a singing quartet. So he decided he would stay all four years, always living at home and re-evaluating his future goals.

Little did Kevin know or even dream that later he would serve on the Roberts governing Board of Trustees, advise two of the school's presidents, and one year be honored as the outstanding Roberts alumnus. By then he would have grown into an outstanding ambassador, although not for the government of the United States but for Jesus Christ. He would have become an aggressive advocate for Christian higher education, particularly in the Wesleyan tradition, and literally all over the world. All that, however, was still far in the future.

Kevin was naturally self-confident, even a bit ambitious he would admit. He remembers that at age nineteen a quite exciting life direction seemed clearly ahead for him. He would land one day in the president's office of some university or maybe be a bishop of his denomination, or maybe even be a leader in the U. S. State Department where some president would spot him and name him the ambassador to a prominent country.

"My upbringing, personality, experiences, and contacts all seemed to provide impeccable qualifications for such things." This rather cocky attitude now embarrasses him a bit. While hardly reflective of the humility of Jesus, it was rather reflective of young Kevin Mannoia. He was bright, full of personality, and surely going somewhere very special. The exact somewhere was still unknown.

Kevin loved the church but wanted to go on to different and maybe bigger and better things. Then it happened, an unexpected meeting with the Lord himself, somewhat like Saul on the road to Damascus. Lord announced to Kevin who he was and that he had other things in mind for this gifted young man. This tap on the shoulder was the Holy Spirit of God saying, "I don't see you in leadership outside the church, Kevin." Well, if not outside mused Kevin, "maybe at least toward the top inside?"

Some new thinking now became necessary. A hard choice was before Kevin. Would he serve himself *or God*? He would reflect this way years later. "I cannot imagine where I would be had I not obediently followed God on *the downward path to servanthood*."[19] He was beginning to learn that God's special way is a self-sacrificing path that, if followed humbly, always tends to lead *upward*. The pivotal day came toward the end of his sophomore year.

In his bedroom at home, guided in part by his father's wise advice, Kevin decided to change his college academic major from sociology to religion and philosophy. This change signaled the beginning of a long journey of church-oriented leadership formation. The goal increasingly would be maturing into the image of Christ and doing whatever naturally flows from that image. Kevin was beginning to think that his future was intended by God to be in top church leadership. President of a school? Bishop of the church? Maybe, likely, at least church-related and high-level.

He began watching college presidents closely when he had the chance and was convinced that, in order to serve effectively, they needed strong theological preparation and pastoral experience. Kevin wondered if it were acceptable spiritually for him to aspire to such top-level leadership, a question that would stay with him well into adulthood. He began to envision a five-year plan for himself involving seminary training and a doctoral degree, maybe leading to a campus presidency for himself (better, *for God*).

Various faculty members were particularly helpful. Harry Anderson taught New Testament, Stanley Magill Greek, and Barbara Rose math. Mike Peterson specialized in philosophy and was young and exciting. Choir was a highlight experience for Kevin over all four of his years at Roberts, easily overcoming his disappointment at losing his run for student body vice-president. He did have an early romance which broke up in his senior year.

---

19   Found in Kevin's personal journal, September, 1998.

Meanwhile, he replaced his 1967 VW Beetle with a Pontiac Catalina convertible. Things were ready to move on.

Kevin's friends were many, natural for him. Terri Douglas was called "Radar" because he was an exact image of the character Radar on *MASH*. Eric Logan was a great vocalist who one day would join Kevin on the school's Board of Trustees. A couple of others would be seminary professors one day, Joel Hunt teaching at Azusa Pacific University and then Fuller Seminary. All of the ministerial students would graduate and go to Asbury Seminary, Kevin being the first to apply but, oddly enough, the only one not to actually go.

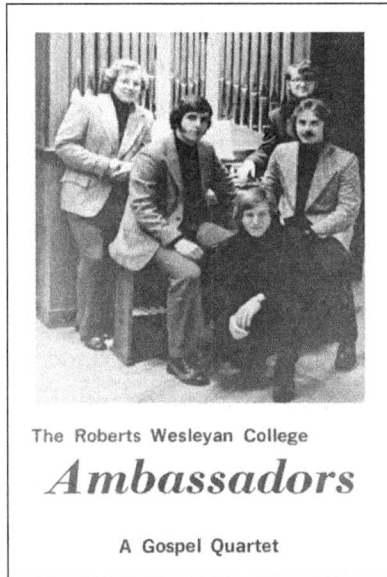

The Roberts Wesleyan College

Ambassadors

A Gospel Quartet

Sideburned Kevin, always musical.

Finally he earned the B.A. with a major in religion and philosophy and a GPA of 3.2. He was satisfied with this academic level. It was good enough and had allowed him time to pursue a "rounded" life—good car, girlfriend, lots of music and friends. "I realized that I wasn't a single-minded academic but enjoyed multi-tasking, like I always have."

The first question to be faced after college was, which seminary for a graduate-level ministerial education? The answer at first was obvious, Asbury Theological Seminary in Wilmore, Kentucky. That was the typical Free Methodist path for emerging ministers. The obvious, however, wouldn't be the eventual reality in Kevin's case. Regardless, quality would mark what was to come in further education and service to the church. Twenty years after Kevin's college graduation, President Crothers of Kevin's Roberts alma mater would be congratulating him as Bishop Kevin Mannoia and Alumnus of the Year. Something had gone very right in the meantime.

The Moses Model

"Pharaoh's Court" reflects Kevin Mannoia's paradigm of Christian leadership development.[20] Moses was the great leader of God's people through decades in the wilderness. He had learned the system of politics and control prevailing in Egypt. He had watched up close as Pharaoh led that great nation, and he learned things not to do and then to do as a leader once God had him leading his people out of slavery to the promised land. Egypt was the best of higher education at the time, at least in a secular sense and with selfishness and power at the core. Servant leadership at first was a foreign concept that Moses would have to learn later, especially when facing the divine flames of a burning bush.

A key context for Kevin's future ministry would be the general deterioration of Christian higher education in America across the twentieth century. As the culture of the nation changed, so did the church's higher education. There was a growing estrangement of faith from learning, a rift between church and academy. Reports a dear friend of Kevin. "The hope in the private, Christian sector is

---

20   See Kevin Mannoia's book *The Integrity Factor.*

that graduates will go out into the world and address the world's needs for leadership in both competence and character after the likeness of Jesus Christ. It is possible for colleges and universities in the Wesleyan-Holiness tradition to reclaim their full heritage in ways that transform *higher* education into *highest* education."[21]

Such reclaiming soon would become a key aspect of Kevin's ministry mission. He would seek to duplicate the Moses model to a significant extent. That is, like Moses he would be privileged to observe great leaders in action. However, like Moses eventually did, he also would learn the proper motives and mechanics of effective divine-style leadership, but only while encountering a burning bush and yielding to becoming a true servant of God and God's people.

How does one lead in God's ways and for God's purposes, not for one's private and selfish ends? The journey toward the answer would be long and not easy for either Moses or Kevin. Young Kevin would find himself turning slowly and by stages toward the fundamental life goal of being a true servant of God, not a puppet anxious to mimic any of today's power-oriented pharaohs.

The primary symbol of proper Christian leadership would be Moses at the burning bush, not Moses admiring the powerful throne of Pharaoh. Like Moses, the big life decision for Kevin would turn out to be having less to do with natural abilities and learned skills, although he has plenty of both, and more with the foundation on which identity is built and out of which God-like leadership activity naturally flows.

Like Moses, Kevin would find himself called to be a servant *of God,* not of state, empire, denomination, para-church religious organization, or even the people to whom he would minister. The "integrity factor" would be his lifelong faithfulness to the divine call to have formed within a "deeper character," that of being "in

---

21   Jonathan S. Raymond, *Higher Higher Education.*

Christ." Out of such character comes "a natural flow of behaviors *after the pattern of Jesus.*"

Moses suffered in the wilderness from the people becoming frustrated, angry, looking to other gods, even wanting to go back to Egyptian slavery. Kevin soon would learn the same about Christian congregations and other institutions that can turn on their leaders. Whatever the cost, he would dedicate himself to being a burning-bush leader Moses. A large part of the goal for Kevin would be working in a servant manner to halt the secular drift and restore the theological understanding and mission integrity of God's people and their institutions of higher education.

Christian colleges and universities clearly can drift and decline. Their Christ-centered priorities subtly can shift to accommodating those who pay the bills and want their own felt needs and standards met. The centeredness of church institutions can slowly change for the worse, going from "in and for Christ" to "by and for the people." This explains much of the history of Christian higher education over the past four centuries. However, Kevin would come to insist that it's possible to avoid the drift from faith as the core institutional commitment. It must happen by rediscovering and reclaiming the first love, the prime commitment to God and his kingdom's presence and transformation of individuals and their societies. It remains possible to go on to new heights of a Christian *higher* higher education.[22]

John Wesley's theology of spiritual formation is central to Kevin's personal church heritage. He would come to value highly how Wesley brings clarity and balance to classic Christian orthodoxy. This eighteenth-century leader was a don at Oxford where he taught Greek. He had his students read and discuss with him the

---

22 Geneva College in Pennsylvania continues to take this matter seriously, saying this. "Starting with the belief that God is the source of all truth, education becomes the exciting adventure of seeking to appropriate knowledge in all its various facets under the guidance of the Holy Spirit. Education that is Christian takes for its perspective the biblical view of God, humankind, and the universe in their mutual relations." Kevin Mannoia would applaud.

writings of the early church fathers like Clement of Rome, Justin Martyr, Irenaeus, Gregory of Nyssa, Vincent of Lerius, Cyril of Alexandria, and others.

Wesley's immersion in the apostolic and patristic writings, discussions, and records of the early councils and synods shaped his "conjunctive" theology of salvation from the darkest of sin to the restoring light of holiness and Christ-likeness. His grasp of Spirit-filled, classic Christian thought makes possible a foundation of orthodoxy on which we can build a *higher* higher learning redirected toward the highest of spiritual ends. This theological vision of spiritual formation and educational philosophy came to Kevin in part through the Free Methodist heritage of B. T. Roberts.

The roots of this vision, of course, lie in the New Testament's revealing of the heart of the Christian faith itself. Paul makes this clear when he prays that the Ephesians will be rooted and established in love so that they may know Christ's love "that surpasses knowledge" (Eph. 3:19a). There is knowledge that integrates the head and heart, and such knowledge can bring a crisis experience of being "filled to the measure of the fullness of God," Christian holiness (Eph. 3:19b).[23]

It's possible, then, even urgently necessary to offer a higher form of Christian higher education, one that stimulates personal and social transformation. Such leads to a purity of heart that engages the broken world with the healing grace of God. In so doing, it's possible and necessary for colleges, universities, and seminaries in the Wesleyan-Holiness tradition of Christianity to reclaim their full heritage in ways that elevate *higher* education into *highest* Christian education. Therein would lie a coming life goal of Kevin Mannoia.

What, then, is the Moses model of faithful leadership? Exodus 3 identifies its basic elements. One must encounter God, remove

---

23   For a contemporary exploration of the biblical roots and social meanings of Christian holiness, see the book commissioned by the Wesleyan Holiness Connection later founded by Kevin Mannoia, Barry L. Callen's *Christian Holiness* (2023).

shoes in humility, hear God's intent to save his people, and accept the "impossible" call to declare to Pharaoh that freedom must come, and putting one's own life on the line to help make it so. The leader to the freedom offered by God must know that it's God who leads and only God who can bring success.

In the years ahead beyond college, Kevin Mannoia would dare to grasp and share this leadership vision and transformation potential worldwide. First, however, his own education had to be completed and his willingness to be a Moses on his knees would have to grow considerably.

CHAPTER FIVE

A SURPRISING SEMINARY

A strategic life plan had invaded the mind and heart of young Kevin Mannoia. It now was the general guiding light if not yet a life-transforming burning bush. Beyond college would come years of deliberate preparation for some key role in church leadership, probably in Christian higher education. Needed would be a three-year seminary education followed by years of graduate study at the doctoral level, ideally while pastoring a church.

The standard first step for a young Free Methodist like Kevin was graduating from Roberts Wesleyan University and going to Asbury Theological Seminary in Kentucky. Despite normal expectations and the plans of many of his ministerial friends at Roberts Wesleyan, Wilmore was not to be for Kevin. His father's earlier teaching contact with another seminary outside the Wesleyan tradition helped lead to a surprising decision. It was made necessary because of a clerical error in Kentucky. God works in the strangest of ways at times!

The educational compass suddenly swung in a most unusual direction for young Kevin Mannoia. It tilted oddly because of a previous poor impression, a father's earlier contacts, a clerical error, and the personal urging of one of the more famous evangelical Christian scholars of the twentieth century. God appeared to have much in mind for Kevin's future. Now a set of unlikely circumstances gathered about him to make it so in a surprising way.

Completing college early, Kevin began to work on his strategic life plan. He enrolled for two graduate classes at a nearby state university campus to get an early start on an eventual Ph.D. after seminary. The classes were in higher education administration and finance, further exciting his interest in such a future for himself. Since these classes weren't that demanding for him, he also began taking flying lessons.

After an introductory ride over Niagara Falls at dusk, he was hooked. Kevin's flying instructor emphasized the "performance edges" of the aircraft and the danger of violating any one of them. Once, being very nervous, he put the plane into a spiral dive and the instructor had to take control from him. After a few more lessons and mastering his nerves, he tested and received his pilot's license. The joy of flying finally had replaced the fear of crashing, a valuable early lesson for his life in general.[24]

Meanwhile, his graduating pre-ministerial friends at Roberts were all heading to Asbury Theological Seminary. Kevin recalls being the first in the group to apply there but something was wrong. His acceptance letter was the only one that never arrived. Would he not be accepted? Why? His grades weren't the very best but clearly not that bad. His father was a prominent minister and former missionary of the Free Methodist Church. What else could the seminary possibly want?

There were no answers. All Kevin knew was that apparently the seminary was still waiting on more information, though never detailing what that was. A clerical problem related to his two graduate classes at the state institution was the culprit, but that wouldn't be learned until much later. It was an accidental and very significant occurrence in an office at Asbury, one critical indeed for Kevin's future.

---

24 Later Kevin would use this learning image to express the better way to live the Christian life and be the church God intends in a hurting world. See his *Church 2K,* chapter four. One must learn to focus on the freedom of the center while not violating the "performance edges."

Meanwhile, Kevin's father convened a Bible Conference in his Pearce Memorial congregation with guest leader Dr. Carl F. H. Henry, who spent four days in the Mannoia home. The men knew each other from the time when Rev. Mannoia had flown weekly from New Jersey to Chicago to teach a class at Trinity Evangelical Divinity School. On hearing about Kevin's frustration at the delayed acceptance at Asbury, Henry suggested that Kevin apply to Trinity.

He did apply to Trinity while still waiting on Asbury, was accepted quickly, then would face the problem of having no financial aid—the Free Methodist Church would have covered the majority of the tuition cost at Asbury but not at Trinity. Regardless, explains Kevin now, shifting seminary plans to Trinity "set my focus on a much bigger view of the church. Providentially, it was the best thing that could have happened to me."

Kenneth Kantzer, founding dean of Trinity Evangelical Divinity School, called his colleague Carl F. H. Henry "the dean of evangelical theologians." Henry, personally encouraging Kevin's future at Trinity, had been one of the founders in 1949 of the Evangelical Theological Society and before that of the National Association of Evangelicals, an organization to be become very important in Kevin Mannoia's future. It likely would not have been had Kevin gone to Asbury Theological Seminary.[25]

To Trinity for Seminary

Since Asbury Seminary had failed for yet-unknown reasons to offer a student acceptance to Kevin, despite his reasonable academic background and prominent Free Methodist identity, Trinity Evangelical Divinity School in Illinois would become his surprising

---

25 Carl F. H. Henry also was key to the founding of Fuller Theological Seminary in California and the major evangelical publication *Christianity Today*. Meeting Henry at this key decisional time in Kevin Mannoia's life was later viewed a true God thing.

seminary home. New problems immediately arose because of this choice, especially financial ones, but none big enough to block progress on Kevin's strategic life plan, now to begin on this surprising Illinois campus.

He first would do a three-year seminary program full-time and then a Ph.D. program while pastoring somewhere for about five years. That presumably would lead to some prominent leadership position in the Free Methodist Church or one of its institutions of higher education. So off he went to Illinois and exposure to a different Christian tradition and some of the best evangelical scholars of the time.

Kevin scrambled, but at least he knew that he had family in Wheaton, Illinois, and of course his father had grown up in the Chicago area and once had taught part-time at Trinity. Kevin would need a job and a place to live, so he contacted an area Free Methodist pastor and landed an assistant pastoral role in youth ministry and outreach at the Evanston Free Methodist Church. After packing his little sports car, he arrived on the seminary campus.

Not able to afford campus housing, Kevin saw and followed up on a bulletin board posting. It was about a widow, Edna Chadwell, who wanted someone to live in and help care for her gorgeous home. It wasn't located far from the Evanston church where Kevin would serve for a year. He interviewed and landed the job and a place to live. It was an excellent beginning to a three-year seminary adventure.

When initially on the Evanston church platform, Kevin experienced something new, a bit strange to him at first before coming to seem quite reasonable. The pastor always wore a black robe when preaching and he had a green one for Kevin to wear. Young Kevin, rather self-conscious, caught himself looking at what people were wearing and realizing that likely they also were examining what he had on. The robes blocked such worship distractions. This church experience was enjoyed greatly by Kevin. It was a good way to begin ministry while also beginning seminary. A first church leadership experience can be critical for a young pastor's entire ministry. In this case, the young minister was blessed.

The Chadwell home was in a very exclusive portion of the Chicago area, with servant's quarters where a guest could live. Kevin had interviewed and hired, receiving free housing in exchange for helping with various tasks and caring for the home when the owner went to Florida for the winter. There's where Kevin would live for three years, with the immediate neighbors being wealthy families in the pharmaceutical (Searle) and food industries (Kraft).

The Chadwell home, Evanston church, and Trinity seminary were relatively close together on the North Shore of Lake Michigan. It was an excellent garden area for the good growing of a young and rather ambitious minister. Culturally and even somewhat theologically, it was quite a distance from Wilmore, Kentucky (Asbury Seminary). God sometimes does seem to work in strange ways, and surely was at work in the ministerial development of a young Mannoia man with considerable potential.

After one seminary year, Kevin went home for the summer and then returned to learn that the Evanston pastor had been moved and his assistant position was no longer available. Fortunately, a Free Methodist denominational leader inquired about Kevin's willingness to work with a group of strong lay leaders who were planting a new congregation in nearby Wheaton. Kevin agreed and shortly would be a "wet-behind-the-ears" seminary student serving part-time as the "pastor" of these venturing believers.

These were exceptionally capable people who treated their part-time seminary pastor well. He would drive there twice a week, visit and arrange the services, often getting guest speakers and sometimes preaching himself. The group met in the recording studio of one of the prominent members. At the end of Kevin's second seminary year, he went home again for the summer and while gone the new congregation employed its first full-time pastor. Some kind of new employment would need to be found for seminary year three.

Randy Discher arrived as a new Trinity student in Kevin's second year of seminary and they quickly became great friends. Randy had a painting background and formed a little company with Kevin agreeing to be his partner—one that knew nothing about painting. They found plenty of work among the rich of the area, pulling snow off steep slate roofs in the winter (the weight could be dangerous) and renewing the beauty of interior walls inside the homes of people prepared to pay well for good work. Randy would do the talking while Kevin would "hide behind his coattails." Randy bid the jobs, bought the paint, and then together they would have a blast earning badly needed money.

"It was really good money," recalls Kevin. How fortunate since he couldn't afford a campus meal plan. Sometimes he would "pig out" on the evening meal, adequate for the whole day. He once suggested to Randy that they call their little company "M. D. Painting," explaining that it stood for Mannoia/Discher. Randy wanted to know why Kevin's name came first. "Because it's a play on words and I have to come first!" That attitude wasn't quite the servanthood model of Moses. Considerable growth was still needed on the front. If Moses was transformed in the presence of God's burning bush, Kevin's bush was still being ignited.

Kevin always has been a natural leader however much he did or did not know about the business at hand. Years later when he would become a seminary dean himself in California, he would explain this to his faculty. "I am a churchman, not a scholar, so I plan to learn much from you folks." As dean, he would be the administrative leader even if those he would supervise were more knowledgeable of aspects of the operation and had been present much longer. This kind of awkward circumstance would be a life-long challenge since often Kevin would wind up being the leader while needing to learn how best to handle the notoriety, challenges, and distractions of being the one "on top."

Thanks especially to Randy, the M/D men were able to do good work most of the time. There was that day when Kevin accidentally bumped a large can of paint off a ladder. It spilled on a dark-wood floor that fortunately was usually under a large throw rug. The two theologs worked frantically to clean it up before the owner came home, managing rather well and covering up any leftovers with the rug. Teasingly, Randy, later the longtime pastor of a large Evangelical Free Church, says he still isn't sure if these two paint-happy representatives of Jesus should confess to the owner, repenting of any damage that was permanent. Kevin thinks they did confess, although admitting that "this could be my mind trying to wash away guilt!"

Kevin later would teasingly be called by some the "Italian Stallion" (the Mannoia family being from Sicily). He had some insecurities but still always seemed confident and influential, dating about anyone he wanted on the Trinity campus and driving like the Italians supposedly do. Once Randy trusted him to teach Debbie to drive a stick-shift car. She was Randy's girl-friend and he could get frustrated with her slow learning. He couldn't manage this without some unwanted tension. He knew, however, that Kevin could manage with a calmness that wouldn't threaten to steal her away for himself. Kevin taught, Debbie learned, and her relationship with Randy was saved. It was early ministry at its best, stick shift, paint brush and all.

The Rich Trinity Experience

The third seminary year for Kevin was mostly about finishing the degree, courting his new friend Kathy, and earning as much as possible to support whatever they would need should they marry. One can't now speak with Kevin long without his raising the subject of Kathy, God's great gift in his life. She and Kevin began dating during his final year in seminary, although he knew her casually for all three years. She was a student at the adjacent Trinity College that shared the dining room with the seminary. Kathleen Ann Knudsen certainly had caught Kevin's eye.

She and Kevin occasionally would joke around over meals in the dining room but didn't start dating formally until her last year in college, his third in seminary. By then Kevin was working as a student in the college development office. One day she came by on her way to chapel and asked him to go with her.

His response? "Clearly, I said yes!" She may not have thought of this chapel occasion as a "date," but he did. Their first real date came shortly after. It was at a dollar theater seeing the movie *The In-laws*. She now comments with a touch of humor, "Maybe a bit prophetic." She was about to meet some real in-laws.

Having his pilot's license, Kevin soon rented a single-engine Cessna airplane so he could attend his niece's baptism back in Winona Lake, Indiana. It was the daughter of his sister Sharla. Kathy agreed to go along. He was concerned afterward that maybe she wasn't overly impressed with his flying. They did have to make an unscheduled stop because she got a little air-sick. Had he kept the cabin too warm? She says no, she's just a bit inclined to motion sickness. Regardless, he was pleased that the lovely Kathy had agreed to a dating relationship and had been willing to take to the air with him to meet his family—a good sign of an even better tomorrow!

Meanwhile, they explored common interests. He loved basketball and football and played tennis. Kathy preferred baseball, especially the Chicago Cubs. Unfortunately, Kevin thought of baseball as "largely a waste of time and space. It's slow-moving and the only good part is the hotdogs." However, over time, his preferences notwithstanding, their relationship would develop and become lifelong. "She's bought into my sports and I grudgingly got along with hers."

A critical mystery in Kevin's early life finally had been solved. No word had ever come from Asbury about its failure to admit him as a seminary student. A church leader finally had contacted the seminary in Kentucky and asked why. During Kevin's second year at Trinity, his parents had moved to Asbury so his father could join that faculty. On a visit to his parents soon after, Kevin was informed that the seminary president, Frank Stanger, wanted to meet with the Mannoia father and son.

Kevin's incomplete admission folder was on the president's desk and immediately a sincere apology was offered to Kevin. Said Dr. Stanger, "It had been a clerical error by one of our staff members who had not checked one required box. Why? Because all transcript information had not been received. Those two graduate courses taken in a nearby state institution in New York were wrongly assumed to have been part of the undergraduate experience and not showing on Kevin's college transcript."

Asked the president, "Kevin, would you transfer to Asbury? We would be delighted to have you!" The answer was a respectful negative. By then Kevin felt that going to Trinity, while merely because of a clerical error, was "hugely providential." That's where he would meet Kathy, his wonderful future wife, and where he would become acquainted with the larger evangelical Christian world, particularly the Evangelical Free Church sponsoring the seminary and the church home of one of its upcoming leaders, his dear friend Randy Discher.

Trinity Evangelical Divinity School also is where Kevin was having opportunity to learn from some of the best minds in the Christian world of the time, names he proudly recalls were "iconic in their fields of specialization." He was sure that he was being more broadly exposed to Christian thought and institutions than Asbury would have been able to provide him at the time.

A young school, Trinity was incorporated in 1963 and located in Deerfield, Illinois. Kenneth Kantzer held a Ph.D. in Philosophy and Religion from Harvard University and was elected the founding Dean. His vision was creating a divinity school that would provide a university environment of biblical studies where world class scholars would produce world class students, the "Harvard" of all the seminaries in the world. Kevin recalled his own father having such a vision for the Free Methodist seminary in Brazil, even if on a much more modest scale.

Affiliated with the Evangelical Free Church of America, Trinity was hardly representative of the Wesleyan church tradition of the Mannoias. Even so, it strongly affirmed biblical authority[26] and offered what it considered the best of academics in all of theological education. Soon its faculty included Gleason Archer, Norman Geisler, Wayne Grudem, Walter Kaiser, Jr., John Warwick Montgomery, John Oswalt, Clark H. Pinnock, D. A. Carson, and Carl F. H. Henry, certainly a first-class line-up!

Although deeply committed to the Wesleyan-Holiness Christian tradition of Free Methodism, Kevin's father was respectful of the highest of academic standards and had taught as an adjunct at Trinity soon after the family's return from Brazil. As pastor of the Pearce Memorial Church in North Chili, New York, Jim and Florence had hosted in their home none other than Carl F. H. Henry, who had engaged young Kevin about where he was intending to go to seminary. He naturally had steered him toward Trinity.

Without question, Trinity was a stimulating academic setting in the 1970s when Kevin was completing his college education. Located north of Chicago, not far from Lake Michigan and O'Hare Airport, one of the busiest in the world, this seminary was a dynamic and influential place, in many ways ideal for Kevin as it would turn out, even if an unusual and unexpected place for a young Free Methodist seminarian.

---

26 The biblical stance included a strong "inerrancy" emphasis, something Kevin signed as an incoming student, "ignorantly" he later would say. Now unwilling to sign such a statement, he muses that likely he couldn't get into Trinity as he did years ago.

This Illinois campus is where theologian Clark Pinnock had just been for five years as a celebrated professor. He at first had been a leading modern-day "fundamentalist," although increasingly was being tempered by his love of new insights, willingness to be creative, and hunger to learn and grow. While at Trinity (1969-1974), Pinnock had moved away from the rigid framework of strict Calvinism to a considerably more dynamic way, a Wesleyan way of doing theology. He was drawn especially to relational thinking about God, clearly away from the all-determining monarch and law enforcer view of the divine. Clark came to understand that the very essence of God is love. Thus, God relates to humans personally, primarily as parent, lover, and covenant partner.

What had dawned on Pinnock while at Trinity, and quite against its institutional grain, was that in our human dealings with God there is "a profound mutuality." Previously he had thought "it would be wonderful to possess absolute truths, based on heavenly oracles, yielding black and white doctrinal and ethical maxims." Once one buys into this framework of thinking, it takes time for doubts about its philosophical validity and theological appropriateness to dawn. Pinnock was finding a different path that would make him a progressive evangelical pioneer in the decades to follow.[27]

Kevin missed being taught personally by Pinnock at Trinity, but later they did become friends, Kevin hosting him at Azusa Pacific University and in his nearby home. They had come to share considerable commonality, including Pinnock's fresh appreciation for the rich Wesleyan theological tradition. Kevin had come to realize that his Free Methodist heritage functions on "more of a track than a rail," more relationally than propositionally, more focused on central truths than insisting on agreement

---

27 See the intellectual biography of Clark H. Pinnock by Barry Callen, *Clark H. Pinnock: Journey Toward Renewal*, especially chapter four. See also *Bible Reading in Wesleyan Ways*, eds. Barry Callen and Richard Thompson.

with narrow views of marginal matters. He loves this about his home denomination.

Kevin had come to Trinity without a thick layer of Calvinistic fundamentalism as did many of the students. He would leave deeply grateful for the experience in general, although struggling with some of its emphases and style. For instance, having joined the Evangelical Theological Society, typical of most Trinity graduates, he later would attend an ETS meeting in Dallas where he then would be pastoring. Norman Geisler of Trinity was prominent there in the effort to "take apart at the knees" people like Robert Gundry and Clark Pinnock for violating the Society's strict stance on biblical "inerrancy." He was doing so, at least in Kevin's eyes, in the most "un-grace-filled" ways. Gundry was forced out of the Society, causing Kevin to quit and never attend again. "What happened was just unfair."

Kevin admits to seeking a "holistic experience" as a seminary student, willing to give up a top grade in order to have time for an active social life, being "a real person," much as he had done in college. He would say that he is a "churchman" rather than an academic scholar. His churchmanship is characterized by a graciousness that allows breadth of thought and insists on a warm relationality in attitudes and thinking. To him, the aggressive narrowness of Norman Geisler in Dallas was a violation of the very person of Jesus. Kevin has hoped to be the opposite of that himself.

God's Special Times and Gifts

It's likely that Kevin Mannoia's seminary experience did cause a modest drift from some aspects of his Free Methodist heritage, although loyalty to that denomination would be strong and lifelong. Since he knew no one at Trinity with enough knowledge of the Wesleyan tradition, he had to go to a faculty member at Greenville University of the Free Methodist Church to complete his required course in the history and polity of his home church body.[28] In the required paper for this course, he testified to searching for the deep meanings of Christian conversion and holiness and finding in this search a life-change for himself.

Dating his own spiritual milestones, like personal conversion and sanctification, is difficult for Kevin, even if expected by many evangelicals. At age eleven during the Illinois-Wisconsin Conference campmeeting was probably the time of his conversion to Christ. As to sanctification, if a date is needed, it most likely was in the middle of his seminary years when he came to understand the need of the deeper spiritual life. He had come to increased personal awareness of "the pervasive work of God," although preferring to leave the precise dating of spiritual experiences ambiguous. Labeling such milestones for him is an imprecise process at best.

To be fair, the non-Wesleyan environment at Trinity was hardly intended to be actively anti-Wesleyan. The experience there was a healthy stretch for Kevin, a definite educational enrichment yielding a broader view of the Christian faith tradition. Having completed the special arrangement course on Free Methodism and nearing graduation, Kevin was ordained an Elder in the Free Methodist Church. His seminary experience on the whole had been in an unexpected location and yet a welcome gift to his future ministry.

In 2003 Kevin would be ministering in Africa and reflecting back on his life journey to that point. He was amazed at the grace and providence of God that he now could see had been shaping him over the decades. Surfacing for him was the principle of "different not better," something "sown into the fiber of my very being from the start." Regardless of being unexpected and unusual, his parents had been pleased with his going to Trinity. He had learned there from major names in the mainstream of the evangelical world, something that later would help his perceived credibility

---

28   For some years later, Kevin's brother Jim would be the president of this Free Methodist campus.

in a coming role like the presidency of the National Association of Evangelicals.

Oddly enough, Kevin's learning and relationships at Trinity also "cemented my understanding of and anchored my commitment to the Wesleyan holiness stream of the faith." He had developed a style of academic excellence and theological positioning that is gracious and allows for an appreciation of diverse thinking. That style would be central in Kevin's future ministry.

CHAPTER SIX

MY HOME A HAVEN

> I remain amazed at the character, faithfulness, and confi-
> dence of Kathy. I know all she has ever wanted was a
> peaceful life for us centered at home. She has worked
> hard to maintain her vow to make our home a haven. The
> rapid and high-profile changes I have walked us through
> certainly have tested that resolve.
>
> While I'm sure she's happy, she has been concerned
> about what my various positions of leadership would do
> to me and the impact they would have on our family. She's
> patient and so trusting in the Lord. She's a gift of God and
> I love her so. Our kids have had their share of growing up
> difficulties, but they now are amazing adults and believ-
> ers in the Lord! How thankful I am for my haven home.[29]

Such private reflections of Kevin Mannoia come after many years
of his completing higher education and filling prominent leadership roles as pastor, superintendent, bishop, president, seminary
dean, and consultant to Christian institutions around the globe.
Stories about the dizzying array of these ministries are still to come.
Seen here first is an important fact about a relationally supportive
context always there for Kevin, whatever he would do and wherever he would do it.

Kathy always has been the loving and supportive wife behind
the scenes, nurturing and assisting her husband and protecting
their home and family from any unnecessary disruptions. The

---

29   Family reflections from the personal journal of Kevin Mannoia.

three Mannoia children soon were part of the family scene, some-times struggling, always stretching, and definitely enriching. Kevin has been blessed to have a home that has been a consistent haven from the storms he would endure and sometimes create.

Kathleen Ann (Knudsen) Mannoia is the lovely Danish girl who was homecoming queen in high school. She had become the apple of Kevin's eye as he was attending seminary. In the busy years to come, she sometimes would travel with him or at least always be there when he got home. She would listen to his anxieties, help with his unanswered questions, and bolster his faith in God no matter the difficult circumstance at hand. She would be a gift of God. No wonder Kevin loves her so.

His love also has been lavished on their children, even on their dog. When Kevin heard that the poor thing had to be put down while he was away, he started to cry. Pepper was so loyal, always there, always so happy to see him. This prominent leader among the Lord's people actually asked God if it would be possible to allow pets into heaven. No answer is reported, but one thing is clear. Kathy has been a heavenly companion over the years, regu-larly securing for Kevin the peace and stability of their home.

Any house of theirs would be a haven for him, in large part because of Kathy. When home came to include the three kids, Kevin would say that they were icing on the cake. Kristyn, Chris-topher, and Corey were sweet and loved additions, sometimes chal-lenging but always sweet and loved. They were high-potential and quite different from each other, such joy while being just kids.

The Heart of the Home

Kathleen Ann Knudsen was born in LaGrange, Illinois, in April, 1958. Since her parents were married in June, 1957, she appar-ently was a honeymoon baby. How good to begin life in the flush of fresh love. The Knudsens were living in Western Springs, IL, in the home where Kathy's father had grown up. They were faithful attenders of LaGrange Bible Church.

The family moved to Nashville, Tennessee, when Kathy was five so her father could produce the monthly magazine of Gideons International. He had technical and advertising skills as well as Christian commitment. They became Southern Baptists for five years, with Kathy baptized at age eight before the family moved back to Wheaton, Illinois, in 1969. Now they were members of Evangel Baptist Church where Kathy finished her growing up and faith formation.

Her dad was the choir director and song leader and her mother the piano player of Evangel Baptist. Dad was still specializing in advertising, now including work for some Christian colleges. One day he was on the campus of nearby Trinity College (now Trinity International University) for business. Kathy was along and on the lookout for a college for herself where she could be comfortable, close to home but not too close. A self-confessed "homebody," Kathy knew for sure that she didn't want Wheaton where her mother had gone to school.

Kathy decided she liked the relatively small Trinity. Now, with decades having passed, and with a warm smile on her face, she says this was a lucky (providential) choice on her part since that's where she would first meet the young seminarian Kevin Mannoia. She left music as a major, deciding it was more work than fun. Instead, she took every history course available. Graduating in 1980, Kathy walked across the platform a few credits short, soon to be completed in Texas by correspondence. Why Texas? That's where Kevin comes back into the picture. She would be in Texas married to him, leaving behind her younger siblings Marybeth, Ginny, and Billy.

Trinity was both a college and seminary campus. Admittedly, it was an odd place for Kevin Mannoia to be a ministerial student since his family were loyal Free Methodists, hardly Baptists, and Trinity had no relationship with either of these traditions. Regardless, that's where Kevin and Kathy met. On only their second date he, with his private pilot's license, rented an airplane and flew to the Warsaw airport near Winona Lake, Indiana, then the North American headquarters of Free Methodism and where the family had lived for a year.

The purpose of this date and destination was the baptism of Yvi Martin, Kevin's niece, daughter of Dave & Sharla Martin. Dave had grown up there and his parents were still there. It also a convenient chance for Kathy to meet Mother and Father Mannoia. Jim and Florence drove up from Wilmore, Kentucky, where by then he was on faculty. Kathy found them all a delight, no problem even though they weren't Baptists and she still was just getting acquainted with their younger son. The senior Mannoias were well-educated people, former Christian missionaries, worthy representatives of a wider world for which Kathy seemed open and quite ready.

There already were hints of a serious relationship already brewing between Kevin and Kathy. Their first kiss came on this occasion in Winona Lake. It was sweet and the baptism of Yvi, daughter of Kevin's sister Sharla, spiritually moving, conducted by Rev. James Mannoia, Sr. It was based on a commitment to Christ that later would mature into a quality Christian leader.[30]

Kevin got Kathy home safely and continued to use his pilot's license on occasion, especially if it meant a chance to go back toward the New York state area that he knows so well from college years. Curt Morgan had married earlier and the couple wanted to honeymoon at Niagara Falls but couldn't afford such a lovely luxury. Kevin knew that area well and personally flew them over the Falls, a lavish generosity gladly offered to good friends.

Meanwhile, Kathy and Kevin dated from September, 1979, until the big proposal day in January, 1980. By then they both were sure this was leading to marriage, although Kevin had told her

---

30   Currently Rev. Yvi Martin is a United Methodist pastor in Kansas City.

that there would be no ring. After all, he was a poor Free Methodist seminarian. They did go shopping once, not to buy a ring but
secretly to allow him to learn what she really liked. Unknown to her,
he proceeded to buy a diamond from a seminary friend, one left
over from a failed relationship. He had it newly set by a jeweler in
her home church, someone trusted to keep the secret. Then Kevin
went to her father, Al Knudsen, who owned a Christian advertising agency and was having an old home updated. Kevin actually
did some paint scraping and clean-up work for him, an echo of his
brief painting "career."

This historic visit between two men was in a little diner across
the tracks in Wheaton. The purpose was for Kevin to announce his
intent to marry Kathy and then to seek her father's blessing. He
makes it clear that he was not asking the father's *permission*, just
his *blessing*. "I was rather full of myself at the time!" The father
readily agreed to the marriage intent but stressed the importance
of an engagement ring in the Knudsen family. Kevin talked of
humility and simplicity and little money in the future of a poor
preacher. Kevin then was offered a loan for an engagement ring (a
recycled one already had been purchased). No funds were needed
or accepted.

Kevin now had what he wanted, except for Kathy's formal
agreement. He selected a key time and asked Kathy out for a nice
dinner date. His request was that she wear a red dress, his favorite
color. Instead of going straight to dinner, however, he took her to
Mrs. Chadwell's home where he lived and worked as a seminarian.
Kathy was directed to a seat in a lovely alcove already prepared with
a vase of roses, one stem carrying the ring. Down on one knee, the
surprise ring was presented and the big question posed. She immediately accepted. Then they went to dinner and a long and wonderful life together that continues to this day.

Many young women known by Kathy on the Trinity campus
were seeking to be wives of pastors. Having to be upfront, speaking

to large groups, and playing the role of active first lady of a church just wasn't for Kathy. She's an admitted introvert, most comfortable one-on-one and with small groups of known friends. There's no apology here, no lack of social skills, just a personality preference. She will rise to whatever the occasion requires, just not always with full comfort and from any felt need to be noticed or in charge.

Kevin's father Jim soon gave Kathy some needed and most welcome advice. "When in a new church as the pastor's wife, you should give things six months. See where you fit with your own gifts and be exactly that and nothing else." This took the pressure off. Kathy would be right there for Kevin in years to come regardless of what God called him to do. She longed for no limelight and would assist him privately after he was on some stage and then need to debrief and experience comfort and understanding.

Father and Mother Mannoia rejoice with
the lovely couple, August 23, 1980.

The couple was married in the Evangel Baptist Church on August 23, 1980, where her father was song leader. It was on the

120th anniversary of the founding of the Free Methodist Church. Kevin's father, Rev. V. James Mannoia, officiated, with Kathy's pastor, Rev. Paul Stenstrom, having a part in the ceremony. Her sister, Marybeth, was the maid of honor. The bridesmaids were another sister, Ginny, and her college roommate Ellen Kogstad. Kevin's best man was his good friend Curt Morgan, with his groomsmen his brother Jim and brother-in-law, Sharla's husband David Martin. Kevin's good friend from seminary, Randy Discher, was head usher, joined by Kathy's little brother Billy as junior usher. Families were joined and soon a future mostly yet unimagined would be forged.

This was Kevin's first real marriage. There had been a mock one when he was a little kid in Spring Arbor, Michigan. Kevin played the little groom (after being bribed with candy) and Debra McKenna was the equally little bride (possible bribe unknown). They spoke their vows in the Mannoia garage in a ceremony arranged by the neighborhood kids and with numerous parents in attendance and dressed for the occasion.

Kevin, although reluctant, must have been convincing because he soon won a part in another wedding. Linda Adams grew up across Harmony Road from the Mannoias. She and Kevin were "best buds." Later she would serve as a Free Methodist bishop, but not before she had "married" Kevin in a little "Tom Thumb" wedding, this time in a play at the church. Two early weddings, not bad for a shy little guy like Kevin. By Kathy's time, the shyness had mostly worn off. A bribe of candy wasn't necessary to get him to this wedding!

Kevin, of course, couldn't have known at the time of that first "wedding" about Kathy Knudsen, one day to be his wonderful and very real bride. Nor could he have known the sudden sorrow being carried into his family's garage on the mock wedding day by none other than President David McKenna of the local Spring Arbor College. Near his presidential inauguration, the youngest college president in the nation, David's beloved father had taken him aside to announce that he was going to divorce his mother!

The shock and pain of this news, along with much more about David's amazing spiritual journey, is now captured in a marvelous little book.[31] At age ninety-four when this biography was being researched, David was pleased to share his memories of Kevin as a garage groom kid and later church pastor, bishop, president, professor, dean, and more. Kevin and Debra McKenna are still friends, though she never was a real rival of the gracious Kathy Knudsen.

Kevin and Kathy, always a loving team.

Twists and Turns

Over the years to come, Kevin and Kathy would be blessed with the three wonderful children. Daughter Kristyn Anne was born in Dallas, Texas, in September, 1983, later marrying Daniel Ng. Son Christopher Reid was born in June, 1987, also in Dallas, Texas, later marrying Victoria Ramirez. Son Corey Andrew would complete the family, born in June, 1991, in Upland, California,

---

31   David L. McKenna, *The Triumphs of His Grace.*

and still available in the marriage marketplace. Grandchildren blessing Kevin and Kathy these days are Maia Anne and Naomi Rose Ng and Vincent James and Camila Grace Mannoia.

These three children and their kids are deeply loved by Kevin and Kathy and all live close enough in Southern California to allow babysitting and other regular grandparent services gladly given. They now are successful professionals, one a vascular surgeon (Kristyn), one the Business Administration Director for *Kingdom One* (Christopher), and Corey a technician for Hyundai Motors, all strong Christians and greatly appreciative of their special parents.

How should one characterize the marriage of Kevin and Kathy? Kristyn explains that they tend not to "compartmentalize." Kevin would become deeply involved with many colleagues on many subjects and even continents over the years. Kathy, although something of an introvert, would be genuinely interested in knowing these people and gaining some understanding of whatever was facing her husband. His ministry is her ministry, his challenges and joys gladly hers. This has been reflective of the earlier ministry mutuality of Kevin's own parents, Jim and Florence.

Although there would be times when money was tight in the Mannoia household, Kathy always would handle the checkbook and keep things in good order at home. She would see to it that home for Kevin would be a safe haven away from the storms that on various occasions would come his way. Kristyn, the oldest child, speculates that her father would seem to be the driving force behind things, while her mother took on his burdens and helped keep things together. Kathy knows Kevin's ways and preferences, down to details like hating refried beans and always wanting ice cream after dinner.

Kevin soon would begin to travel in ministry, at times it seemed almost constantly. Kathy would go with him on occasion, genuinely interested in what he was doing while not wanting to be pushed up front herself. An example of her personal involvement was the 2012 trip to Varshets, Bulgaria, for the annual meeting of the International Council for Higher Education. She joined Kevin in experiencing the very difficult road required to get to the meeting resort. The Soviet Union had pulled out of the country, leaving the local infrastructure to collapse. She sat with the observers, knowing none of them and, despite being an introvert, was most interested in the actual meeting agenda.

Once the meeting had concluded, Kevin fulfilled one of her life dreams. She had been a college history major with her favorite class being ancient history. At the top of her list of desired visits was Greece, especially Athens. So they went there for a three-day vacation and she was very excited. Over the years the whole Mannoia family has traveled and played together on a range of occasions and in some of the most enviable locations.

A clear highlight among them was the 2004 summer trip to the Mannoia family origins in Sicily. It was in celebration the 80th birthday of Kevin's mother, Florence. His father unfortunately already had passed away. Everyone else went, Kevin, Kathy and their three children, and Kevin's brother Jim and wife Ellen and his sister Sharla, her husband David, and their families. It was all about connecting with family roots.

They went to Palermo and found the church where the grandparents were married and Maria had sung in the choir. They found the house lived in and talked to people who remembered the family. It was nostalgic personal enrichment and great fun, all Jim's original idea and mostly his planning. Mother Florence already was losing her memory but responded with the affectionate hugs of some local ladies who were curious about what this crowd of Americans was doing on their little street.

They rented three cars and a villa with several buildings right on the Mediterranean, "absolutely gorgeous." Kristyn remembers the family parading along twisting streets, Uncle Jim leading the way and father Kevin coming up the rear. That was because David, Sharla's husband, was a more cautious driver, not a real Mannoia. Kevin made sure he didn't lose sight of the group because of his hesitancy. They stopped by a roadside to buy some yellow melons. It was a local delight but a mistake since nearly everyone got sick! Sharla notes that she didn't because she had skipped the melons while busy preparing the evening meal for the group. Teasingly, they blamed everything on her cooking!

What they learned in Sicily, apart from some historic details of family roots, was always to be proud of being a Mannoia. Kristyn heard that admonition often as a kid, and when marrying Daniel decided to keep her original name. She is and always will be a proud *Mannoia*! Kevin's sister Sharla struggled with the married name choice in the 1970s and finally decided to become a "Martin," with her daughters deciding different ways at their marriages. There's something about the "immigrant mentality," says Sharla, that passes through more than one generation.

Kevin would make a short video in 2023 for the launching of various religious meetings, speaking of the "holy river of God" and how important it is for leaders in this river to each know their names, particularly "Wesleyan" in this case. That doesn't make them better than other streams feeding into the one river but does highlight the distinctiveness of it and anchors one's identity and important contribution to the whole.[32] This is true of the Mannoia family and the Wesleyan church tradition.

Not surprisingly, and even with great times together, it wouldn't always be easy rearing three high-capacity Mannoia children over the years, including when Kevin was holding a series of high-profile positions and often away on long trips. Kathy was the key, but only part of it. Says son Corey, "my parents are a team with very distinct and different roles. She is his safety net. If he is the tower,

---

32   See Barry Callen, ed., *The Holy River of God* (Aldersgate Press, 2016).

she is the cables that keep it upright. Daily they challenge each other to be better."

On their thirty-first wedding anniversary Kevin announced: "I have never loved Kathy more than I do now. Thank you, Lord, for the most amazing gift of a life partner. Have I been a good husband and good father? I think I have done okay in fulfilling my call. Lately I have been thinking how much I didn't know early in my marriage, how much I strove for accomplishment. Early I was driven. I hope that did not take me away from Kathy or the family more than it should have."

The twists and turns pulling at the home of Kevin and Kathy would occasionally strain but never come close to disrupting their relationship. He readily admits that "the rapid and high-profile changes I have walked us through sometimes have been stressful for her." Just his schedule would be more than most wives could tolerate.

Take the example of one month recorded in Kevin's personal journal. That month he had consulted with church leaders, taught in two universities, and hosted large gatherings in Taiwan, Canada, Ethiopia, Brazil, Chili, and the United States (separate occasions in North Carolina, New Jersey, and Indiana), with a quick family vacation in the Dominican Republic squeezed in somehow. And this wasn't a rare month!

Says Kathy, "the Dominican was great!" She admits that sometimes she has had to take a deep breath and say, "OK, God, I'm going to just have to trust you!" She's always has been sure that God has his hand on Kevin's life and she's been determined never to get in the way of that. She pained a little defensively each time someone wrongly criticized him. "Church people can hurt way worse than others. Kevin's willing to make hard decisions, confronts misbehavior, and faces openly hard issues that divide the church."

One criticism of Kevin came on occasion and probably was justified. As an aggressive leader, he sometimes got too far ahead, allowing some to begin shooting him in the back. "Even so," concludes Kathy, "he's tried to learn from this along the way and I wouldn't trade anything we've been through. Each hard thing has seemed to prepare us for what was to come next."

Kathy recalls with a bit of amusement that she had not planned to marry a pastor, but did marry Kevin. So, by her surprising choice, his ministry in a sense has been hers. She has felt called to make a home for her family and a haven for her husband. Yes, she admits, "sometimes there has been a lot to keep track of, and often the kids and I would hide notes and even little gifts somewhere in his packing to keep in touch." On occasion he and Kathy would go off alone, like once on a cruise among the Greek islands, with Kevin excitedly pointing, "Look, I think the Apostle Paul once sailed right over there!"

There certainly have been memorable times, often Kevin's doing, showing his romantic side. For milestone occasions Kathy prefers a lovely meal around the home table with a few close friends and family. Kevin loves throwing big parties in her honor that bring many people together with lots of color and live music played in some stunning setting. At her fortieth birthday it was a band under a gazebo next to a large pool at a friend's wonderful home. "I got her there under some pretense, with the crowd suddenly jiving to *YMCA* and then *Jeremiah Was a Bullfrog*. At her 50th we started at a Club House with a professional musician before I played my guitar and sang to her a Brazilian love samba in Portuguese."

He did more. On one occasion Kathy cried when her father suddenly arrived—her mother having died and Kevin secretly flying her dad across the country from Wheaton, Illinois. Kevin decided on a different direction for her 60th, flying his family to Arizona to celebrate in the pristine Karchner Caverns and then on to an exciting performance at the *OK Corral*. Granddaughter Maia was frightened when a gunman on horseback shot another out of the saddle—she thought it was real.

Concerning to Kathy more than Kevin's occasional extravagance on her behalf were the times when he had to be very careful on the ground in China, Nigeria, and once especially in Ethiopia. It was there that he was taken from the airport to the hotel in an armored vehicle. Still, setting aside the occasional struggles and danger, Kevin reports this:

> Kathy was thinking the other afternoon how she is where she had hoped to be at this point in life—a nice house, comfortably able to pay the bills, and with three great adult children with good hearts. I had to agree. It's amazing how God has been so good to us. In spite of all the twists and turns I have put her through and taken our family through, things are basically as she had hoped.[33]

Then There Were Five

What about the three kids who soon were growing up in the Mannoia household? Was Kevin an absent father when it seemed the whole world had become his workplace? Not according to the youngest son Corey. "Mom and Dad did a good job of helping us understand why he was going away. He was needed where he was going. His task was bigger even than we were. He always wanted to be with us, we knew that, but still he went where God wanted him to be. Here's the important thing. When he was home he was *really with us.*"

Kristyn, the oldest, never felt her father was absent from the family. She was not insecure as a kid. Now a skilled surgeon, she has worked 80+ hours some weeks and hopes not to be the absent mother. Kevin and Kathy insisted that Sunday was worship and family day, always eating together. When Kevin had to travel

---

33   Found in Kevin's personal journal, June, 2011.

around the western region of the United States as a Free Methodist bishop, he arranged for the family to join him on the road when possible, squeezing in a national park here and there between business stops. Such joyous exposures together were intentional and memorable.

Kevin would braid his daughter's hair, staying in her life in practical ways, usually bringing something home after being far away. When grandkids came along, Kevin knew how to turn off the business concerns when at home and do flips with the kids in the swimming pool. "He could be just a crazy kid." Kristyn even attributes to her parents her own staying in church when friends drifted away. Why did she stay? In the Mannoia household, when appropriate, the kids were included in knowing about and understanding some tension-filled things going on in churches—not always good things, but things they were helped to see happen to real people, things that could be healed if approached properly. That helped her not to be driven away by the human side of churches.

A growing and loving family.

Kevin's part in holding the family together, while necessarily sporadic, was very real. When asked to describe their father in one word, one surprising response from all three kids was "goofy!" He could be silly, tumble on the floor, tickle, act or even dress stupidly just for fun. Whenever possible, he enjoyed putting his kids to bed at night. He would tell them stories and make up songs. "It was one of my favorite times," says Christopher. Kevin's love of the TV series *Star Trek* influenced some of the bedtime stories. Tales of adventure stretched the imagination that led these kids to sleep—maybe in some other world but happily asleep.

Kristyn recalls the nighttime stories as "fables tailored to each of us. If Christopher got octo-spiders, I got character-building vignettes that always ended in an inspirational mantra. Dad had special songs he'd sing to us every night. Some were standards ('Over the Rainbow' and 'Edelweiss'), some hymns, others he just made up.

Special ones go to the tune of "Love and Marriage." One features "Daddy and Kristyn, they go together like a motor and a piston." He has one for each kid and grandkid: Daddy and Kippers (Christopher's nickname) go together like a diver and flippers, Daddy and Corey (a motor and lorry), and now Grandpa and Maia (mangos and papaya), Grandpa and Naomi (pistachios and spumoni), Grandpa and Camila (chicken and tortillas), and Grandpa and Vincent (cheese and blintzes)." Kristyn admits that now she's doing much the same with her girls.

Corey says his favorite dinners at home were when food was placed on a tablecloth on the floor with all seated, eating and watching some sci-fi episode. One of these episodes was later used by Kevin as an image for how Christians today must perceive the multiple dimensions of God's kingdom, learning how to distinguish kingdom principles from human standards.[34]

---

34   See "The Star Gate Effect" in Kevin's *Church 2K*, chapter three. Also see in chapter twelve below.

Kristyn remembers very clearly when Kevin first taught her to drive. He finally got her on one of those dreaded California freeways and home safely. Like the sci-fi TV episodes, he also turned this awkward process of teaching Kristyn to drive into an image of how best to live the Christian life. It was his cloverleaf image.

When Kristyn was trying to handle the cloverleaf to get on a freeway, her driving was particularly erratic. Why? Because she was watching the road's edge and trying not to hit it. Observed Kevin, inclined to spiritual lessons from practical events, "We tend to be drawn to where we look." This creates the very danger we so much are trying to avoid.

"Setting your mind on the things of the Spirit results in living according to the Spirit. Christian disciplines are behaviors intended to train the mind to focus on Christ, the kingdom, the center."[35] When focused on the center, the marginal matters seem to care for themselves.

The lessons were more than spiritual, adds Kristyn. "Dad also insisted on teaching the basics before we could go on. We sat in my first car, a manual transmission Jetta, for at least thirty minutes while he explained the clutch and the flywheel and the principles of an engine before he let me try to drive it. He'd have us bounce the racquetball against the wall forever until we'd actually play a game. He said we had to understand the way something worked to eventually become good at it. His approach to every challenge was that it builds character."

Especially when the kids were small, the family had annual passes to Disneyland. When the boys were older they and their father worked hard to accomplish a beautiful rebuilding of a Cougar, the car that Kristyn and Christopher later used as their wedding get-aways, something Corey still hopes to do some day.

---

35   See "The Cloverleaf Lesson" in Kevin's *Church 2K,* chapter four and in chapter twelve below.

Each drove it when first getting a driver's license. Once Kristyn took it to a dance and scraped the side panel rather badly in a little accident. Kathy said to her, "You'll have to tell your dad."

Dreading it, she did on the phone (he was on another trip) and surprisingly Kevin laughed despite injury to this proud vehicle, almost a fourth child in the family. "Why are you laughing?" she asked, relieved but puzzled. "Because it's only a car!" It was repaired and he didn't even make her pay. His explanation: "I never want my kids to think that they are less important than any piece of machinery. Now if she had been drunk and done it, maybe that would have been a different story!"

Kristyn has even more to report about her beloved father. "He was pretty relentless when it came to pushing us when he thought we had potential. Most of the time it was good, but sometimes we'd push back and it took some intervention from Mom to break the impasse." Kevin was picky about what the kids wore to church (no tennis shoes and for the daughter a dress). Then there was Kristyn's learning to ride a bike.

"I was pretty stubborn and cautious and didn't want to risk falling once they took my training wheels off. Dad would push and I'd refuse to even try, and he'd get pretty frustrated. When I was about seven he went out of the country for several weeks and Mom cleverly let slip that Dad didn't think I'd ever learn how to ride a bike. I took the bait and she and I practiced up and down the street for weeks to prove Dad wrong. It worked!"

Kevin is a car man, although things haven't always gone as planned. He once tried to build a bridge to the younger family members with a key purchase that collapsed before finished. He bought a four-wheel-drive Jeep "because I really wanted to enjoy the summer with the boys and with Daniel and Kristyn off-roading." Unfortunately, the vehicle chosen had been "rebuilt" by a guy who turned out to be a shyster. The man had done a quick fix to cover an engine problem that came back while Kevin was driving it home. This junker was donated to the Salvation Army before the frustrated new owner even had managed to register it.

The kids all got a chance to laugh at their father when he once really embarrassed himself. He loved to play with words, twisting them around for dramatic effect. Once it went badly wrong. He tried to play with "If the shoe fits" and it came out "If the foo shits!" Oops. However, when the kids stopped laughing they knew they were truly proud of him. He would shine far more often than fumble. Usually the shoe did fit.

When Kevin stuck his neck out in public on the dignity rights of LGBTQ people, he made a real effort to help his kids understand the complex whats and whys of his controversial action. Corey judges: "Dad was doing only what Jesus would've done. Given the motivation behind his action, there's no regret on our part." More on this later.

By the time the three children were young adults, each had experienced her or his own personal challenges. Kevin typically would intervene when things got tense, trying to understand and fix the problem. He's a fixer. Occasionally he would become frustrated and even a bit angry, maybe a few times unintentionally making the situation worse. He once reflected:

> I never thought I would know the depths of love like I do now. I feel more deeply than I knew I could, for Kathy, the gift she is to me, also for the kids through whatever the season of struggle. It's amazing that when they are struggling, I feel it so deeply. I think I'm beginning to understand compassion. I think I've been so shaped by the circumstances of my position or task that I've missed the deeper nuances of compassion, emotion, embracing the moment. But *they are alive in me.* I continue to learn and grow. Thank you, Lord![36]

---

36 Found in Kevin's personal journal, 2009.

Growth or not, Kevin admits a failure here and there. He regrets "tying my kid's shoelaces too tight before school—maybe insensitivity." Had he pressed his sons inadvertently about the importance of college, pressing too hard, tying too tight? After all, he had a masters and doctoral degree, as had his father before him from Michigan State University. Was that subtle pressure for the new boys in the family to measure up? What if that's not who they were being called by God to be? "Oh for the insight of compassion!" Both sons did have their difficulties in college. It wasn't quite their thing.

Kevin once admitted, "I find myself sometimes feeling inadequate, disrespected, frustrated. Why do both of my sons have such a struggle with school? How did I not help to prepare them? Did I force something on them they are now rebelling against? Do I keep encouraging? Do I lay down the law?"[37] The answer could be yes and no—how it is with parental dilemmas. The struggles in school certainly were beyond Kevin's doing or fixing. They would get sorted out later.

Kristyn remembers the shoe-tying problem very well. "Dad was rather stubborn about my clothes as a kid, hard on a little tomboy. Once I sat on a half-wall while he tied my shoes for school, always so tight, saying it was good for my arch support. I said there was sand in the shoes. He took them off and there wasn't. I complained still and finally off they came again. No sand still. Actually, my feet were "sandy" asleep from lack of blood circulation!"

This circulation memory is from a future vascular surgeon. Kevin's sister Sharla offers helpful perspective. Her brother had to wear shoe inserts as a child and was quite conscious of adequate arch supports. Now he's learning about the possible evils of "projection" on a new generation that may not need such support. Kristyn did know some insecurity when young, but not necessarily from stumbling around with numb feet.

---

37   Found in Kevin's personal journal, 2012.

Moved to high school in a neighboring town, at first she knew no one and was more comfortable skipping many of the school dances. Kevin didn't quite understand this—he had found his way socially while attending four different high schools. It's worth noting that whatever the insecurity during high school, it changed for Kristyn over time. She now is an adult surgeon functioning well in a male-dominated profession. This requires more than the typical amount of inner strength and self-esteem. She is just something of an introvert like her mother, preferring a smaller group of really good friends to relishing crowds and big parties.

Corey suffered some bullying at school and would retreat inward on occasion. College was quite the struggle for him at times. Often he wouldn't focus and follow through. He tried, his dad disciplined, and things went up and down emotionally, although finally he did graduate. There certainly was no lack of intelligence, just no real awareness yet of who he was and was meant to be. Kevin struggled through this erratic behavior, finally adjusted to what he couldn't fix—a difficult adjustment for this fixer. He loves Corey deeply, and now with increased understanding.

Regarding Corey's huge beard worn these days, his mother insists that it "covers such a lovely face." He's much more comfortable with himself now and functions very well as a skilled auto technician. He cautiously announces that he is open to the right woman coming along eventually. Meanwhile, Hyundai is fortunate in getting most of his quality attention. He now speaks of considering getting a masters degree. Who knows what the future holds? Whatever it is, his mother speaks of his being an introvert like herself, this not being a liability but a special approach to life. "He'd be a great leader, not the forceful one always needing to be upfront, but the enabling one encouraging others forward."

Even in a highly educated household constantly on a university campus for something or other, school somehow just wasn't quite right for son Christopher. He was perfectly capable of managing reasonable grades with the least work possible, satisfied at being more hands-on in his approach to life. He did what had to be done and sometimes little more. He struggled somewhat like his brother, particularly when in college at Azusa Pacific University. Christopher didn't respect some of the campus people and resisted aspects of the general campus culture, so he transferred to Greenville University in Illinois where his Uncle Jim was president.

This school was out in the country, at least compared to the Azusa Pacific setting. He was "moving from big bustle to cows and cornfields." Kathy and Kevin drove him back to this campus in Illinois, hoping for the best for their precious son. The problem persisted, although somewhat lessened. Christopher finally was given a proper medication and improved considerably. He also graduated successfully.

Helpful indeed was the chance on occasion for Christopher to hang out with his Uncle Jim, the university president. This support was needed especially when Christopher was faced with a difficult situation. He needed to support a prominent young man on campus who was quite troubled and even threatening to end his life. Stressful or not, Christopher managed to rise to this difficult challenge. Like so many college students, he was gaining the stability and wisdom of young adulthood. None of us, however, grows up all the way and all at once.

One summer, with Christopher home from Illinois on summer break, his mother Kathy worked hard to prepare a really nice steak dinner. He suggested eating on the floor and watching TV, a favorite family activity on occasion. Kathy already had set up everything on the patio and so understandably said no, not this time. He wasn't happy about this decision but, with some encouragement from his father, was willing to stay home and enjoy the steaks on the patio. It helps to have a nurturing and loving home like the Mannoias to cover the rough spots. Christopher would instantly and gratefully agree with this today. He knows he has great parents and is anxious to duplicate that the best he can in his own home.

If growing up isn't always easy, neither is parenting, even for the finest and most well-intentioned people. God is faithful and love covers much that's less than perfect. There was a lot of love in the Mannoia home. Currently Christopher is a man of strong Christian faith serving capably as the Business Administration Director for *Kingdom One*, a church resourcing ministry. His hands are happily on many practical matters, apparently where they belong. So are the hearts and hands of his brother and sister in very different settings, one in a hospital operating room and the other in the technical world of a modern auto-repair facility. The parents are as proud of all three as they could be—and for good reason.

Victoria, now the wife of Christopher, is the Account Director for a fundraising agency serving non-profits. Kevin clearly rejoices. "It's such an amazing thing to watch Christopher flower with Victoria. He has truly found his path and rhythm."[38] A similar glowing report could be made about the other couple. Kristyn's husband Daniel is a physician in emergency medicine while she is a highly skilled surgeon. The wife of Corey is yet to be named. Whoever she turns out to be, she'll be lucky to have him.

All the Mannoia kids eventually got through college, two at Azusa Pacific University, Kristyn in 2005 with degrees in biology and philosophy and Corey in 2018 as a communications major. Christopher finished at Greenville University in 2011 with a focus in business management. Kristyn went on to Loma Linda Medical School. Her husband Daniel finished his three-year residency in Emergency Medicine and Kristyn enjoyed a two-year fellowship at Baylor Hospital in Dallas, Texas—ironic since that's where her father Kevin had begun his ministry after seminary. Kathy and Kevin love dearly the two new family members, Daniel and

---

38   Found in Kevin's personal journal, May, 2018.

Victoria, to say nothing of the four grandchildren, Maia Anne, Naomi Rose, Vincent James, Camila Grace.

In the summer of 2018 a great family vacation was planned for Kauai, Hawaii. Kevin reflected afterwards, "It was simply outstanding. Daniel & Kristyn with Maia, Christopher & Victoria, Kathy and me. We really missed having Corey along but he stayed to work. I think he would've liked it better than he thought. We rented a nice condo in Poipu and two Jeeps. We hung out together for everything, meals, hikes, beaches, and coffee stops. The last day was Victoria's birthday. Daniel and Kristyn made reservations for a really nice Luau."

Yes, fun and family, love and joy, that's Kevin and Kathy. Like any family, there also have been moments that are otherwise. Kevin will never forget what happened in December, 2013. He was losing sleep because of high anxiety over the dog Tucker. It had rather viciously bitten the neighbor's dog. Kathy had been injured trying to intervene. Even though Kevin had successfully gotten the mess under control, he had lost all trust in the family pet. What if it would attack a child? He was paralyzed with this thought. "I find that my mind goes to the worst possible scenario. Is that simply my low emotional levels reacting in lack of faith? Am I allowing anxiety to take control? Or is that just a function of aging?" We'll leave those questions unanswered, as he had to do.

Apart from the negative times all families face, the Mannoias are a family full of faith and fun. There has been pain over the years, much of it coming from outside the home itself. Always it's been accompanied by lots of trust in the God who seems to make good possible whatever the circumstance. Fortunate for Kevin, and thanks mainly to Kathy, home has been a haven, a welcome place to retreat, renew, and rejoice. It's also been a place of music.

Kevin loves music. So does son Corey who found a welcome outlet in music, as his father had done in high school and college. Corey toured for a couple summers with an Azusa Pacific men's ensemble called *The Saints,* and he also was a member of the *Chamber Singers Ensemble.* This excellent group won an international choir competition in Corey's time, his quality bass voice a welcome addition. Kevin's singing or his hands on a guitar are happily remembered things by all who have known him well.

A Strong Sense of Family Legacy

Sharla, Kevin's sister, speaks gratefully about the father-to-son legacy in their family. "Daddy connected easily with people, and Kevin is very much like him. They both drove themselves, traveling widely around the world, first Daddy as World Fellowship Secretary of the Free Methodist Church for a couple of years after we returned from Brazil. Kevin now acts like he's World Secretary for Evangelical Christianity in general, no geographic limitations. They both have a passion for preaching and family."

"When we were kids," Sharla recalls, "Daddy taught at Spring Arbor University, but in the summertime everybody packed in the car and off we went to some camp meeting where he was evangelist. We crisscrossed the country in our old Plymouth, Daddy trying to pick spots of beauty that we could visit along the way, so that's how we vacationed. Both Daddy and now son Kevin were seminary and college professors with PhDs and wonderfully supportive wives, Florence and Kathy. Much moved from father to son, and most of it was really good!"

That's to say nothing of son James, Kevin's big brother. Greenville University has great significance for his family. His father and several of his siblings graduated there. For relatively poor Chicago Sicilian immigrants, Jim proudly reports, "this says a great deal about my grandmother Maria and her commitment to Christian character."

There now is a prominent lectureship on this Illinois campus named in Maria's honor. Jim says, "My sister Sharla, her husband

David, and two children graduated there. One of the newest halls on campus is named for my late wife Ellen who died from cancer during our term as president and first lady."[39] Of course, nephew Christopher, son of Kevin and Kathy, also completed college there, with Uncle Jim as president.

"Remember that you are a *Mannoia*." All of Kevin's kids often heard this family mantra from him. He is intentional about memory making, the resource of yesterday's roots intending to enable productivity in the tomorrows. For daughter Kristyn, the strong family tradition was elevated even more by her Aunt Sharla. "She's a force of nature," says Kristyn, "one who helped me be proud of being a woman as well as a Mannoia."

The greatly expanded family.

Kevin's family has some rituals that have been highly valued. At the birthday celebration of any one of the kids or grandkids, a birthday litany is read aloud. It says much about the believing and parenting priorities of Kevin and Kathy. Picture the Mannoia family circled and taking turns reading lines of holy blessing, for daughter Kristyn in this case.

---

39   V. James Mannoia, Jr., *Paradox and Virtue.*

We gather to celebrate and give thanks for Kristyn's life and days now woven into ours, that we might share the joys and burdens of life together, delighting in the ways God's glory are reflected in the unrepeatable gift of her being. So we celebrate and honor your image, O God, uniquely reflected in the life and personhood of Kristyn. Bless this Your child in the year to come. May she know the comfort of Your presence, the certainty of Your purpose, and the consolation of Your love at work in her life. Grant her wisdom, maturity, vision, and passion in increasing measure so that she might be an instrument well-honed for the building of Your kingdom. AMEN![40]

In April, 2012, Kathy and Kevin made a big decision. They would buy a "legacy home" in the mountains where their kids would like to gather and then their kids, keeping all connected as a family over time. Their parents now had all passed away and they used the inheritance to make a substantial down payment. It was considered a final blessing from their parents, a lovely mountain home in Big Bear, California, with easy access to lovely Big Bear Lake. In July, 2012, they headed to this new home to celebrate Corey's birthday. Kristyn, her husband Daniel, and Christopher also were there. There were only one folding table and four chairs, so everyone moved close to the hearth where the others could be seated.

Kevin then asked them to circle in the kitchen for a dedication service for the new family home. Kathy read a passage from the Psalms about going to the mountains to find peace. Kevin made clear that the deceased parents were involved in this too. Then he asked each person to pray a brief prayer of dedication and thanks.

---

40 Adapted from *Every Moment Holy*. More recently, shortened adaptations have been necessary because little grandkids just won't hold still long enough for solemn formalities!

Five years later, Kevin wrote in his personal journal about consequences of these precious family moments: "Big Bear has come to be what I prayed it would, a family point of reference. Daniel and Kristyn have had special times there and Christopher proposed marriage to Victoria in this family center."

Kathy remembers having an early Thanksgiving celebration there before any grandkids had come along. The boys, Christopher and Corey (and maybe "the bigger boy," Kevin), couldn't imagine such a day without a TV. So a big flat-screen had been bought and gotten up there in the car. It now was put on the floor leaning up against the wall—there wasn't a table or time to affix it to the wall.

Dinner was ready in another room. All were there and bowed to pray. Suddenly an awful crash was heard! The TV had collapsed, smashed, and the family day of thanks would have to proceed without it—it had been bought used, rather cheap, no big loss. That was then. Now there are grandkids learning to love Big Bear, including going to the lake with adoring grandparents to watch the local fireworks on July 4. They would snuggle under blankets in their boat since even in July it's still only in the 40s at night in the mountains. The closer the better. Kathy was so glad they had this beautiful place "to escape and let Kevin just unwind from his crazy schedule."

Sometimes on a warm summer day they would drop anchor in a little cove and Kevin would turn on his Brazilian samba music and read. If time allowed, he might switch to the mellow tones of Natalie or her father Nat King Cole. Kathy tries to relax out there even though the water makes her a little nervous, especially when the boat traffic gets heavy. "The jet skis are like scary little mosquitoes buzzing about." Despite such momentary distractions, and with tears in her eyes, she says this about her marriage to Kevin. "I watch and listen to him and I'm blown away that I get to share life with him!"

When the cove is quiet and the sun warm, the legacy lounging in Big Bear is a perfect time and place to reflect on Kevin's life and ministry to this point in time. Home has been a haven. From what? Answering that requires the big story now to follow. After seminary, Kevin's Christian ministry was to begin in Texas, eventually shift to California, and then appear all over the globe that we call Earth. It would remain deeply rooted in his Free Methodist church heritage, although soon it would cross church lines in multiple directions, even working hard to turn those dividing walls into more porous picket fences. His relational nature would be constant.

CHAPTER SEVEN

IN A TEXAS SADDLE

A strategic life plan was now well underway for Kevin Mannoia. The first phase was the seminary years, now complete on a surprising campus in Illinois. The second phase now would occur in another surprising location, in a Texas saddle. It would be quite a ride! The goal of the plan beyond seminary was to gain pastoral experience, then supervisory experience with pastors, and also the earning of a doctoral degree in some field of church leadership. Once all these were successfully accomplished, presumably they would prepare Kevin for whatever God was intending, likely a major leadership position in the Free Methodist Church.

The next phase of the life and ministry plan was now ready to unfold. The scene would be Dallas, Texas, the big cattle country. The rush of initial ministry activities to be carried on there would be quite a practical learning experience for Kevin, together forming a foundation for much to come later.

In the Lone Star saddle soon would be a confident and aggressive if somewhat immature carrier of God's good news. A friend of Kevin's from their seminary years called him the "Italian Stallion." The reference was affectionately meant to picture a particularly strong leader of a team of horses that's unfettered and on the move to somewhere important. In Kevin's case, the lead horse was young, fast, and had sturdy Italian heritage and high hopes for the future.

Exhibited by this cowboy minister would be a sense of confidence, activism, and leadership. Although not the Sicilian Mafia, at least this stallion would be a sturdy Italian quite other than the stereotype of corruption seen in *The Godfather* (1972 movie). He would exhibit more the elements of passion and adventurousness seen in *Roman Holiday* (1953 movie). This young minister would exude a clear confidence sometimes mistaken for arrogance. Kevin was ambitious, to be sure, although meaning and hoping it would be directed more on behalf of his Lord than himself.

If the seminary scene for Kevin had been surprisingly northern Illinois, not central Kentucky, the place of his first pastorate after seminary would be equally surprising. It would be Dallas, Texas. Considerably more prominent places in the world of American Free Methodism had been possibilities. Representatives of various church bodies had come to Trinity Evangelical Divinity School to interview graduates for possible placement, but none came from the Free Methodist Church so far as Kevin remembers. This graduate school was hardly in the Wesleyan tradition. Free Methodist seminarians typically went to Asbury Theological Seminary in Kentucky on scholarships from their denomination.

Kevin, brother James, sister Sharla, and spouses.

Kevin naturally joined conversations about placement interviews his friends were having, and he wasn't comfortable with the standards he was hearing from some. One friend didn't accept an offer because the parsonage was too small, another because he wanted a more competitive salary than was being offered. Free Methodist leadership obviously knew Kevin apart from the seminary. He had pastored one church and helped plant another while a seminarian, and his parents were widely known and highly respected in the denomination. A few informal possibilities were mentioned to him, ones located in Illinois, Wisconsin, New York, and Arizona. While none of these were pursued actively, Kevin had every intention of staying within his home church, not being drawn away to the Evangelical Free Church of America of the seminary.

Why finally Texas? Kevin's father Jim, then a faculty member at Asbury Seminary in Kentucky, had been in Texas as the speaker at a men's conference of the Free Methodist Church. Present there were men from its Kimball, Texas, congregation located in the greater Dallas area. That church just happened to be looking for a pastor.

Dr. Mannoia mentioned that his son was just finishing seminary and might be a real possibility despite his not being a student at Asbury Seminary, as were the typical new candidates of the denomination. Kevin and Kathy weren't married yet. Even so, the Kimball leaders were attracted to the possibility and invited them both to fly to Dallas to get acquainted. They agreed and Kevin preached on a Sunday morning.

They met the people, toured the community, and then flew back north not sure that anything would come of it. Nor were those who did the interviewing. Texas was a small and weak conference in Free Methodism, and the Kimball leaders, while impressed with this young couple, were not sure they could attract someone like Kevin, a gifted young man now well educated and from a prominent FM family. Even so, they had to try. The other conferences presumably in the picture for Kevin's placement had multiple candidates available and Texas didn't.

Oddly enough, it was that very fact of need that drew Kevin's interest. Texas was where he felt really needed. "I want to go to the place that other people overlook and help as much as I can." So that was it, first a surprising seminary for his ministerial preparation and now a surprising decision that was the beginning of the Mannoia's "Lone Star" years.

The couple was married on August 23, 1980. Kevin and Kathy took one week of honeymoon in the Caribbean, came back and loaded a moving truck. They towed Kevin's little Mazda car and headed south into one of the hottest summers in the history of Dallas. He had a good education, a little pastoral experience, a marvelous new wife, and big hopes and dreams. One was to gain a doctoral degree that likely one day would help secure a major leadership role in one of the institutions of higher education in Free Methodism. He would have to look around Dallas, Texas, for a campus offering such a program in some appropriate field of study. That would turn out to be the University of North Texas located in the Dallas-Fort Worth metroplex.

Building a Church that Multiplies

The Mannoias moved into the Kimball parsonage and would serve in Texas for nine years. The church was small and struggling, called "Kimball" because it was close to the Kimball High School, although the church actually sits within the Dallas city limits. It had only about forty people, with at least some of them wanting to congregation to grow. So did the superintendent of the conference who frankly was surprised that a seminary graduate "of that caliber" would seriously consider getting in a Texas saddle. Kevin did come, and with excitement, although soon he admits having "hit a wall." He soon began wondering who he was to think that he could do as well or even better than Rev. Charlie Brown, the pastor he followed at Kimball. The new Kimball pastor was a mixture of ambition and insecurity.

Kevin wasn't shy about seeking personal assistance with his concern. Bob Briner, family friend and prominent Free Methodist businessman locally, was asked about this personal issue. What Kevin was told impacted and inspired him. "It comes down to your gifting, Kevin, your particular skills of leadership. There can be a very godly person who is not competent in leadership and little growth will happen. On the other hand, a skilled leader lacking godliness can become arrogant and misleading. The challenge for you will be managing a careful integration of the two." Such balancing would be a significant challenge for the remainder of Kevin's ministry in Texas and then elsewhere.

This wise piece of friendly advice sent Kevin to Ephesians 4:1-3. There believers are told to walk "worthy of the calling," meaning for Kevin a careful blending of his apparent competence, needed spiritual depth, humility blended with a strategic activation of his gift of leadership. With this wisdom in hand, he focused consciously on this and other challenges as he began his pastorate, and the Kimball church began to grow.

By 1987, he was on the radio with his *New Wineskins* weekly program, introducing his congregation and the gospel of Christ to the wider Dallas area. Assistants for the ministry had been hired over time, with two ministers soon being sent out to plant new congregations nearby, one Spanish. The needed blending worthy of the calling seemed well on its way.

The goal of Pastor Mannoia was "not to build the church *big* but healthy and strong so that it could *multiply*." The two church plants were evidence of initial success. He also was gaining a recognized voice and appreciated presence in the religious community in Dallas/Ft. Worth. He was coming to think of himself as part of a new wave of church leaders then entering the ministry.

"We are trying new things, taking bold steps, testing new ideas, not out of rebellion but out of passion for the church's relevance. We are not interested in building *great* churches as much as building *the* church." The question was understood not so much as "Who has the biggest church?" but "Where is there real Kingdom effectiveness happening?"[41]

In 1983 Kevin had found the doctoral program he wanted and began at North Texas State University. By 1986, the last year of his doctoral studies, a real turn came in the scope of his ministry. He was asked by the Free Methodist Texas Conference to retain his pastorate and also become the part-time superintendent of the Conference, thus a "stationed" superintendent. Despite being a relatively small conference of twenty-three congregations, it was quite spread out across a very big state, reaching west from Kimball in Dallas to Midland and Abilene and south to San Antonio, Houston, and McAllen on the Mexican border.

Kevin agreed to this big new challenge and served in the dual role for three years, traveling widely as necessary and writing regular superintendent editorials in *THE COURIER,* publication of the Texas Conference. He was completing elements of his strategic life plan for this initial stage of his professional career—seminary preparation, pastoral experience, supervisory experience of pastors, and doctoral work in higher education. These were expansive and sometimes exhausting years, but right on target for his future ministry goals.

While this sounds highly planned and almost automatic, it wasn't by any means. Times were not easy financially in the Mannoia home. Two of the three children came along in Texas. Even before the first child, daughter Kristyn, was born in 1983, Kevin and Kathy were living in a parsonage in Dallas and drawing a modest salary. Soon there were car and then home mortgage payments. They had moved out of the parsonage when an assistant pastor was hired. Kevin and Kathy could hardly dream that one day they would be able to put all of their children (eventually

---

41   Kevin Mannoia, *Church 2K: Leading Forward.*

three) through college without accumulating considerable debt. Much would have to happen before that could be possible.

Son Christopher was born in 1987. He recalls the little family house just after they had moved from Texas to California. He had his own room, but his father had nowhere to keep and use his computer except in the little boy's bedroom closet. There was a small table in there but no room for a chair in addition to the clothes. Something would happen on occasion as Kevin worked on a sermon, article, or book. When he thought Christopher was asleep, he would slip into the room carrying a chair to be placed facing the computer in the open doorway of the closet.

Kevin needed to work for hours while, unknown to him, Christopher sometimes was awake and fascinated by the green glow in his closet coming from the computer face. Was some strange wisdom from another world appearing on that screen and filling his dad's papers? After all, just minutes before Dad had helped him to sleep (not quite) by telling him a made-up tale of the "Octo-Spider," a crawling alien arrived from outer space! Christopher says "My father has quite the imagination and, I suppose, also quite the greenish sermons and articles!"

Kathy was a relatively introverted person in those early years of their marriage. Beyond the need for a second income, Kevin wanted her to flourish by having something of her own not connected to him and the church. She found excellent employment, "making I think twice as much as I was, executive assistant to a plant manager and potentially soon to be the H. R. Director." With the eventual two kids and their own home, her excellent employment was a necessary blessing she gladly supplied. She worked right up to the time of the family move to California. Kevin recalls that "she never made a point of where we lived, she just made everything we had better, no matter how humble it was."

When the area bishop of the Free Methodist Church would come to visit the conference, Rev. Clyde VanValin, he would stay with the Mannoias. Kathy had some of her father's artistic skill, "that creative gene," an eye for color and arrangement in the home. Kevin had her father do some things for the church, like develop a logo.

Once Kathy had samples of new wallpaper up on a wall and asked Clyde which he liked best. He pondered and finally selected one, which she agreed likely was the right choice. Then, as he left the room, he was overheard saying quietly to himself, "but of course I'm colorblind!" Kathy thought this was hilarious but went with his choice as a possible word from God. How wide-ranging are bishopric skills?

The denomination's national publication, *Light and Life*, ran a major story titled "Free Methodism's Youngest Superintendent."[42] It was reported to the national readership that the unusually young leader of the Texas Conference starts his day looking at his personal calendar, "which reads like a train schedule from Grand Central Station." Thirty-one and already serving his third year as Super-intendent, Mannoia "sprints from place to place." He was seeking to fulfill the daring goal of helping the Texas Conference become "one of the leading conferences in the Free Methodist denomina-tion." His working assumption was this. God has not called us to maintain. The minute we just sort of exist, we might as well cash it in and close the place down."

Note was made in this article of this young superintendent having an impressive educational background, including by 1986 a Ph.D. in higher education administration from North Texas State University.[43] The campus was about forty-five minutes north of Dallas in Denton, Texas. Rev. Mannoia had attended classes once or twice a week, having tested out of a research language

---

42 In the publication *Light and Life,* February, 1988.

43 Kevin's doctoral colors are blue (Ph.D., higher education) and green (UNT). His father's are also blue and green (Michigan State University). In loving memory of his father, to this day Kevin wears his deceased father's regalia on formal occasions.

because of his Portuguese fluency. Other curriculum advantages were gained because of the educational emphases in Trinity's Master of Divinity program.

Mother and Father celebrate Kevin's doctorate.

Kevin's doctoral dissertation was "Perception of Faculty Concerning the Integration of Faith and Learning at Free Methodist Colleges." This subject, the integration of faith and learning, would surface often in his consulting ministries around the world in years to come, often in Christian institutions of higher education far beyond those of his home denomination. His 2023 book *Expressing Life* highlights key emphases of his dating back to this dissertation of the 1980s.

Kevin was assuming that completing this doctoral program, along with his Texas pastoral and church supervisory experiences, might lead him one day into the presidency of one of the Free Methodist institutions of higher education. This young pastor, now holder of a doctorate, was very denominationally loyal. If one of the FM schools called, his answer probably would have been "Yes." This church "was my family." In years to come there would be such calls, but without "yes" answers. Each of these instances is a story in itself.

The Language of "World Speak"

While pastoring in Dallas, Kevin certainly wasn't confined to a university classroom or pastor's office. He served as a member of the Evangelical Alliance of Greater Dallas, the YMCA, and the Lion's Club of south Dallas, largest in the country with some five-hundred members. He loved this kind of public involvement. It got him "out of the shell," connected him in the city at large, and taught him the language of "world speak."

Lion's Club members included City Council representatives and the Chief of Police, all becoming well known to Kevin. Even the Mayor of Dallas became a good friend. Kevin was club chaplain at one point, an officer and ticket sales chair for the club's annual gala event. Not typical of most pastors, such extensive "secular" involvement was, as Kevin says, "a blast, so much fun!"

Kevin served as chaplain of one sub-station of the Dallas Police Department, leading seminars for them on the spiritual dimensions of the use of deadly force. One policeman killed someone in the line of duty and, although fully justified, was guilt-ridden.

Dallas was in the Bible Belt and the Bible says not to kill. Kevin tried to explain to this officer the difference between "killing" and "murder." Meanwhile, Pastor Mannoia became a lifetime member of the Texas Camp for Crippled Children because of time and energy invested there through the Lion's Club. He helped with the Dallas County's "Future's Program," learning much about the skills of strategic planning.

For a few years Kevin served as the chair of the board of a regional YMCA. In the mid-1980s, he was one of a dozen persons representing the USA in an exchange/friendship program with the USSR. He got to watch Russian people go to the ballot box for the first time and vote for or against Mikhail Gorbachev as mayor of Moscow. He was amazed to see these people grip their paper ballots with two hands, knowing the special privilege it was. The group visited various cities, always accompanied by a Russian guide and party official.

Once the group was in a parking lot after seeing a statue of Lenin and his wife. Kevin had forgotten the name of that famous Russian's wife and asked the guide. The Russian man quickly responded with a twinkle in his eye, "Yoko Ono!" The American group burst out laughing while a nearby party official stared rather critically at the guide. The husband was *Lenin*, not *Lennon*! The impact of western culture, especially through the modern music of the Beatles, apparently had trumped the indoctrination of communist political theory. Recalls Kevin, "What an amazing moment of Eureka that was!"

Obviously, the last thing Rev. Mannoia wanted in Dallas was to be an isolated pastor known as a "maintenance manager." There was strong motivation in him to plan, strategize, activate, and broaden the reach and fronts of Christian ministry. Already showing were some dynamics that would characterize his later ministry in numerous other settings. He's quoted this way in that 1988 *Light and Life* article about him. "Bringing change where there is long history and tradition will cause some people to be upset with you. Old thought patterns and ways are hard to give up." One characteristic of Kevin's whole ministry would be an occasional suffering from this truth being aimed at him.

Kevin learned this lesson early. "*Efficiency* is doing things right. *Effectiveness* is doing the right things." God's on the move and not to be locked in any past. The church is supposed to be following the divine movement. It must expand, experiment, and occasionally risk, determined to do the *right things* as well as doing them well.

There was some discussion with Kevin about the possibility of the denomination bringing its next General Conference to Dallas, Texas. Such a major event would have to be heavily dependent on this young pastor's planning skills and wide connections in the city.

Such would not happen as things turned out since Kevin would not be remaining much longer in his fast-riding Texas saddle. Even so, church leaders just broaching such a consideration was quite an honor for Kevin. Apparently he was being viewed as both efficient and effective in his ministry, and that in a difficult area which lay on the fringe of the denomination's national life.

A Turning Point

Kevin's sister Sharla graduated from Greenville University of the Free Methodist Church, where her other brother Jim later would be the president. She married David Martin who worked for IBM in nearby St. Louis, introduced to her by Jim when he was a graduate student. In 1984, with Kevin now well-established in his Texas pastorate, the Martins decided to move to Dallas to accept an advancement opportunity for David. Having family in Texas made this move easier for them. They located their home between David's new work and the Kimball congregation where they started attending. Soon Sharla was aware of some tensions her brother was experiencing in the church and helped as much as possible.

Texas is so spread out that often Kevin, in his role as Superintendent, would fly commercially to visit the churches not located near the Dallas area. On occasion the family would go with him by car on long tours to a series of congregations in a given area of Texas. By 1989, however, trouble was in the wind. Kevin had come to feel increasingly overloaded by his dual Texas ministry. He had completed his doctorate, was pastoring the most prominent congregation in the Texas Conference, Kimball in Dallas where his sister Sharla now was attending, and he had planted two new congregations out of that church.

Kevin was a multiplication man, but one soon under considerable stress because of also superintending the Texas Conference while still pastoring. He sensed that his calling was to include and maybe focus on pastoral oversight, the reason he already had turned down offers to top leadership positions in two of the colleges of Free Methodism. This dual role in Texas, however, was burdensome enough that he realized increasingly that it was unworkable.

He was wanting to move forward aggressively both in the local Kimball congregation and in the Texas Conference, with one always seeming to restrict the possibilities of the other. There also was his clear priority on family. He would take them with him on trips around Texas whenever possible. Sister Sharla urged her brother to think even more carefully about his family priorities. She and Kevin came from a missionary family in which there was a tendency to go where called. They were servants of the church. They also had to be good stewards of themselves and their homes.

Becoming known across the denomination, options for Kevin to move were increasingly available. Bishop VanValin wanted Kevin to stay in Texas, reminding him that the big conferences always had good candidates and he had come to Texas initially because it was the place that really needed him. It still did and Kevin cared about that. He also needed to admit to himself the growing tension that was bothering him more and more. Trying to be both a pastor and conference superintendent, and do both aggressively and well, was just untenable. His problem was "a divided heart." He wanted to pastor his people but was drawn strongly to supervising pastors and building the conference. Something had to change.

Especially had this necessity grown when an assistant pastor of the Kimball congregation began pulling in a direction opposite of Kevin's. He had been given increased responsibility to allow Kevin's larger ministry in the state, but now his presence and personality and larger leadership platform was creating division of loyalty and even direct criticism of Kevin—for reasons Kevin still doesn't understand. The circumstances of one couple in the Kimball church certainly compounded the problem. They had large personal issues. Kevin counseled both separately trying to help, but mistrust grew from suspicions and misunderstandings. They fueled these in a group of the disgruntled, quietly undermining the pastor's leadership.

By 1989 Kevin knew something had to change. Should he resign the superintendent role and focus on solving the local issues? Unknown to him, the end of the entire Mannoia ministry in Texas was nearing. There were two young children in the family now, with Kevin and Kathy in the kitchen one day watching them when an unexpected call came. Would he be open to being considered for the Free Methodist superintendency in Southern California? Rev. Denny Wayman was calling for the search committee, possibly encouraged by his brother Danny, a Texas pastor very appreciative of Kevin's apparent potential for greater responsibilities.

The Mannoias weren't actively looking for a new deployment despite the frustrations in Texas. They were quite cautious, having their biases about California not being a good place to raise a family. Kevin had only been to Southern California a couple of times to visit his brother Jim who was teaching at Westmont College. A second call came, however, pressing the invitation. Kevin now agreed to be considered. Something significant had happened to him recently that refueled his ministry passion and made it at least conceivable that he could accept a new and even greater challenge.

A Personal Revival

Kevin had agreed to go to the Greenville University campus in Illinois to speak at religious emphasis week. He almost canceled at the last minute. He didn't because he just couldn't disappoint them like that. On his way to Illinois, he had an extended layover at the Houston airport, a time of his feeling so low, having "a pity party." He was drained, distracted, and disillusioned about "my once ideal sense of destiny in ministry. The power was absent, the passion diffused."[44] The Italian Stallion had been reduced to a sickly pony. He found his way to the InterFaith Chapel in a neighboring terminal, just wanting to be quiet and alone while he waited, wishing he were back home.[45]

Confused about not being able to please his people, a big question soon captured him. "Who was Jesus trying to please when he emptied and humbled himself (Phil. 2:5-11)?" Jesus came as a servant *of God*, not of the people. Who then was Kevin Mannoia supposed to be serving? He pondered deeply. It's so easy to design all of one's vocational activities in a way that supposedly will please the people. That creates a "performance identity," the minister becoming a slave to the needs and expectations of the people. Rather, like Jesus, we are called to be servants *of God*, ministers who perform acts of humble service *for* people, but not as *their servants*.

Kevin now was grasped by the paradigm of *servanthood*—Jesus did not come to serve people but to serve his Father on behalf of the people. This subtle distinction can be life changing. If one is being faithful to God, there is no need to crumble under the criticism of people. This insight suddenly seemed to be coming directly from the mouth of God in an airport chapel. God was saying, "Serve *me*, Kevin, then minister to people as an expression of that service. Stop feeling sorry for yourself!"

The plane was caught and shortly the renewed servant of God was standing in the pulpit of the Greenville chapel beginning his sermon with this: "I'm Kevin Mannoia, *a servant of God*, nothing more, nothing less, and my particular mission in this session is to . . . ." More than a simple slogan, here was the announcement of a fresh ministerial identity that would be used on other occasions

---

44   Kevin writes about this pivotal life incident in chapter one of his *The Integrity Factor* and in chapter five of his *Church 2K*.

45   See chapter twelve for Kevin's pivotal image of "The Stick Figure with Bent Knees."

over the years, especially after Kevin would hear a glowing introduction to himself.

He explains, "I don't want to listen to my own PR." He no longer would be controlled by how people judged him or what they expected of him. He was on the world's playing field being supervised by and responsible to one alone, *God*. Such commitment was symbolized by a simple creation of Kevin's father.

Kevin recalled this in 2024, and with deep emotion. "In my first year of full-time ministry at Kimball, Father brought me a kneeler he had made in his basement woodshop. It's been in every office of mine ever since. It's the centerpiece of my 'ready room.' I've begun many of my days at that kneeler for more than forty years now. Kathy has recovered the kneeler pad many times. It's where I am most comfortable." It's where he refreshes his commitment to God alone.

It's worth noting that the Greenville chapel session in the fall of 1988, a planned 50-minute period between classes, ended with the speaker, Kevin, offering an altar opportunity for anyone who wished to confess anything—confession the subject of his presentation. The chapel period lasted for sixteen hours! It was a spontaneous revival that caused class cancellations to allow attention to very important matters of the Spirit. The whole week at Greenville was amazing, a highlight of Kevin's life. They were days of going from "the hollow of the well to the burning bush," from a pity party in Houston to rejoicing in Illinois.

Now there was renewed confidence in a young pastor who was determined to wrap this confidence in a deep humility. Kevin later would suggest that God seems to allow circumstances in our lives to force us into a position of surrender. Not until there is a voluntary choice made to let go of selfishness and become a humble servant will there be experienced a new Jesus-like identity. It will be one of a courageous servant of God gaining the mind of Christ.

Leaders are called to serve God, not be slaves to God's people. Knowing this and daring to be faithful to it, one can navigate and survive the structures of the institutional church and the demands of its very human members.[46] Kevin now was committed to this without having knowledge of how much navigating and surviving still lay ahead for him.

Kevin's brother Jim observes that their parents, Jim and Florence, were especially gifted and yet unusually humble people, with Kevin inheriting much of this critical combination. Says sister Sharla, "Dad would face criticism and misunderstanding for his being an active visionary and change-agent. He would be inclined to 'suck it up' and not fight back, absorbing the blows and moving on. That has happened numerous times in Kevin's life." His years in Texas had been learning ones, growing ones, ones forcing him to be a leader after the model of Jesus. He now was better positioned for a larger field of ministry.

Confidence in a strong leader certainly can be misunderstood, something Kevin would face on occasion. There is a subtle but real difference in perception between *confidence* and *arrogance*. The latter is ego-centered, the asserting of oneself. The former is knowing who is being served and what makes God smile, regardless of the frowns of some who wish to be served themselves.

So Kevin agreed to the unexpected invitation. He would fly to California and meet with the search committee. If not anxious, at least he was ready to consider a new challenge beyond Texas. The subsequent interview went well. Kevin would be recommended to the annual conference in southern California for election as the new superintendent. He alerted the Texas leaders of this major development. Preparing to leave Texas, Kevin reflected on the Kimball church. "The people were amazing, extremely generous in blessing our move. We love that congregation and were shaped by them in our lives and ministry."

---

46   See Kevin's *Church 2K*, 76-77.

Kimball without Kevin

Kevin immediately set about empowering the Texas conference appointments committee to find a good successor to pastor the Kimball congregation in Dallas. Once the Mannoias were off to California, a sad departure for all, Kevin's sister Sharla and her family remained in the Kimball congregation for some years. Kevin soon was mentoring in California a Rev. John Richardson, an African-American Pentecostal from the Church of God in Christ denomination. John's role first was to pastor a troubled Free Methodist congregation and, given his success there, then to encourage increased African-American leadership within Free Methodism in the United States.

The Kimball congregation, soon in a racially-changing Dallas neighborhood, eventually came on John Richardson's schedule. Kevin by this time was transitioning from being a bishop to a national evangelical presidency and knew little about what was happening in Texas. Some in the Kimball congregation felt that John's consultation with them involved his calling them "racist," and they pushed back. His advice was only that they should rethink their place as an essentially White congregation in a growing multi-ethnic and multi-racial neighborhood. They should seek new leadership appropriate to the setting.

Kevin no longer was available to "do interference" for John, who began to feel that the door of Free Methodism was closing around him. Kimball would make its own decisions and John would head back to the Church of God in Christ. He had fulfilled his original agreement to stay with the Free Methodist Church for at least two years and leave behind at least two new black pastors. He had stayed a decade and left behind a series of such pastors.

Judges Kevin now, "That's all acceptable in God's economy. It's all Kingdom." Years later, Kevin would act again on John's behalf, still believing in him and drawing him into participation and then leadership of an ecumenical ministry Kevin by then would have launched called the Wesleyan Holiness Connection. Meanwhile, sister Sharla and her husband David were left behind at Kimball "hanging on" for several years, serving out of necessity in multiple roles.

The congregation kept declining and the Martins grew tired of "propping it up." The few members left were all driving to a church no longer related to its neighborhood. In fact, the area Free Methodist conference no longer was Texas only but one administered from afar, unable to offer much help to this congregation. Finally, as Kevin and Kathy had done years before, Sharla and David left Kimball. This was particularly hard for Sharla. She had decided sadly that "my church had left me." They would find their place nearby as United Methodists, with daughter Yvi eventually becoming a prominent UMC pastor in Kansas City. She's the one Kevin had flown Kathy to Indiana to see baptized by his father. The Kimball congregation, Kevin's first pastorate out of seminary, closed in 2000 but since has been reconstituted much as John Richardson had suggested years earlier. Church plants that now meet in the building are multi-ethnic, much more with a neighborhood flavor than Kevin or his sister Sharla ever knew there. One welcome tie to Kevin's family did come along later. With the family of Kevin and Kathy settled in California and the Martin's still in the Dallas area, Kevin and Kathy's daughter Kristyn, born in Dallas, returned there for a two-year fellowship as part of her advanced medical training.

Soon Kristyn would encounter some real stress of her own, partly from her multiple responsibilities (herself a new mother) and partly from working in vascular surgery, a male-dominated profession. She received welcome encouragement and advice from her Aunt Sharla.

"I have no place to go to nurse my baby when on duty," Kristyn complained to her aunt. The response? "Then speak up! Tell them you may be the first but you won't be the last woman in the program, so you people need to think about these things. Women are as good or even better than men in many things!"

That gave the young woman the self-esteem needed to speak up and move on. The medical fellowship would be completed successfully and this young doctor would head back to practice in California near Kevin and Kathy and her two brothers, all very proud of her. She was indeed *a Mannoia*. In coming years, far from Texas, her father would be an outspoken advocate for the divine rights of women clergy.

CHAPTER EIGHT

GO WEST YOUNG MAN!

Home base for the coming decades would not be Texas but California. The new ministries would be natural outgrowths of the Texas experiences, pastoral, educational, supervisory, and spiritual. One big difference would be that southern California was not in the Bible Belt as was Texas. At first Rev. Dr. Mannoia would continue to serve the Free Methodist Church directly, although later the settings would be well beyond. Immediately ahead would be nearly seven years as an area superintendent in California, then three years as a denominational bishop. This would be before so much more that wasn't even imagined as the family left Dallas and traveled west.

Kevin Mannoia had accepted a call to be the chosen candidate for Superintendent of the Southern California/Arizona Free Methodist Conference beginning in July, 1989. In contrast to Texas, the oversight responsibilities wouldn't be "stationed" (coupled with a pastoral responsibility) but full-time and not of a small conference but of a primary one in the whole Free Methodist denomination in the United States.

At the time of Kevin's initial arrival in Southern California, in progress was a personnel and philosophic transition in the church. A new generation of Free Methodist pastors was rising and many were having some difficulty with the "old traditionalisms." Worship "wars" were in progress and there was strong interest in bringing new and particularly innovative leadership with an expansionist mentality. That's apparently how Kevin was being perceived, a change agent in fresh directions.

One unusual mover in new directions was Rev. Marty Edwards who was leading a non-traditional church plant. Recalls Kevin, "He and others formed an amazing cadre of high capacity, effective leaders in the church whom I discovered and actively nurtured for years." Soon Kevin would be having meetings with prominent area Christians like Robert Schuller of the Crystal Cathedral and *Ted Engstrom*, head of Youth for Christ and World Vision International. Ted had assumed the role of interim president of Azusa Pacific University after the resignation of Paul E. Sago.

Ted and Kevin would form a close personal relationship and work at redefining the relational connection between Azusa Pacific and the Free Methodist Church. Kevin had been warned when first elected Superintendent that the denomination was planning to sever its tie with this school. He asked for a year to address the situation and would manage to avoid that drastic action. Gratefully recalling all this, Kevin says, "I was blessed over the years by Ted's mentoring influence." A major new phase of Kevin's ministry was quickly in full swing.

A Superintendent Again

Rev. Dr. Kevin Mannoia had first returned to California for a special sitting of the annual conference convened at the Mountainview Free Methodist Church in Upland, with Bishop Robert Andrews presiding. It had been the time for his formal election as Superintendent, presumably a process to go rather quickly. The meeting, however, had "a bit of a rocky start," he recalls, "as the committee got bogged down for a couple of hours in heated discussion about worship wars and power in the church, reflecting the divided nature of the conference."

He managed to endure the discouraging tenor of this meeting and was elected to a three-year term, being assured privately that he should not take personally this meeting hassle. Regardless, it now was clear that the situation into which he was stepping would hardly be a panacea of perfection. He had become the regional overseer for churches, schools, and a conference center in southern California and Arizona, most in some degree of transition. The Mannoia family would settle in southern California and make the best of it.

As initial arrangements were being established at that electing conference meeting, wife Kathy was trying to locate a home for the family to rent or buy "in a really hot market." She had one big obstacle, not knowing what the new family income was going to be. She was willing to work if necessary, as in Texas. They now had the two children, Kristyn and Christopher.

Kevin had an unusual complicating attitude. He didn't want to know in advance what his compensation was, having accepted this new leadership role on its own merits. He only had hoped that it would be full-time so Kathy wouldn't need to provide supplemental income, and that he wouldn't again have to minister with a divided heart, dealing with both local and regional responsibilities. He yielded to Kathy's need, asking privately for the income number being offered.

Years later, given everything in between, good and bad, Kevin would be able to say this of his experience in the California superintendency. "What a blast! What an exhilarating ride!" It started with a most unusual ride indeed. A significant voice of the new ministerial thinking was Rev. Denny Wayman, Free Methodist pastor in Santa Barbara. He would be a valued assistant of Kevin's who would help him connect quickly with some of the "young movers." They certainly included Marty Edwards.

Marty rode his put-put motor scooter right into the first annual conference being held in a large open-air setting! He had planted

"The Lamb's Fellowship" and soon would begin a motorcycle riding ministry among the congregation's "Black Sheep," Christians spoken of in the New Testament as outcasts, aliens, and foreigners. They were the proud "HOGS" (Harley Owners Group) riding for Jesus Christ, soon to have club chapters nationwide and even internationally.

Marty and Kevin became close friends. People loved him. "Marty is the kind of person who's interested creatively in the future of the church's mission. He and a handful of other pastors were those in whom I would invest heavily as a superintendent in my attempt to alter the trajectory of the conference."

At an annual conference when Kevin was presiding, Marty (who had been to clown school and was "Luther" on occasion) passed out a coloring book filled with caricatures he had drawn of many of the church leaders—some with crazy looks on our faces. Presumably, like Martin Luther nailing his Ninety-Five Theses to the church door in Germany, Free Methodists needed reminding that their leaders and structures should never be allowed to stunt the growth of God's Kingdom with any dry institutionalism. If the conference proceedings were to get overly boring and irrelevant, at least they could color in their little books. I leave to your imagination what Marty gave Kevin to wear on his head when elected a bishop!

The most painful issues near the beginning of Kevin's new superintendency would hardly be encountering creative ministries like Marty's, things he'd welcome and by which he'd be energized. The problem issues would be his having to deal with a series of ministerial moral failures. There were enough of them that other denominational leaders began calling Kevin for advice on how best to handle such crises, not exactly what Kevin in his thirties wished to be known for. He encouraged his conference in this regard by instituting psychological programs and marriage counseling offered at church expense and bringing retreat speakers to address healthy marriages. Out of this context came Kevin's 2006 book *The Integrity Factor*.

A Sense of Joy and Inadequacy

Apart from the occasional moral crises, what Kevin calls "a horrible time that forever changed me," he determined to set a path for conference renewal marked by a new direction and a fresh conference culture, hopefully relating constructively to both the old guard and the new innovators. The building of relational trust was a priority for the superintendent, as was structuring for aggressive mission growth in whatever ways possible.

By Kevin's side were key individuals like Denny Wayman, Bill McKinney, eventually Steve Fitch, and others. A process was initiated to separate Arizona's thirteen congregations into a new conference. There soon was clear movement forward, shifting away from eighty percent problem solving to a focus on leadership formation of "next generation" pastors achieving aggressive mission growth. God began blessing richly. "What a place! Kathy and I felt so very blessed to be part of it all."

Even so, Kevin admits that during this time he realized that he was living with a constant sense of inadequacy. Given all his gifts and opportunities, he had feet of clay like any of the pastors. Having dealt with several moral failures in the conference, he admitted humbly to Kathy that so easily it could be him as well one day. "This sense of vulnerability is very frightening. How fragile life is! And yet, how amazing that with it, by God's grace, there comes confidence and success." Much success indeed was coming, and fast.

An international dimension to Kevin's ministry developed rapidly in this new California setting. As Superintendent in Southern California and Arizona, arguably the flagship conference of the denomination, he was blessed with various new international contacts, largely in Asia. These led quickly to new friendships for Kevin, and even part-time teaching assignments at the Asian Graduate School of Theology in Bangalore, India, and the Holy Light Theological Seminary in Taiwan. From the California base, the wider world was poised to open to Kevin. He had leadership and teaching skills that propelled him forward with fresh visioning and lots of energy and opportunities.

Kevin with ministerial colleague and friend Robert Schuller.

Kevin soon became known as anything but "conservative." He was progressive and activistic, although not quite to the dramatic extent of his new California ministerial colleague Robert Schuller. Bob was proclaiming a "theology of self-esteem" enlivened by "possibility thinking."[47] He had come to California from the East, like Kevin, and began by preaching from the roof of the refreshment center of a drive-in movie theater. His ministry soon ballooned into a landmark megachurch, what some would call a religious empire housed in the "Crystal Cathedral." It's 14-story Tower of Hope could be seen from nearby Disneyland.

---

47   Robert Schuller was influenced greatly by Rev. Norman Vincent Peale and his best-selling book, *The Power of Positive Thinking.*

Kevin and Bob became friends and shared a mutual respect and common willingness to cross fresh ministry frontiers. They were not quite mirror images, however. Kevin was more than willing to experiment progressively, but minus most of the dramatic theatrics and massive expenditure of dollars characteristic of Bob's big operation. After all, Kevin was a Free Methodist and his denomination had humble roots and an historic commitment of frugality and ministry to the poor. Kevin always would be a loyal Free Methodist, on the cutting edge of things or not.

Even so, Kevin was finding himself serving in places where great wealth was obvious alongside poverty. His style with individuals and institutions was energy-packed and frontier-crossing. This reached even to his parenting at home. His oldest child, daughter Kristyn, describes her father like this. "He can be stubborn in good and bad ways, but mostly in good ones. He insists that you can do anything and helps you believe it. He holds himself to such high standards."

Kristyn continues. "He'll make friends with anybody and they will be taller for the meeting. He tends to see what could be and often even sees how to get there, and he'll pay the personal price to help somebody else reach their potential. He pushes toward higher ground. He's always looking forward, sometimes farther than some people are ready to look. That's when he gets hurt."

An example his positive mentoring is Rev. John Mark Richardson who had visited the Kimball, Texas, church after Kevin had left. In 1992 John had been a young pastor in the Church of God in Christ denomination, serving in the Watts area of Los Angeles. The place was wrecked by recent riots and many in the local Black population were moving to places like Hawthorne, California. John's wife Renita was blessed to have a father in Hawthorne who was a major businessman. He arranged for John to speak at the city Rotary Club about his vision of planting a new church in Hawthorne.

The Richardsons soon moved there, began worship services in the YMCA, and struggled until they became acquainted with the local Free Methodist congregation that was on the brink of closure. Kevin Mannoia, then the young Free Methodist superintendent, became acquainted with John, and John quickly began to think of Kevin as "idealistic, wanting to change the world!" Kevin's initial view of John was "a God-send to help revive a dying little Free Methodist church in a changing community." The superintendent proposed something a bit revolutionary for the time.

Would John associate with the Free Methodist Church and rebuild its troubled little congregation as a supply pastor, while retaining ministerial credentials in the Church of God in Christ? John identified himself as a "true African-American Pentecostal," someone rarely known in Free Methodism. Even so, he was open to the possibility and with Kevin's active support was approved by the 1993 Conference as an Free Methodist supply pastor.

That required some "blocking and tackling" on Kevin's part which he was more than willing to do. This was a first in the denomination, an African-American Pentecostal taking the formally approved leadership of a Free Methodist congregation. Kevin was beginning to specialize in firsts when he judged them valuable for church health and mission.

John served in Hawthorne for a decade, soon enjoying multiple services on a Sunday. The growth was mostly with young people, bringing both excitement and frustration. Now there were lots of people but very little money. Kevin intervened with a special refinancing grant enabling larger facilities and opening a new conversation. The denomination as a whole, announced Kevin, needed many new African-American pastors and he was an "out-of-the-box" superintendent. Not knowing it yet, Kevin soon to be a bishop overseeing the western United States and parts of Asia while John would be a counselor to Free Methodist congregations across the nation struggling in changing neighborhoods.

Rev. Richardson, a respected friend of Kevin, would be sharing his vision of aggressive church planting on a national basis, including racial integration, even with admitted "charismatics." The Urban Planning Director of the Free Methodist Church learned of John's success in Hawthorne and recruited his help. They began traveling together, John doing research for local Free Methodist congregations in radically changing communities, proposing ways forward, even identifying African-American pastors who might come and help. He was doing exactly what his friend Kevin was promoting.

That's when the difficulty in Kimball, Texas, had developed, with John soon ending his relationship with the Free Methodist Church. By then Kevin had moved on to other things and felt very sad that this denomination and probably his own successors "likely had caused John's departure." Soon John would be a bishop in his home denomination, the Church of God in Christ, having no contact with Kevin for many years.

He was never forgotten, however. In 2023 John would replace Kevin as the Executive Director of the Wesleyan Holiness Connection founded by Kevin. Says John, "Kevin was always looking for a "Kevin Mannoia 2.0" and it turned out to be me!" That's getting way ahead of our story, however. The point here is that, as Kevin progressed in his own ministerial career, he was pleased to mentor others who could come along with him. In fact, mentoring young Christian leaders would be a Mannoia life passion. As his daughter said about Kevin, "He insists that you can do anything and helps you believe it." He did that for John Richardson and now for so many others.

Elected a Free Methodist Bishop

Dr. David McKenna, renowned leader of higher education in the Free Methodist denomination, observes this. "Kevin and I hit it off when he was the forward-looking Superintendent of the Southern California Conference. I identified him as one of God's choicest young men with an unlimited future in leadership. He integrated well in his presentations his faith with the latest and best of leadership theory."

That "unlimited" was about to move Kevin beyond being the superintendent in California. At the annual meeting of the denomination's Board of Administration meeting in Indianapolis in October, 1996, Kevin was elected to succeed the retiring Bishop David Foster. He now would serve the nine-conference western area of the United States and the overseas conferences of the Pacific Rim. In only a few short years, he had come a long way from pastoring the small congregation in Kimball, Texas.

In 1998 Kevin wrote in his personal journal private reflections on first being elected bishop in 1996. He recalled talking about his future plans with his father back in his college days at Roberts Wesleyan University. He already had begun to think back then about someday being a college president and/or a bishop if he went into Christian ministry. He had wanted to know if that desire was acceptable to God. It wasn't wrong, his father had said, although Kevin admits that "My father may have qualified this comment somehow." It now was amazing for Kevin to realize "how God took my personal ambition and rewired me and affirmed me in ministry and has fulfilled me in the very things I had set out to do in my own strength."

Kevin's new bishop role would be more vision casting through writing and speaking than the superintendency had been. Rather than making regular decisions that immediately affect people's ministry careers, "I now am to make multi-generational decisions which will affect the nature and life of the whole church for decades to come." What a high calling and a humbling realization.

After a year and a half of being a bishop, Kevin finally would have adjusted to the new role. Even so, he admitted that again he had "come face to face with the same issues which occasionally rear their heads in my personal life. It's my *confidence* perceived as my *ambition*. I need to remain humble before God and gentle in my presentation of the vision and message God has given me."

Election day to the bishop role had stunned a bit Kevin's wife Kathy. She was in the workroom of a California school when a call was transferred to her. Kevin said, "They've just elected me a bishop!" She recalls being a little "terrified." Bishops have territories. Is the family suddenly going to have to take the kids out of school and move across country? He quickly reassured her. He had told the other bishops that he had three children in three different schools, the ages of some of their grandchildren. The Mannoias couldn't move. This limitation had been readily understood. Kevin was a serious family man.

He even suggested successfully to his new bishop colleagues that retreat planning meetings of the Board of Bishops should convene in Southern California whenever possible. Family was a priority. Kevin would not do as the other bishops had been doing, being away from home some 200 nights per year. He would limit himself to 85 unless he managed on occasion to have his family travel with him. He also had posed to the other bishops what to him was a very important question.

"How much of who I was as superintendent do I bring to who I am now as bishop?" They said, "Bring as much as you can because that's why you were elected." He was pleased at this open door and soon observed to his colleagues that he saw a major frontier needing to be crossed by the denomination. There was no cohesive vision from the denominational level motivating the average Free Methodist pastor. It soon was agreed that addressing this problem would be a group priority of the bishops. Soon they began calling people to the overarching denominational vision of "Knowing God and Making God Known." That came from the new Bishop Mannoia.

The new bishop and his colleagues developed together "The Cascading Flow" framework of thinking. It was to be encouraged of all pastors. The slogan "Knowing God and Making God Known" should be conceived as a pool that fills up and overflows into the mission pool, and then into the pool of values, all natural overflowings. With this thinking framework came an action plan—three columns on a projected chart. On the left were non-negotiables (stay with denominational beliefs, be loyal to the *Book of Discipline*, etc.). The right column listed the desired outcomes (we want to be faithful to our holiness tradition, be a multiplying church, etc.).

The middle column was particularly important. It was left deliberately blank—that's where others would put the hows of getting from left to right. Methods would not be determined in advance "from the top" but be left to individual leaders in different contexts and with different gifts of service. The bishops determined not to tell pastors and other church leaders exactly what to do, only that they were to get *there* (the outcomes) without compromising *these* (the non-negotiables). This was understood to be servant leadership, providing the vision and respecting individual insights and callings.

The bishops proceeded to lead a series of three-day "Schools of Renewal" to convey and encourage all this. They were aggressively setting the pace, establishing the goals and guidelines, but not micro-managing the process and details of implementation. It was very Kevin-like. At one of the schools, he was pressed with a pastor's question. "Can I allow a non-Christian man to be a drummer on the platform of my church?" Kevin declined to answer with a simple yes or no. That was to be the pastor's decision, filling in the middle column.[48]

---

48 That answer was quite "progressive" for the time. In 1963 I married a Free Methodist woman from the conservative Pittsburgh Conference of the Free Methodist Church. In her home congregation, and although I was an honor graduate of a Christian college on my way to seminary, I was not allowed on the platform of that church to do anything. Why? Because I wore a wedding ring. Free Methodist frugality? The combined cost of hers and mine was $30.

On one occasion Kevin made a bishop's presentation in which he commented that the Free Methodist Church is not an "inerrantist" body (not affirming the inerrancy theory of biblical inspiration championed by fundamentalists). He quickly made what to him was the "amazing discovery" that this comment shocked some pastors in the room who didn't know this about their own church. Recently Kevin has produced a podcast on "God's Word More than Words." Divine inspiration and infallibility of biblical revelation in relation to intended teachings, yes, but not the wooden, questionable, and unnecessary fundamentalist theory of inerrancy which the Bible does not claim for itself.[49]

Mildly unsettling for some leaders was another initiative of the Board of Bishops, one many believed was directed from within the Board mainly by the new Bishop Mannoia. The denomination was being administered in part by a series of Commissions. Kevin came to Chair the ones on Evangelism and Higher Education. Mostly for reasons of cost effectiveness, the bishops began to move away from this organizational system.

Given these changes and initiatives in the denomination, Kevin admits to struggling with the demands of learning how to be the leader he had always been, "but now in concert with my fellow bishops." He was accustomed to being the primary vision caster and head of the group. "Perhaps I am not cut out for this. I may be perceived as too assertive and aggressive." He became aware that some in the church were thinking that the Board of Bishops was grabbing excessive control for itself. Kevin's particular problem was that "I am being perceived as the culprit."

He admits to thinking that in previous years the bishops had abdicated their rightful leadership responsibilities. Still, "my sense

---

49 Soon Kevin Mannoia would accept the presidency of the National Association of Evangelicals. One reason that move was possible for him was that "inerrancy" did not appear in the NAE's statement of faith, even though various of its constituencies would affirm this vigorously. Kevin would be appreciative of the major exploration of this subject co-authored by his friends Clark Pinnock and myself *(The Scripture Principle)*.

of rightful control is limited to vision, values, and purpose. Some think I want more than that, driven by the need to control." His fear was that "I may be expending all my leadership capital in short order and will find that my effectiveness in this office is limited." His tenure as bishop would indeed be limited, but only because soon he would accept a major new responsibility outside the Free Methodist Church.

A great deal was accomplished in the first two years of Kevin's time as bishop, or at least much had been changed. "I realize that many view the organizational adjustments and changes in staffing as my responsibility personally. I have spent hours in prayer and thought considering my motives as I bring initiatives to build the Board of Bishops. I will accept the risk that some will misunderstand my intentions. I cannot help but feel responsible for some of the criticism which has come to the other bishops because of me."

One Free Methodist superintendent made a side comment that seemed to imply that Bishop Mannoia was *arrogant*. Kevin immediately went to one of his fellow bishops and asked, "Am I arrogant?" The diplomatic response was, "You are very *confident*, and for some that can be read easily as arrogance." This has been an issue for Kevin over the years, regardless of his leadership role. He is well aware of it and when possible counters what to him is a major misunderstanding of his inner motives.

"I do wonder what will become of me when I leave office or am voted out for being too aggressive. Should I back off? I am trying to soften the edge. I am yoked with the weight of leading a church that desperately needs to be rewired, though only a few within it desire the path required for that to occur. What if arrogance and impatience do overtake the grace-filled spirit within me?" Although some have wondered otherwise, Kevin insists that he never feared not being re-elected as bishop because of negative perceptions of his leadership. He occasionally wondered more than often worried.

Surprise Invitation to the NAE

A big invitation suddenly came to serve elsewhere and Kevin broached the subject with his son Corey, who may have put best what his father ought to do. Her was putting Corey to bed. After singing some songs, a story and prayer, he asked the eight-year-old boy what he thought the decision should be about his going to the National Association of Evangelicals. Corey responded, "Well, you've led one denomination, so now maybe it's good you will do it with a lot of them." This was received as a good stewardship perspective that Kevin will never forget.

Here are Kevin's words, countering what some wrongly presumed. "I've always *gone to* something, never *run from* anything. When the invitation from the National Association of Evangelicals came up, it was not a matter of my resigning my bishop position, only of my notifying the general church that I would not be available for new-term consideration." At the key General Conference convened at Anderson University in 1999, a group of delegates approached Kevin and urged that he reconsider his decision to leave the bishop role. It was a hard moment because Kevin has always loved his home denomination.

His response was a simple. "I'm sorry but my heart already has turned to the larger evangelical world." Delegates went on to the balloting and later the General Conference held for Kevin and Kathy a commissioning ceremony to the new NAE role. On behalf of the Board of Bishops, Kevin delivered a "pastoral address" to the gathered delegates. The early sentences clearly came from a dedicated, proud, and grateful visionary, one about to assume the helm of the NAE.

> What glorious works God has wrought among us in these recent years. Some have said that the Free Methodist Church must find a new vision, that staying on the path of the past fifty years was doom or at least irrelevancy. We rejoice in the

evidence all around that we have turned a corner. We are not in crisis but in God-directed transition. The shroud of uncertainty and irrelevancy is lifting rapidly. Praise be to God!

We find exhilaration in redefining ourselves as a *movement*. We encourage those churches that venture to "weigh anchor" and "head out to sea" rather than staying in the harbor, enjoying safety but going nowhere. Such a "movement" mindset demonstrates progress toward mission. Always it will meet with resistance and create waves—but we embrace it gladly because it is of God.

Kevin's personal journal reports this of that transitional time for himself and his beloved church. "I watched as God brought into place virtually all of the goals I had envisioned as a bishop of the church, not in refined detail but at least the basic directions, reorganization, and ownership of the vision. It was a wonderful event in Anderson, Indiana, and very emotional for Kathy and me. We knew that it would be our last official act in the Free Methodist Church."[50] The General Conference granted Kevin the title "Bishop Emeritus," which means a lot to him.

Beloved Free Methodist leader Dr. David McKenna, once himself vice-president in the National Association of Evangelicals, offered his reflection. "When Kevin was Superintendent of the Southern California Conference, he asked me to come as a consultant during the time he was assessing the direction of the conference. A survey was done, with each respondent indicating what readiness they had for a new direction. Many were ready for change and the conference became an example of dynamic growth and vitality under Kevin's leadership."

Such leadership "vaulted Kevin into candidacy for bishop," reports McKenna further. "After his election, he and his fellow

---

50   Kevin's personal journal, September, 1999.

bishops launched a vision for growth and change in the general denomination based on the latest model for organizational change. Again, I was asked to be a consultant, viewing the process and assessing its effectiveness. To my knowledge, the results were minimal, partly because Kevin left the position as bishop before some of the changes could be enacted."

This was not meant to be criticism, just an observation of apparent fact by an admiring friend of Kevin's. At least there was little question about a new tone having been set and new thinking established. Future leaders would decide to complete the implementation or let the progress lapse. Either way, Kevin was moving on, called to a larger arena of Christian service.

Perspectives are limited, of course, to one's angle of sight. Kevin was sure that he had helped set the right course for his church even if many others would have to do much of the future implementation. Left and right columns on that bishop's chart were well set. The blank middle column, the "hows" of getting from left to right, was still to be developed. Hopefully the "Cascading Flow" framework of thinking would continue regardless of Kevin's departure.

The years of Kevin Mannoia's denominational leadership in Texas, California, the western United States, and parts of Asia were for him times of stretching, experimenting, and sometimes soul searching. There were many changes made and numerous international contacts enjoyed that would influence the future greatly. The 1980s and 1990s had been seasons of growth both for Free Methodism generally and Kevin Mannoia particularly, accompanied by times of critical self-examination.

All the related seriousness occasionally had was accompanied by the relief of a little humor. Kathy remembers her husband preaching at a camp meeting on Lake Ontario in Canada. The couple had walked around the lake prior to one service and Kevin was very impressed with the many boats perched in the air to protect them when not in use for long periods of time. His sermon that evening began by his commenting on the beauty of the place and the wisdom of how boats are cared for in Canada. "They are lifted in the air by . . . what?" Kevin wasn't sure. A voice called out from the auditorium, "Boat lifts!" Even church leaders still have much to learn.

The preacher laughed heartily at his own ignorance of the obvious. But to the Free Methodist denomination as a whole, his vision and skill were quite obvious, even if a little unsettling for some. He had lifted up its boats for a time of fresh thinking and needed directional change, protecting them and preparing them for a new day. He would leave denominational leadership in 1999 with much still perched in the air, waiting for others to determine what would be next.

Including the Family

When first elected a Free Methodist bishop, and with eighth-grade daughter Kristyn along, Kevin Mannoia had done a tour of the Philippines, Japan, Hong Kong, and China. Originally, when yet superintendent, the intent in planning this trip was to learn how to be a better ministry partner with the Free Methodists in these nations. Now in 1998 as Bishop Mannoia, he was responsible for overseeing this area and his perspective had to change. How could he best supervise and assist them and their work? He was anxious to "shrink the Rim," get more synergy going among the several Free Methodist bodies of the Pacific Rim.

Regardless of which role he was serving, superintendent or bishop, Kevin always had a sturdy family focus. He wished to expose his children to multiple cultures and ministry opportunities, especially in underdeveloped nations. In addition, they were meant to see what their father does in these settings when often gone from home.

On this particular 1998 Asian journey, Kevin believes, is when Kristyn's call to a medical career began to take shape.[51] They visited and served for a time in leper villages of south China. People with this disease had their identity papers taken. As virtual non-persons, they were sent to very isolated villages and survived there as they could.

Ruth Winslow, veteran missionary, had an arrangement with the government to serve as a nurse (not missionary), taking care of persons in these leper villages. Ruth, Kevin, and Kristyn traveled by train and then motorcycle to reach these desperate people. The three participated in giving some glasses and for others cutting nasty calluses off their feet. These visiting servants weren't allowed to talk about religion, of course, always watched carefully by a communist party official.

The international dimension of Kevin's ministry would keep broadening, especially in Asia, although he never has forgotten or neglected his childhood roots in Brazil. Eventually he would become president of the International Council for Higher Education, a global body that accredits and supports over one hundred Christian institutions of education around the world. A clear ICHE focus is integrating Christian faith and quality education. In the midst of this work, Kevin also has cared about the maturing and world perspective of his children.

He took sons Christopher and Corey on trips to developing nations, wanting them to see the church as something bringing them special privileges and not just taking their father far away. Many things can be learned only by direct experience. Christopher went with Kevin to Taiwan, Hong Kong, China, and India. In India they went to a large church service in a remodeled and very long chicken coup, Kevin trying to make sure that Christopher

---

51   Kristyn now is a prominent vascular surgeon in Southern California and says that at least the seeds of her calling were planted then, especially in the leper villages of China.

didn't drink the wrong water. He discovered too late that the locals were refilling communion cups without washing them! Fortunately, Christopher is still with us, even having been at the Table of our Lord in India.

Corey once went with his father to Mexico for a pastor's retreat. They stayed in a small trailer that was very cold inside, Kevin even risking lighting the stove-top burners to keep Corey warm. The boy played with kids in piles of rubble like Kevin had done as a kid in Brazil. Then he went with his father to Ethiopia when he was about twelve. He helped Kevin's teaching role by passing out papers.

"He was a trooper!" recalls his father. Corey was very fair-haired then. They visited a monastery and a monk said to Kevin, "For men only. She can't come in." She? Corey's substantial and very dark beard these days discourages any such gender confusion.

Such deliberate multi-cultural exposures of the Mannoia children accomplished their purpose. Kevin would schedule conferences on the West Coast of the United States back-to-back when possible and take the family with him in a large mini-van, squeezing visits to national parks into the schedule on free days. The family sometimes was on the road together for four or five weeks in the summer, with a TV rigged inside the van for the kids before any were ever built in.

Once elected to the NAE presidency, the whole Mannoia family went in 2000 to Amsterdam, Netherlands, with Kevin a prominent NAE representative. This nine-day conference was for preaching evangelists and convened by evangelist Billy Graham's association. One of the most internationally representative Christian gatherings ever, the attendance exceeded 10,000, with the United States sending nearly 3,000 of them. Evangelists from the developing world were there in large numbers. The city, crowd, and ministry excitement were great for the Mannoia kids. At times on the home scene, however, things were hardly perfect for these kids.

Kevin generally is quite gentle with his beloved wife Kathy. Once, however, his yelling at her was startling. Corey and his father were replacing the coil springs as part of their big rebuild of a Cougar car. The new coil needed to be compressed under great pressure to be installed. The Mannoia men had one lying horizontally on a table in the garage facing the door into the house. It had been compressed with about 3,000 pounds of pressure, like a poised bomb.

Suddenly the door opened and there stood Kathy right in the line of possible fire should the spring break loose. Kevin "was scared spitless" that it would uncoil violently and shoot at her like a cannonball. So he shouted, "GET OUT!!" She was saved, he explained, and she forgave his apparent rudeness. The men, father and son, gave up on the coil business and a mechanic friend finished the job for them.

Then had come that big NAE invitation, seemingly out of the blue, or was it from God? Kevin was being invited to the presidency. He called aside his respected friend John Mark Richardson. "Here's what happening, John. What do you think I should do?" John had heard that some Free Methodist pastors were thinking of Kevin as "a bull in a China shop." Some who were leading smaller FM churches were rumored to be worried that if growth didn't come soon Bishop Mannoia might have them replaced. Others were claimed to be thinking that Kevin might not be re-elected and the invitation was a convenient way out.

Kevin reports that he told the head of the NAE search process that he was perfectly happy where he was. They initiated the call to him. He did not seek or pursue it. "I never have pursued ANY position nor was I at all worried about being re-elected."

Richardson encouraged Kevin to take seriously the opportunity. It would be a feather in the cap of the Free Methodist denomination, he observed, maybe even encourage more unity in the whole Christian cause, and certainly it would bring increased visibility to the Wesleyan-Holiness stream of the faith within the larger Evangelical world. Kevin heard and agreed with all that. He would accept the invitation believing that it was "about the maximum impact available for the Kingdom through my calling." Hopefully, he also could make it an asset and not a troubling development for his family.

CHAPTER NINE

SQUARE PEG IN A ROUND HOLE

The common method of securing the steel rails of a train track to the timber sleepers was to drive square-cut spikes into pre-drilled round holes. This difficult process became an idiomatic expression describing an individual who fails to fit into the niche of a society. Kevin Mannoia seems to have been ahead of his time, something of a square peg in a round hole.

"Failure," however, would be too strong a word for Kevin's short period of leading the National Association of Evangelicals. There was positive movement and fresh wind that he caused to blow. Major "refocus" was attempted. Some organizational identity shift and ministry priorities did happen, but with growing resistance that cut short the length of the young reformer's attempts.

Kevin Mannoia's tenure as president of the National Association of Evangelicals was only from 1999 to 2001. He was the youngest president ever and assumed office at a time when the NAE was aging and its annual meeting attendance down. He came bristling with fresh vision for a new day. The question would be whether the organization was ready for such big shifts. He was an activist and certainly would find out.

David McKenna, highly respected and longtime member and NAE officer, now concludes this. "Kevin cast a vision for an organization of denominational members who were held together by good will more than organizational commitment. Kevin may have misread their readiness and even ability for significant change." Ready of not, he would press on quickly with vision and determination.

Kevin's coming to the NAE as president was much like his father going to Brazil as missionary and seminary head nearly three decades before. The vision of both son and father was focused on church health and growth, more openness to understanding, reconciliation, and contemporary relevance. Father Jim Mannoia would move the Brazilian seminary to a dramatically new location, countryside to large city, and open its doors to a much wider range of students. Son Kevin would seek similar goals, moving the NAE headquarters from the traditional Chicago area to California and altering its bylaws to allow a broader range of membership.

Although the resulting turmoil of Kevin's few NAE years would be awkward for him and the organization, they both would survive. Having completed his NAE years, Kevin would conclude this. "I see the amazing grace of God that allows me to find meaning and purpose apart from position, title, and institution. It's like watching a caterpillar shed its outward skin and become something new." He could see more than the struggles he had faced and victories he had hoped for but were largely delayed. He would characterize his time this way. "While with the NAE, I did get accomplished about everything I had hoped, although some of it was not well consolidated and got reversed later." Such reversal would be the responsibility of others. He had fulfilled his calling.

Because of this sensed divine graciousness, Kevin would later see troubled paths somehow finding their ways into greener meadows of opportunity and ministry well beyond his few NAE years. This hardly eliminates the pain and sadness from his tenure's early ending. What it does do is keep him looking forward and remaining encouraged and productive regardless of frustrations. Faith should never falter because of institutional reversal that's beyond a leader's control. God's church transcends the life cycles of its institutions. Leaders must find ways to absorb reversal and move on. President Mannoia would do just that.

The Ecumenical Century

The twentieth is called the "ecumenical century" when Christian leaders worldwide were freshly sensitized to the evangelistic hurtfulness of the badly divided body of Christ's followers. How can Christians who can't manage well their own households bring a credible message of Christ's new community to a dangerously divided world? There arose various national councils of churches and a World Council of Churches formed in 1948. In the United States, the Federal Council of Churches began in 1908, followed by the National Council of Churches in 1950. Increased unity was in the wind despite the considerable diversity among world Christians.

The National Association of Evangelicals was founded in 1942, in large part to resist what it considered the "liberal" ecumenical trend. The NAE would stand for "classic" Christianity undiluted by modern theological compromises seen as often encouraged by unification efforts. It was a middle way between the "fundamentalist" American Council of Christian Churches and the "progressive" Federal Council of Churches.[52] While most Christians were generally agreed about the need for Christian unity, understandings of proper ways to it were anything but unified.

When Kevin Mannoia was elected president of the NAE in 1999, the "ecumenical" organization had weakened. Its previous president had tried to revitalize the membership, calling it "too old, too white, and too male." New NAE Chair Edward Foggs had

---

52   Carl F. H. Henry's classic *The Uneasy Conscience of Modern Fundamentalism* (1947) had served as the manifesto of "evangelical" Christians serious about bringing the fundamentals of the Christian faith to bear in contemporary culture. This seriousness was much of what brought Kevin Mannoia to the NAE, although without Henry's overlay of theological fundamentalism which for many was militant. At the first meeting of the NAE in 1942, Harold Ockenga warned his fellow "lone wolves" of the ominous clouds on the horizon that spelled "annihilation" unless they decided to "run in a pack."

nearly written off the organization himself, saying "it was dying or at least under the oxygen tent." For many inside the organization, the coming of Kevin Mannoia as president was a breath of fresh air, new hope for a more viable NAE future.

With active membership down, it seemed time for the organization to reinvent itself, and Mannoia was named the active agent of change. His personal vision was to shift the priority focus from "fighting the liberals" to church planting and enhancing the health and cultural impact of member churches and their pastors. At the same time, many vocal members weren't done with the liberals or comfortable with someone seemingly like them in their own ranks. Who is to define a "liberal"?

The governing board of the NAE was a large group, representatives of all affiliated bodies. The Executive Committee was the guiding and decisional body. Kevin Mannoia had been the Free Methodist bishop designated to represent his denomination in this body. He had developed key relationships, including with Lamar Vest of the Church of God (Cleveland), Chair of the Executive Committee from 1998 to 2000. Vest began talking with Kevin about the potential of his being considered as the next president when an opening emerged.

It soon did emerge and the coordinator of the search process also expressed clear interest in Kevin being a presidential candidate. Kevin's response? "I'm stunned by your interest, I'm not ready to leave the Free Methodist bishopric, so I need time to think and pray about this." He did and finally expressed a guarded openness to the consideration. He had a series of additional conversations with Vest and was flown to Chicago for a formal interview.

The initial decision of the Executive Committee was reported to favor another candidate. This unexpected decision caused Kevin some pain, his being human enough not to like the feeling of apparent rejection even if he hadn't been aggressively seeking the position. However, he soon received a call from Vest saying that "the urging of the Holy Spirit" had prevailed and the Executive Committee had reversed itself and now was affirming Kevin as God's choice.

Why the sharp change? Presumably the Executive Committee wanted someone with a more compelling vision to empower and encourage denominations and bring some unity to the evangelical movement in America. As a Board member, Kevin already was known as a man with exceptional relational skills, high vision, and the ability to inspire others. That's exactly what the NAE now needed.

Kevin realized that to accept this presidency would involve some personal redefinition. "My whole life had been defined by the Free Methodist Church. My radar screen never was larger than in terms of my future leadership there. Over the past few months the Lord has helped me expand that view so that going to the NAE can be seen not so much as leaving the FMC as broadening my ministry platform and vision to include many more groups. The NAE has a good heritage, very high profile, and huge influence. I would need to give it a vision to support all that before it collapsed for lack of substance."

Shortly after Kevin assumed office, Vest left the role of Chair and was replaced by Edward Foggs of the Church of God (Anderson), an African-American man Kevin soon came to respect highly. "Ed was a giant of a man in my book!" He relied on Ed and others on the Executive Committee whom he trusted. However, there remained a few "old school power brokers" who grated against Kevin's style, strength, and direction of leadership, something boding ill for the future.

Billy Melvin had been the long-term NAE president (1967 to 1995). Any differing vision and fresh priorities from a new and aggressive young man on the block likely would be resisted by Billy. Nor was Kevin totally sure of himself. He admitted this after a short time in office. "I am discovering the lack of momentum in the NAE and the huge amount I have to learn. I don't know how to go from where I am to where we should be. I'm not even sure what 'where we should be' looks like. I have never felt so inadequate or uncertain in my life."

There was more, a genuine self-doubt. "It seems that every time I turn around there is something else I find in the NAE which is a disillusionment. Have I made a mistake?" These were real but momentary cautions. He was prepared to move ahead.

Vigorous New Vision

Hardly one to back off, President Mannoia indeed did plow forward. About 350 registered participants were at the NAE's annual convention in March, 2000. They heard their new leader report that the organization now would reach out to mainline churches, charismatics, women, youth, and people of color in an effort to "embrace the whole body of Christ." The NAE should be "a river of healthy churches moving in unity to transform culture." As far as Kevin was concerned, the organization's very reason for existence would be shifting.

The shift would be from the reactionary, providing an alternative to the threatening theological liberalism, to more of a calling for churches to be agents of personal and community transformation. "The identity of NAE has to be seen as leaning into culture, not an enclave of evangelicalism." These rather dramatic announcements of Kevin were welcomed by some and of clear concern to others at this 2000 convention.

The young president told this to *Christianity Today*, evangelicalism's leading publication. "The NAE has perhaps drawn the circle too closely. We don't need to be looking for theological litmus tests. We should be replacing block walls with picket fences." Kevin obviously was intending the NAE to stop defining itself as those opposed to the faulty beliefs of "the other guys." Too often it had been shaped more by opposing others rather than by the center of biblical revelation, relationship with the person of Jesus Christ and engagement with Christ's ministry to the culture of the time. Kevin tended to be "relational" in his leadership style and theological approach. Both were quite new in this setting, joining to bring fresh hope and growing internal opposition.

Prominent United Methodist theologian Thomas Oden was among those attending the NAE for the first time. "There is a real evangelical ecumenism," he told *Christianity Today*. "This new leadership of Kevin Mannoia could signal a convergence of the NAE and mainline evangelicals." Actually, a bold step soon was taken in just that direction, newly allowing a denomination with membership in the National Council of Churches to also be a member body of the NAE if it wished. This friendly overture raised eyebrows among many NAE supporters, as did a parallel effort to forge cooperative ties with Roman Catholic bishops. Under Kevin's prompting, the NAE soon rewrote its bylaws to formalize these "softened" and broadened relationship stances.

With clear confidence in the rightness of such forward thrusts, Kevin still was unsure. "Who am I to say that now is the time to change and totally rewire and redefine evangelicalism in America?" Even so, he moved on, believing that it was God and not himself setting this fresh course of unifying a broader range of Christ's body. An address he gave in several locations in 2001 included this fresh way of defining "evangelicalism":

The New Evangelical Church is . . .
Centered in Christian orthodoxy;
Oriented in Christian community;
Concerned with Christian character;
Engaged with the world;
Characterized by mission;
Described by works of the Holy Spirit;
Active in multiplication.

Kevin certainly had charged out of the gate at full speed following his presidential election in 1999. Shortly after assuming leadership he had taken a very big step indeed, moving NAE's headquarters from Illinois to California, with a government affairs office in Washington, D.C. This dramatic move was intended to give the NAE a "bi-coastal national image."[53] It also was very symbolic for Kevin. It was separating the organization from its established roots in a suburban, white, largely male traditionalism, despite he and Kathy having strong family identification with Wheaton, Illinois. He was interested in "rewriting the nature of evangelicalism, painful but rewarding."

Billy Melvin, former president, sent a letter of opposition to all Board members slamming this proposal for moving the headquarters. The letter hit hard at the aggressive new leadership. Kevin responded this way in his personal journal. "On one thing I am as sure as a bell. I do not care much for what impact this has on my leadership. I will serve God in ways that I believe are right and good. I cannot afford nor do I have the ability to be more complicated than that." This was a reflection of that great insight he had received years before in that Houston airport. His call was to serve God, *not please people*.

The big move west was made, uprooting some of the key physical symbols of NAE's historic heritage. When first elected president, Kevin's daughter Kristyn remembers a discussion at home about the feared necessity of a family move to Chicago if Kevin went to the NAE. The kids had made it plain that they wanted no part of such a move way back east. Even so, Kevin is anxious for it to be clear that his family situation was not the motivation for the move of the headquarters to California.

Kevin did make it a habit of allowing his children to weigh in on decisions of his big ministry shifts, although it's unknown if

---

53   While NAE president, Kevin Mannoia spent considerably less time "on the hill" in Washington pressing for restrictive legislation and much more with denominational leaders.

they had any real influence this time. What is known is that Kevin was criticized sharply by some NAE people for even contemplating such a drastic move, some even suggesting openly that it was being done for personal and selfish reasons—so he could work from home in California and please his family. He insisted that it was for the good of the organization and was pleased when the Chair of the Executive Committee, Edward Foggs, stood tall and supported the move and the selling of the Wheaton, Illinois, property.

Another significant decision was made, this time clearly without regard for consequences to Kevin personally. The National Council of Churches was celebrating its 50th anniversary by staging what it called the "Great Conversation." Kevin realized that some of his NAE constituents wouldn't like his participating. In Billy Melvin's words, "it's consorting with the enemy. The NAE exists to beat down the liberals, and they are it!" Kevin participated anyway. He always was open to serious conversation with anyone, especially on behalf of the church's well-being, and he saw the church as much bigger than the members bodies of the NAE. For a few years Kevin would become quite active personally with the Faith and Order division of the National Council of Churches.

Such innovative and questionable initiatives of the young president kept coming. Kevin reached out and managed to convene in Dallas, Texas, a group of about thirty of the nation's mega-church pastors, people like Robert Schuller, Jack Hayford, John Perkins, Ted Haggard, Charles Blake, and T. D. Jakes. The intention of this "Thirty-Six Hours" gathering was to provide a safe place (no press allowed or minutes taken) for this unusual group to talk frankly with each other about their most intimate hopes, concerns, and the substantial influence they were having on so many young pastors in all denominations in and beyond the NAE.

Kevin knew that denominational heads could push the brakes on things they didn't like in their own circles, but this was the group that had its foot on the accelerator of God-ward change.

Only in this intimate setting could one event ever have happened. Bob Schuller shared very vulnerably about something and the group gathered around him and, with hands on this special brother, prayed for his acknowledged need. Even today, when Kevin recalls that scene, his eyes fill with tears. No details were recorded, necessary for it to have ever happened.

These pastors were frank indeed, reports Kevin, being brought together by someone they obviously trusted. They shared common concerns and came to know and support and even love each other as never before. Actions of Kevin like convening this private gathering left some long-time NAE members feeling overlooked, even compromised. "What was Mannoia doing? Is he really on our side?"

Kevin and T. D. Jakes became good friends. Later he turned to Kevin for help. Moody Bible Institute had pulled all of his books off its shelves, accusing him of being unorthodox in theology. Pleaded Jakes, "Kevin, help me understand the white evangelical mind!" Kevin did. Here's one key point he made. "The evangelicals are uncomfortable with your coming to understand God as seen through the historic suffering of your people rather than in the context of their classic propositional theology. Your contextual approach stimulates their theological defensiveness."

Afterwards, Kevin then wrote to Moody on behalf of T. D. and its decision about the books was reversed, maybe because of his letter, but Kevin isn't sure. He so wishes that this incident would teach people "not to codify Christian faith into rigid doctrinal precepts that become exclusive and isolating. God is inherently relational and our faith is in pursuit of a *Person* and not a *proposition*." That lesson comes hard to those with a fundamentalistic bent.

The National Religious Broadcasters broke its historic ties with the NAE for reasons beyond merely Kevin's leadership. Kevin couldn't respect what he judged the NRB's somewhat selfish anti-unity decision. He believes it wanted to grow its membership in an underhanded way, using the NAE change of bylaws (allowing dual membership, NCC and NAE) to say that the NAE was planning a merger with the NCC and thereby losing its evangelical moorings. Kevin pained over this. "I really cannot believe that such a self-serving false claim goes on in the name of Christ."[54]

Kevin's conviction was strong indeed. "Accepting one another without diluting our faith will not weaken the well-tempered character of the church nor will it alter the centralized message of the Lordship of Christ. In fact, it will be strengthened. Church unity is predicated especially on submission to Jesus Christ who is full and final expression of the nature of the Godhead."[55] No merger with the NCC had ever been contemplated. The very suggestion, in Kevin's view, was judged to be just more of the old fortress mentality, a cover for what some wanted for their own organizational purposes.

For years Kevin would serve in numerous planning meetings of the NCC's Faith and Order division with Dr. Bill Rusch, Director of Ecumenical Affairs, and then with his successor, the Quaker Ann K. Riggs for whom he developed high respect. Later, Kevin was requested to deliver a major paper that appeared in the 2012 book *Ecumenical Directions in the United States Today*. His chapter was titled "Kingdom Chaos: The Joy of Finding Unity: An Evangelical Perspective on the Future of Ecumenism." Of course, it had direct reference to his earlier years as president of the NAE.

The evangelical movement, according to President Mannoia, is a positive force of God in today's divine work in the world. It can't be defined precisely, ignored, or minimized. "Those who try to codify it, organize it, define it, control it, direct it, or in any way manipulate it as a whole do so at their own peril" (Kevin's personal

---

54 Robert Schuller of the Reformed Church of America was thrilled at the change to allow dual membership, ending an unnecessary exclusivity, and was deeply upset when, after Kevin Mannoia's presidency, the NAE reversed this decision.

55 This comes from Kevin's personal journal. Often he could say privately to himself more than was wise to announce bluntly in public.

experience with the NAE!). He continues. Often present is a "fortress mentality, the logical expression of a fear-based existence that leads to an enclave of exclusivism." Nonetheless, envisioned beyond this evangelical problem is, at least in Kevin Mannoia's mind, the hope among evangelicals for a fresh focus on realizing Christian unity for the sake of church mission.

If such is to happen, it will be characterized by "relationships established through networks, described experientially, celebrating diversity, driven by mission, and centered on Jesus Christ." The obstacles to this do seem insurmountable. Ironically, for Kevin, "that's the joy of it. It is impossible *for us*, but not *for God*. Our God is not ordered according to our patterns or contained by our structures. In God there is energy that surpasses our ability to confine. In that I take hope. Only God in the divine transcendent 'chaos' can bring the unity for which Jesus prayed."[56]

A fresh motto now was being heard occasionally from Kevin. It was "*Anchored and Reaching*."[57] The evangelical church, to have the integrity God intends, will have both deep roots in the revealed gospel of Jesus *and* deep involvement in the current mission of Jesus. Kevin began the habit when he traveled of taking along bungee cords for exercise use in a hotel room. When hooked solidly on a door knob, both ends can be stretched to the middle of the room to worked to strengthen muscles. The cord, to fulfill its mission however, must be anchored *and* reaching. Being anchored to the knob but hanging limp to the floor is a useless situation. To not be anchored is worse than useless.

Kevin had found far too much identity and action limpness in the NAE, and real resistance to the perceived dangers of any

---

56   Kevin Mannoia, "Kingdom Chaos: The Joy of Finding Unity: An Evangelical Perspective on the Future of Ecumenism," in *Ecumenical Directions in the United States Today* (Paulist Press, 2012). It was in the context of these NCC meetings that Kevin built a relationship with Bill Eerdmans and convinced him to publish *The Holiness Manifesto* book (Kevin and Don Thorsen, eds.).

57   More recently, this phrase has become the name of Kevin's personal podcast.

meaningful change. While this was a persistent problem, what finally broke the camel's back of Kevin's relatively brief NAE presidency probably was the lack of money. Financial woes of the organization had worsened and now were hindering the viability of Kevin's reforming causes. The headquarters had a faulty administrative system, worsened by the new necessity of having to layoff some key staff members.

Total income to the NAE dropped by a third from 1999 to 2000. Expenses now exceeded income considerably, requiring the painful staff layoffs. The impetus for "ecumenism" among Christians was declining generally. As a counter force, Kevin was seeking to enlarge the circle and increase the initiatives of the whole evangelical Christian world in North America. He was an active networker at a time when the odds seemed against such noble efforts. Add to that the decline of available operating dollars and the end of Kevin's presidency would come in 2001.

Trouble Clouds Gather

A common criticism of President Mannoia was that he had "gone soft" on liberalism. In fact, he was thoroughly orthodox in theology and strong on biblical commitment—although admittedly not an "inerrantist." He was following through on his 1999 pledge to broaden the circle of the NAE to include evangelicals in the old-line Protestant churches and also in "charismatic" circles. He had done both. These changes had nothing to do with being "liberal" or "conservative." They were more an issue of shifting the NAE's center of gravity from what it was *against* to what it hoped to accomplish together, more relationally, in church health and mission.

President Bob Brower of Point Loma Nazarene University says, "Exploration and protection are not good cousins." Kevin had relaxed the protective fists of the NAE and gone relationship exploring with open hands. He was looking for the growing edges of truth and mission while many of the evangelicals in the NAE still were focused on protecting God's reputation and revelation from what they saw as encroaching contemporary heretics.

This clash of central aims had caused trouble clouds to gather. Admitted Kevin, "I'm trusting God to protect us from our own conservative constituency. I don't fear the press, the public, the NCC, or the Roman Catholic Church. I fear some of our own people. I have already pushed them to the edge by moving the organization to Los Angeles and changing our bylaws. My efforts to stay above the fray and not condemn the NCC or close the door soundly on any future dialogue is perceived by our conservative people as compromise and playing a 'footsies' game."

Kevin once conveyed his analysis and related anxiety with a biblical analogy. "I have never lived or worked like this before. Faith has deepened. Dependence and transparency have grown. But there is the frightening side. It sometimes feels as though I live on the edge of ineffectiveness and collapse emotionally. I'm impressed that we are definitely out of Egypt and across the Red Sea. I have no road map save the pillar of God, and now I feel like the supplies we brought with us from Egypt have run out. I pray now for manna from heaven!"

Supplies running out? Kevin finally had gotten some reliable information from the NAE's most undependable operating data system. He learned that the financial situation was worse than anyone realized. The organization was deficit spending by some $40,000 per month and the total debt was approaching one-half million dollars. Kevin had to make some unpopular personnel reductions. High hopes had to be reduced because of lowered implementation ability. This frustrated everyone.

Meanwhile, Robert Pearson was running into the same negative whirlwind. Having served as Kevin's colleague in California for their respective denominations, Bob had assumed the top leadership role in the Church of God (Anderson) at about the same time as Kevin had begun heading the NAE. He offered the commissioning prayer when Kevin was on the Anderson University campus and transitioning from his role as FM Bishop to NAE President. Like Kevin, Bob was a natural networker with high vision for Christian unity and aggressive church growth. Quickly, however, there came a similar resistance to his aggressive moves for change and then a realization that he had inherited a large debt load.

Such a set of negative circumstances brought an early resignation from Pearson and another was coming for Mannoia in the immediate future. During what was Kevin's final meeting of the Executive Committee of the NAE in Washington D.C., he realized that increasingly he was stressing the organization to the breaking point. The mood seemed to be toward much slower and very bureaucratic approaches to the organization's identity and mission. That was naturally very uncomfortable for Kevin.

At a key moment, Kevin made what for him was a strong "power statement" of quite a bureaucratic nature. At the coffee break one man tapped hard on Kevin's chest with two fingers, got close to his face, and said, "Kevin, what you just said is not who you are." The toxic environment was trying to twist him away from his true self.

Based on his own writing in *The Integrity Factor* and constant preaching about character and leadership formation, Kevin realized that this criticism was sadly correct. His very identity was in danger of being compromised in this deteriorating and even toxic environment. "I realized that my leadership capital was exhausted. The conservative Christian world appeared unready for significant change, at least not to the degree and at the pace that Bob Pearson and I had in mind." Both decided reluctantly that it was time to step aside.

Said Kevin: "For me it boils down to this. I have moved very fast in effecting changes. In the process I have not brought things along in order to support that change. These things include the administrative structures and finances and the people on whom we have depended. I recognize this and accept it."[58]

To Be Judged a Failure?

President Mannoia was quite plain in his personal journal. "Evangelicals have a long way to go in understanding Christian grace and the mind of Jesus. I need to get out! I'll just walk away and let people think I'm a failure if they want. Recognizing that support had eroded, the best thing for the NAE Executive Committee and for me was simply to step away and let the organization breathe."[59]

Whatever breathing was needed, the NAE Chair at the time, Edward Foggs, praised Mannoia for leading the NAE "with courage and conviction through important changes. He was willing to take risks. The pace of change was just more rapid than many could embrace. There were divergent perspectives about certain operational and fiscal matters that led to the resignation." It was a mixed bag, an unfortunate set of circumstances, probably a presidential square peg in a round hole, a visionary man of God in too much of a hurry.

Reads Kevin's resignation statement: "I have invested heavily in creating a climate for change in the NAE and am pleased at the significant changes that were necessary for stepping into the new day. In the process, however, I have 'spent my capital' and come to a point where I cannot be effective in moving it forward in the ways necessary to assimilate that change into the broad and corporate mind of the NAE."

Had Kevin's accepting the NAE helm been a mistake? Reading things in such a negative way is certainly uncharacteristic of Kevin. "The call of God is something far deeper than a position. For me,

---

58   In Kevin's personal journal, June, 2001.

59   In Kevin's personal journal, February, 2001.

this was a stewardship issue. I felt at the time that it was the best deployment of the assets that God had entrusted to my care for His Kingdom's sake." Kevin had done what he could with the considerable number of negative factors he had inherited. Now he was open to the stewardship of some redeployment as God would choose to direct and provide.

Denny Wayman, Kevin's valued ministerial colleague in California, has it right. "Setting out to alter the DNA of the NAE was a difficult task, but to some meaningful degree Kevin did succeed." There is one night Kevin will never forget. He had hoped to influence the evangelical community in new directions, including a fresh focus away from political influence to Kingdom influence on the culture. The memorable sight was a strong indication that it had happened, at least in part.

It happened at the NAE conference where Kevin, in the face of some criticism, had arranged for the organization to award to African-Americans Andrae and Sandra Crouch the *Reconciliation Award of the Year*. They received it gladly and then, as requested, began singing his signature song, "My Tribute: To God be the Glory." This already was a gospel classic. Andrae had just been inducted into the Gospel Hall of Fame. Kevin was seated on the front row next to his close friend Ted Haggard and was emotionally moved. The music being quite loud, Ted suddenly shouted something in Kevin's ear. "You Win! You Win!" Kevin looked behind him and began crying, and said to Ted, "No, God wins!"

What was the unforgettable sight behind Kevin? He saw most of the evangelical leaders and denominational heads in the ballroom on their feet, arms raised in praise to God! They weren't fighting liberals or fussing over doctrinal incidentals but were praising God together! A new image for the NAE? Was it coming into a new day just as Kevin hoped? Major newspapers carried headlines like, "EVANGELICALS—NO LONGER MONOLITHIC" and "NOT THE NAE OF YOUR FATHERS." Kevin sensed God on the move.

Yes, Kevin had won for that grand moment but not overall. Too few dollars and too much opposition from some brought things to a head for President Mannoia. Kevin's wife Kathy recalls the pain involved in the departure transition. "The database of the NAE was a wreck and I knew something had to change."

She was at home reading, quietly waiting for her husband to return from a tense NAE meeting. He appeared, leaned against the door jamb, and announced, "I resigned!" Kathy responded with "YEA!" knowing that it had to happen, and probably the sooner the better. "It was," she now says, "both a huge relief and a little scary." After all, what would be next? Whatever it would be, Kevin admits this about his NAE years. "It was wonderful. I loved it! Yes, there was lots of pain, but pain is part of growth, and there was growth even if only by a few degrees."

Recently, the NAE website has announced that "Evangelicals are a vibrant and diverse group, including believers found in many churches, denominations, and nations. Our community brings together Reformed, Holiness, Anabaptist, Pentecostal, Charismatic, and other traditions." A headline on the site reads, "Evangelicals—Shared Faith in Broad Diversity," meaning that "our core theological convictions provide unity in the midst of our diversity."

This sounds almost like Kevin had written it. When asked if this sense of breadth and openness to diversity reflects his lingering positive influence on the NAE after many years, he responded humbly.

> I am really happy with this statement. Any influence I may have had on it or the NAE is completely unknown to me. Perhaps a ripple effect could be traced to me, my contemporary work being known to them and therefore influencing them, but only God knows. The thing that might be a continuation of what I committed to is the matter of unity amidst diversity. God uses what we've done to inform what we are doing. I have always taken everything I have into my next thing.

CHAPTER TEN

AZUSA THE KEY HOMEBASE

A Southern California Christian school was begun in 1899 by the area Quaker community. It was intended to be "God First" from the beginning, a Training School for Christian Workers. In the 1960s Los Angeles Pacific College of the Free Methodist Church and Arlington College of the Church of God (Anderson) merged with the expanding Azusa campus. By the 1990s the school was supported by five affiliated religious bodies, now including the Brethren in Christ, the Missionary Church, and the Salvation Army.

Azusa Pacific University became the scene of many years of ministry for Kevin Mannoia at the staff, faculty, and academic administrative levels. It was the welcome harbor that followed the NAE storm that Kevin had endured. This would be his redeployment homebase. For many years to come he would benefit from its many resources and seek to enrich its Wesleyan heritage and growing world outreach.

Numerous references to Azusa Pacific University must be made in any telling of the story of Kevin Mannoia. They will be of various kinds, some on the negative side. On balance, the positives definitely will prevail. When Kevin's daughter Kristyn was first enrolling as an undergraduate freshman on this campus, Jon R. Wallace was president. The faculty discount deriving from her father's new employment there, plus scholarships, covered her basic educational cost.

Looking back now, Kevin and Kathy are so grateful. "It blows our minds!" They sensed a divine orchestration of things that allowed the future to unfold in fruitful ways. The campus of APU would be central for their family and for Kevin's ministerial career for years to come. In 2023, then newly retired from Azusa, Kevin would look back and characterize the memories of his long experience on the Azusa campus.

> APU was a fabulous ministry platform for me in many ways. I am indeed grateful to God for it. Although fraught with bumps here and there, something bound to occur with any institution over time, especially when one's serving in rather high-profile roles, this university was a true gift of God to me. Key campus leaders were aware of my larger ministry well beyond the university and could see how it was a benefit to APU.

Kevin would become a prominent and trusted voice on the Azusa campus. He would be a nurturer and networker of numerous faculty and staff persons, and a valued presidential confidant. This was especially true with President Wallace for whom Kevin was received as a source of wisdom and vision. Whatever the shifting titles and various campus roles at Azusa over the years, Kevin would work hard at adding to the university a clearer Wesleyan identity and developing a dramatic international footprint. The years, however, did bring some significant difficulties to Kevin's door.

Redeployment to Haggard

Azusa Pacific was unknown to Kevin Mannoia until his arriving in Southern California from Texas as a new Free Methodist superintendent. His first awareness was awkward. "I got a call from Bruce Kline, the Free Methodist Director of Higher Education.

He wanted me to know that there would be a recommendation coming to sever the denomination's tie with Azusa. I didn't know all the reasons but simply asked, 'Can you please delay that and give me a year to sort things out?'"

Kevin thought that reasonable and it was agreed. He soon set up a meeting with Ted Engstrom who had become interim president of APU. They spent a lot of time talking about the brokenness of the relationship and future possibilities. It was agreed that a joint committee would be formed to explore rebuilding the relationship. It was successful.

Years passed, Kevin moved to the bishop role, then to the NAE presidency, and finally to the necessary search for a redeployment after his resignation. Within a short two months he would be finalizing a new plan, assuming the deanship of Haggard School of Theology at Azusa Pacific University. October 1, 2001, was the official beginning date. His office would be only 150 yards from the dorm room of his daughter Kristyn, a beginning freshman.

He recalls, "It's amazing how God has worked all this out! As tough as the work with the NAE was in many ways, it was absolutely wonderful, and now I'm grateful to God for the privilege of those experiences." Being faced at Azusa now was a new set of challenges and exciting opportunities.

APU's President Wallace said this about Kevin's arrival on campus as the new seminary dean. "Dr. Mannoia loves the church and we wanted a dean who would strengthen the outreach ministry and training of Haggard School of Theology." One institutional goal was assisting with the building of healthy churches, not being hampered by the isolation of an ivory tower seminary judged not relevant to the churches.

Earlier Kevin had helped rebuild the relationship between the Free Methodist Church and this campus when denominational superintendent, and a major goal of Kevin's time at the NAE had been revitalizing churches across the nation for fresh mission. The resourcing and nurturing of church leadership for relevant mission in today's world was in the Mannoia blood.

Jon Wallace would be a key figure in Kevin's professional life for nearly all of his coming years at Azusa. Jon would serve as president from 2000 to 2019. He earned degrees from Azusa in the 1970s and served in various positions on campus, including Dean of Students before his becoming president. He cared about healthy campus-church relations and had a strong appreciation of internationalism, key to many aspects of Kevin's coming activities on and from the Azusa base.

Once Jon joined other Christian college presidents in sending a letter to the White House concerning an executive order on immigration: "Many in our diverse communities come to our campuses on the shoulders of immigrants. Indeed, we all share pages in that American heritage of welcoming the vulnerable, extending hospitality, and inviting participation in the great experiment of these United States." Campus programming under Jon would reflect this generous perspective, and soon Kevin would be a presidential right arm in this and other regards.

Kevin recalls with pleasure the key part his children were allowed to play in the big decision process about his future ministry deployment after the NAE resignation. "I love the fact that my children basically set the trajectory of our lives from 2001 onward. They are awesome!"

Six redeployment options had come Kevin's way quickly. He and Kathy had decided to ask the three children to think and pray with them during a declared 45-day beach interim period (Kevin would be on the California beach with his family as much as possible). The big question before the family was, "Which of the options would the children advise, some being on the East Coast of the United States. Kristyn had just graduated from high school, Christopher was entering high school, with Corey was in fifth grade. Kevin thinks he actually told them he would do what they decided.

Finally, Kristyn responded for the three kids, saying essentially this. "If it's all the same to you guys, we'd like to stay in Southern California. Other than that, we think any of the three California options would be fine." With that, Kevin proceeded to choose the invitation to Azusa Pacific University. On September 11, 2001, on his drive to Azusa to carry his decision to President Jon Wallace, he called Robert Schuller at his Crystal Cathedral and turned down Bob's gracious offer for him to work closely with Bob in an expanding international ministry, basically designing the strategic future of his amazing church. These two progressive church leaders had come to know and respect each other before and during Kevin's NAE years.

Now ahead would be many years of Kevin being based at Azusa and functioning in various roles, beginning with the deanship of Haggard Graduate School of Theology, the role he would fill from September, 2001, to August, 2004. He would long carry the title "Professor of Ministry." Initially he judged this graduate school to have a wonderful faculty. He looked forward to "listening, learning, and leading there, preparing disciples and scholars to advance the work of God's kingdom."

Dean Mannoia launched his seminary leadership with a set of assumptions that appeared to fit well the desires of President Wallace. Recent years had seen many denominations taking a close and often critical look at their seminaries. They tended to see a general lack of apparent relevance to what congregations were needing in their new leaders. Church efforts to reach their communities and multiply their ministries were not being aided by the academic rigor and inflexibility of institutions educating ministers. The gulf between them had become quite wide.

Churches increasingly were beginning to do their own ministerial training, stressing practical preparation for specific functions in modern church life. Kevin recognized the reasons for this but only in part did he affirm its wisdom. There had to be a workable middle ground. Serious learning beyond immediate practical function is required in rapidly changing circumstances. "The discipline of the mind, pursuit of truth, and hunger for education calls for reconsideration of the once-abandoned academy. As for the seminaries, we must maintain high accountability to the guilds *and* high commitment to the church and its mission."[60] The tension of faith and learning would become a priority consideration for Kevin in coming years.[61] It clearly was reflective of his father's ministry at Spring Arbor and in Brazil.

Asked the new Dean Mannoia, "An ivory tower isolation of academics from practical church life? No! Does the practical life of the church have any real need of the academy? Yes!" Finding that essential connection was a core goal of the new seminary dean. Kevin saw the evangelical Christian community beginning to grow up. He had helped that growth as much as he could through his previous NAE post. The life of the church was now being shaped too much by the current microwave culture where value was being placed heavily on sound-byte education for specialized skills and immediate results. Believed the new Azusa dean, this circumstance

---

60　See the Mannoia article found in *IN TRUST* (Spring, 2003).

61　Just before the beginning of Kevin's deanship, his brother Jim had authored a major volume on this very subject, *Christian Liberal Arts: An Education that Goes Beyond.*

must be understood, honored for the good it is, and also judged inadequate for the weakness it also has.

Kevin believed that a new adulthood was slowly settling in for the evangelical Christian community. There was rising awareness of a need for mentoring new leaders in *depth spirituality*, contemplation for wisdom beyond the moment, and character formation in addition to being "saved" and well informed. Today's church needs its leaders to be mature disciples of Jesus motivated and able to engage constructively today's culture. They must know how to be as clever as serpents and as gentle as doves (Matt. 10:16). Needed was an "integrative" adulthood for the church and its leaders. Nurturing such adulthood was surely one role of the seminary.

Kevin was very much in a learning mode personally as a new dean at the graduate-school level. Inspired particularly by faculty colleague Don Thorsen, church history became a new passion. The dean soon funded an artist to paint the portraits of the founders of several of the holiness denominations associated with Azusa, all now hanging impressively in Azusa's "Founders Hall." "As I learned from Don Thorsen," Kevin explains, "I brought to vision the history of the school rooted in orthodox Christianity, and especially in its Wesleyan identity."

Kevin became supportive of Dr. Thorsen's program called *The Word Made Fresh*. It was a Friday-night lectureship held annually for sixteen years, co-led by Stanley Grenz, Roger Olson, and Don Thorsen. Invited to Azusa were prominent evangelical scholars, sometimes ones marginalized by the larger evangelical world. Clark Pinnock, Tom Oden, Ron Sider, and Billy Abraham were among them. Thorsen coordinated these lectures from 2002-2019, always encouraged by Dean Mannoia.

Being a school dean brings its difficult personnel decisions. In January, 2002, Kevin had to look carefully at the continuation as a faculty member of former seminary dean Les Blank. He decided to not renew this contract, making Blank clearly unhappy and yet knowing that it needed to be done. Kevin tried hard not to demean this good man, talking to President Wallace about his decision in advance. With the president's support, Kevin proceeded with the termination, commenting, "I have a hunch this marks the beginning of the end of my honeymoon period as dean." One particular faculty appointment of his soon made that ending quite clear.

A Big Bump in the Road

One of the more difficult episodes of Kevin Mannoia's entire ministry would occur while he was heading the School of Theology of Azusa Pacific University. Although highly educated himself, he openly admits to not being a pure "academic" in the research and certainly ivory-tower sense. He was and remains more of a churchman with high educational ideals. That was made clear to the Azusa seminary faculty. It's what the school wanted and needed at the time of his coming.

Soon the new dean chose to emphasize the "scholarly" phase of his vision by bringing Dr. Donald Dayton to the faculty. By such an appointment Kevin hoped to introduce more of an academic focus to the seminary. Don was superbly prepared to enhance that focus, especially in faculty and student understanding of scholarship related to the Wesleyan-Holiness tradition of the Christian faith, some of which Don had authored himself. This particular tradition of the faith was key to Kevin's personal identity, and he hoped it also would become more so for Azusa's conscious institutional self-understanding. As Haggard dean, he took personal initiative for Don's faculty appointment. It would, he hoped, bring a welcome face of academic respectability to the eyes of the school's academic accreditors. It also, unfortunately, would bring much pain to the seminary dean.

The hope was to highlight the Wesleyan-Holiness tradition in part by launching a new Ph.D. program in Wesleyan Theology.

With the encouragement of faculty colleague Don Thorsen, Kevin brought to the Azusa faculty this especially well-known scholar in the field, widely recognized for holding impeccable academic credentials and the presumed ability to anchor the new doctoral program Kevin envisioned.[62] This strategic appointment of Dr. Dayton was made despite his having some personal eccentricities that might have to be managed with considerable care by the dean. Kevin knew about these and thought he could handle any awkwardness out of the public eye, something worth the risk given all the positives.

Church historian Bill Kostlevy now observes this. "Since both Don Dayton and Kevin Mannoia are visionaries, but with different educational backgrounds and somewhat different goals, it was inevitable that they would clash. Don was a graduate of Yale and the University of Chicago. Kevin was a graduate of Trinity, outside the Wesleyan-Holiness tradition, and a state university in Texas. Kevin's leadership roles had been in the church, not the academy." True, Don had some qualifications Kevin lacked, which is partly why Kevin brought him.

Don came to Azusa as a "golden egg" for the campus during re-accreditation years. He and his background would look great on paper. Soon, however, Don decided that the campus was not capable of establishing a new graduate program that met his high standards. He found the library seriously inadequate, the faculty largely unqualified, and campus politics quite unintelligible to him. Even so, Kevin was grateful that Don was willing at least to think with him in some aggressive academic planning. While Don was willing to try, frustration and failure were ahead.

Don's frustration seemed to ignite his personal eccentricities. There came spurts of anger at staff and faculty colleagues,

---

62   Two celebrated books by Dr. Dayton were *Celebrating an Evangelical Heritage* and *Theological Roots of Pentecostalism.*

sometimes in the open. He was delinquent in his routine responsibilities for grading student performance and sloppy at best in caring for his personal and office appearances. Once his office was actually deemed an institutional fire hazard! While greatly frustrated, Dean Mannoia continued trying to keep the mounting negatives out of sight as much as possible.

It wasn't long, however, until awareness of some of Don's problems widened and Kevin had to apologize to top university officials for failing to report everything and act decisively to end the problems. "As much as I wanted to keep Don on the faculty, all of his idiosyncrasies notwithstanding, I now realized that I did not have the institutional capital to win the day." The trigger for Don's final firing probably was an angry fit that involved throwing a pile of papers on the desk of Kevin's administrative assistant, an act judged by the school as unacceptable harassment.

Don was summarily separated from the school. His friend and colleague Don Thorsen wasn't surprised but was deeply grieved by the apparent necessity. Not long after, Kevin, also deeply grieved, was himself separated from his seminary leadership and offered the newly formed position of University Chaplain. This was a role he had himself designed earlier as an institutional need without it being implemented until after this crisis. He could have remained in the seminary as a full-time faculty member, of course, but he wasn't comfortable with that idea. His continuing presence might be a problem for a new dean, and he had strong pastoral instincts and caring for the spiritual needs of his many campus colleagues.

Kevin continued to consider Dr. Dayton a highly respected friend despite the troubling Azusa failure. He never felt that he and Don were really at odds personally. Without question, however, his having to move out of the dean's role at APU was very painful for Kevin. He recalls asking this of the Lord. "Just tell me that you love me and I'll be OK."

It's clear that Kevin deserved some of the blame. "I had not told the whole truth to the Provost about things related to Don Dayton. Why? Because I didn't want Don to be impugned and I didn't want to think I couldn't handle this." But Don's issues were more than Kevin could manage well and always out of sight. Bringing Don to campus had been an honorable dream that just went sour.

The guilt came from a mixture of Kevin's having so much respect for Don as a scholar and his own presumed self-sufficiency rearing its old head. He knew APU "would have run Don in the mud if they had known some things about Don that I knew." Kevin soon did confess to the Provost and members of his own family for having not reported the whole truth and having hoped for more than he could deliver. All understood and Kevin was given an opportunity for a new future on campus, one he certainly would capitalize on in quite amazing ways in future years.

Kevin has reflected often on these painful days of failure and transition. "It was probably when the academic and ecclesial forces came into engagement most visibly and were most tension-filled for me." The engagement had been full of friction for reasons largely although not wholly beyond his control. For a visionary activist, the abrupt ending of the NAE presidency and then this departure from the seminary deanship joined to be a difficult double blow hard to absorb. They might have been ministry ending for most people. Not for Kevin.

Kevin has a way of moving on in hope and even gratitude, regardless of circumstance. Part of the explanation for this ability is the great support of his wife at home. Part also is his deep belief that he is doing the Lord's work faithfully, serving God and *not people*. Whatever failures may frustrate, God will see to it that there will arise a favorable way forward.

Dean Mannoia had envisioned well in the Dayton situation, but with intervening forces disrupting vision fulfillment. Included at a point or two was Kevin's own pride and inadequacy that needed more of the transforming work of God. The new chaplaincy role that would come next for Kevin at Azusa would blossom into a highly productive base for future ministry on campus, and from there to much of the wider world. God is so good!

The institutional weight of detailed administrative responsibility hadn't proven an ideal fit for Kevin's gifts and calling. He is a creator, activist, traveler, connector with people, personal mentor of future church leaders. He's a flying missionary to the churches and schools of the world. Fortunately for him, Azusa Pacific came to see value for itself in enabling such a ministry for Kevin—a missionary educator who would be well funded and without geographic boundaries.

Kevin now would experience Azusa as an ongoing and gracious host base for his future ministry. In return, he would enrich a range of its programs and nurture numerous of his colleagues academically and spiritually. He would do this with fresh curricular designs and spiritual ministries, and he would connect many of them helpfully with numerous institutions of Christian higher education worldwide. Various denominational bodies would become involved in this process and Kevin would sense ways to penetrate their organizational needs with rays of fresh hope.

Rev. Dr. Mannoia now was poised to move on from being a pastor, superintendent, bishop, president, faculty member and dean—well beyond. While carrying some scars with him, they would not obstruct much that God still had in mind for this gifted servant of the Kingdom of God.

Completing a Wonderful Relationship

There was wide-ranging new ministry ahead for Kevin Mannoia, still based on the Azusa campus despite his troubling departure from its seminary deanship. It would be accomplished in part around the world without Kevin neglecting the original impetus for his new, post-dean chaplaincy role. Azusa's president, provost, and even board of trustees already had been very concerned that there existed no campus-sponsored spiritual care focused on Azusa's many graduate and professional students, nor for that matter was there any particular spiritual care being provided for faculty and staff.

Celebrating with a group of MBA graduates.

Consequently, Kevin set about developing and fulfilling the new chaplaincy role between 2004 and 2020. It came to be all of the following and more:

- Spiritual care for graduate & professional students (approx. 10,000)—*Soul Quest.*[63]

- Spiritual care for faculty & staff, including events, emphases, etc. (approx. 2,500).

- Counsel to the president, administration, and Board on matters of institutional identity.

---

63   By 2016 Kevin had a network of regional chaplains, one for each of Azusa's regional centers and schools. He wrote weekly emails to all graduate students. Most of these now are on his website and YouTube channel in video format. He reports introducing more people to Jesus through this program than in his earlier roles as church superintendent and bishop.

- Oversight of one associate chaplain and thirteen part-time regional chaplains.

In 2010, for instance, as APU's campus Chaplain, Kevin would note this in his personal journal:

> This is a year of expansion, taking things to the next level. The *Soul Quest* program is moving forward in the School of Nursing and beyond; in the School of Business I will be taking for the first time MBA's to Brazil; faculty chaplaincy efforts are expanding with an orientation and a reformed faculty spiritual-care retreat; the Spiritual Emphasis Committee is coordinating well the Day of Prayer, Spiritual Emphasis Day, Faculty/Staff Chapels, and the prayer ministry. I'm investing personally in the deans.

To get into the detail of all this would take volume two of any Mannoia biography! Kevin's post-dean campus ministry opportunities were being maximized marvelously. He was doing innovative pastoring in an academic setting.

Chaplain Mannoia would leave Azusa in 2020, framing it publicly as "retiring" to make sure there was projected no hint of "bad blood." In fact, he was full of gratitude. His central functions on campus had seemed to run their course and the lead pastor at the Rock Church in San Diego had been urging him to come on staff there and actively mentor his young associates.

Kevin did stay at Azusa long enough to assist President Wallace complete his long tenure. The president's dying of cancer was creating a leadership vacuum setting off unfortunate campus dynamics among aspiring future leaders. It soon was hurting many people. Kevin loved Jon Wallace but wanted no part of more administrative chaos, other than privately counseling with various individuals caught unfairly in the transitional dynamics.

A few of these "victims" would leave Azusa and become significant professors and administrators in other Christian universities.[64] They went with Kevin's blessing and sometimes even direct assistance. He certainly wished no harm to Azusa that had been so good to him. Even so, he is a highly relational individual who is quick to assist persons in need. He always was connected with a network of such persons.

Kevin's daughter Kristyn, by then a vascular surgeon, recalls all this campus confusion clearly and still struggles to forgive. She's amazed that her father could go on at Azusa as long as he did, not only go on but be a healing agent even for some who in her view clearly didn't deserve it. Kevin came to realize that he and the new president following Wallace were not on the same wavelength, so he decided to complete his contract and not renew, calling it retirement and moving on to big new challenges.

He now would shift his gifts and energies initially to the Rock Church in San Diego, functioning very effectively there for two years. In this mega-congregation, he was the "Pastoral Coach" before the lead pastor seemed to shift his leadership philosophy away from that of Kevin's. Despite this philosophic rift between himself and Rev. Miles McPherson, former NFL football player, Kevin invited Miles to stand with him as he received the Pastor-Preacher-Scholar Award from the Wesleyan Theological Society. He gladly did so and delivered a moving tribute to Kevin's ministry.

In August, 2022, Kevin chose to be free of institutional commitments, free to roam the world as a freelance ambassador of Christ and his Kingdom. Many new doors were opening to him. God was guiding and is so good! On the table now were the Wesleyan

---

64 Dr. Katy Tangenberg was a colleague of Kevin's at APU who had been mentored helpfully by him over the years. She found herself caught in the middle of a campus turmoil and now serves effectively and happily at Seattle Pacific University under the new presidency of Deana Porterfield, also once at APU and very appreciative of Kevin's friendship and mentoring over the years. Many others were served in this manner by Chaplain Mannoia.

Holiness Connection, Aldersgate Press, and Aldersgate School of Ministry, all founded by Kevin, the International Council of Higher Education with Kevin as president, his *Anchored and Reaching* podcast, and more, much more—including grandchildren.

In fact, by 2024 Kevin's assistance was being sought again for continuing service to Azusa Pacific University, especially related to its large School of Nursing. The former office of University Chaplain had been closed, but there was no end to the urgent need for faculty understanding of faith-learning integration. Numerous nursing faculty members were facing promotion or extended contract decisions and expected to write wisely on such integration. Kevin's assistance was urgently sought and he was more than pleased to re-engage. Retirement had not altered his passion for this need or his love for this campus and its faculty.

CHAPTER ELEVEN

REACHING A DIVERSE WORLD

Attempting to gain a clear focus on the Kingdom of God will be a partial failure because we all view it from our limited contexts. We tend to assume that what we know of the Kingdom is fully what it is, even concluding that anyone who doesn't see the Kingdom as we do is misguided. Kevin Mannoia is still traveling the world, seeing the Kingdom from multiple angles, and encouraging theological roots that enhance Kingdom fruits. Is his view limited? Yes, but much less so than most. John Wesley said that the world was his parish. Kevin Mannoia represents this tradition, having himself become a true world Christian. He actively seeks to overcome the typical bias by consciously being part of the global Christian family.

Just as multiple reference points are required to accurately pinpoint a target in space, so multiple perspectives will aid in gaining a fuller understanding of the Kingdom and what constitutes a healthy church engaged in world mission. Guiding a new generation of believers today must be a multi-cultural effort, seeing diversity within the body of Christ as more an asset than an obstacle.

While Kevin Mannoia has been finding real benefit in the diversity of the Christian family, he has not been pushing some pluralism that gives spiritual credence to any opinion or religion. For him the center always remains the Kingdom of God where Jesus Christ is absolute Lord. The task is to lead in a way that guides people to new insights and perspectives on the Kingdom while maintaining the foundation firmly in the center, Jesus Christ. There indeed may be multiple reference points, but only one target, one center, only one Son of the most high God.

Such unity in diversity is the life and mission context of the church in this new millennium. The door that God is opening before the church is one that requires bold steps ahead in discriminating between the bias of individual perspectives and the inherent nature of the Kingdom that transcends all human variables. Failure to see this richness will result in missing the wave of God in the world today.[65]

Kevin regularly expresses the need for the Christian "liberal arts."[66] This vision supports his ongoing effort to help Christian schools in many countries gain or regain their rich Christian heritages in ways relevant to their own distinctive settings. Azusa Pacific University itself had been critiqued for theologically straying from its Christian Holiness tradition. Kevin had gone into action.[67]

In late January, 2018, the APU Board of Trustees invited Kevin to be with them to talk about the school's Wesleyan Holiness heritage. He sensed that after two years of talking with them about this, they finally had come to a common commitment to ensuring that Azusa truly intended to be a Christian university consciously in the Wesleyan-Holiness tradition. This has been Kevin's goal for many years in many settings. "I feel like my time at APU was well worth it and my original desire to anchor the university theologically is truly coming to reality after seventeen years of a long and arduous journey."

Such an effort to theologically grounding churches and their schools now is being repeated by Kevin on campuses and in board rooms across the United States and literally around the world. This

---

65   Kevin Mannoia, *Church 2K*.

66   See his book *Expressing Life* (2023).

67   See James Burtchaell's book *The Dying of the Light*.

effort reflects the concerns expressed well by Kevin's brother Jim. He has resisted an unfortunate and yet seemingly inevitable trend in American higher education. Many Christian educational institutions that traditionally had been "points of the spear" for character education and Christian citizenship had been squeezed into market-driven programming that emphasizes career preparation, often to the virtual ignoring of faith and character formation.

Numerous Christian institutions have been strangled by government, political, and parental pressures to dilute the Christian foundations of virtue and the connections of Christian faith to these virtues.[68] Accordingly, Kevin and his brother Jim share much the same passion for the recovery of Christian integrity and relevance. Jim, college professor, dean, and president in several Christian institutions over the years, now consults on these and related matters. Kevin is doing the same worldwide and at an aggressive rate indeed.

The World My Stage

When Kevin first went to Azusa Pacific University, it was offering a masters degree program called "Operation Impact" and designed for Christian missionaries to study organizational leadership without leaving their countries of service. Operating in some twenty countries, Kevin was asked to help teach some of these courses. As time allowed, he did so enthusiastically. Eventually this program was reduced and then shut down, presumably because it didn't make money.

Kevin felt badly about this demise. He saw this program as less a business investment and more an outreach of the university on behalf of the Christian world mission. One of his students in this program was the immediate past president of Ethiopia. Kevin

---

68   See V. James Mannoia, Jr., *Paradox and Virtue: Talks to My Students.*

was able to lead to the Lord another prominent person of that nation. Disappointed or not by this program's ending, he tried to stay out of administrative politics. Campus Crusade began filling the gap left by the demise of Operation Impact. Ironically, later it would seek program accreditation from the International Council for Higher Education of which Kevin then would be president.

Kevin became known at Azusa as a specialist on faith in the academy, whether at home or among his numerous international contacts. Being good friends with several of the campus deans, various program partnerships evolved. The Dean of Business sought his curricular design help with a masters program, especially with a course in "World View and Christian Formation" that soon included student travel enabled by Kevin's connections in Brazil. He took Ph.D. students abroad. He was contacted by the Dean of Nursing who was aggressive about the internationalization of her majors. He then took nursing students to China and got this Azusa program connected in Brazil.

Kevin and an Azusa University String Quartet in China.

The Dean of the School of Music had a great string quartet and Kevin arranged for a church tour in China, his going along to do the preaching. Wherever he went, he met people and drew them into ministries he envisioned or already had created. For instance,

Kevin first met Dr. David Han in Columbia in 2018 at an ecumenical meeting. Impressed by him, he broached the need for new leadership of Aldersgate Press, publishing arm of the Wesleyan Holiness Connection that Kevin had launched a few years earlier, and soon that was accomplished.

Kevin became deeply involved in higher education internationally, with two universities in particular, although there were numerous others in Latin America, Africa, Europe, and across Asia, especially in India, China, and even the University of Central Asia in Kyrgyzstan. Many of these institutions would be served by him personally, often through his presidency of the International Council for Higher Education.

The relentless pace of Kevin's ministry activity can be glimpsed by a short entry in his personal journal.[69] He had gone to Duke University in North Carolina for meetings of the Wesleyan Theological Society and Society for Pentecostal Studies, then to Taiwan to address leaders of a collection of Asian Christian universities. After one day home in California, it was off to Ethiopia before returning to speak at Greenville University in Illinois, just before hosting regional networks of the Wesleyan Holiness Connection in New Jersey and Indiana, and moving on to Canada, Brazil, and Chili to teach, squeezing in a quick family vacation in the Dominican Republic. This was all in one month! He says his home ministry base at the time, Azusa Pacific University, "is OK with it, actually likes it. I love having so much to do."

More recently, Kevin agreed to serve particular needs of the worldwide ministries of World Gospel Mission. He had brought its president, Dan Schafer, into leadership roles in the Wesleyan Holiness Connection and now Dan was drawing on Kevin's considerable expertise for his own mission organization. He would be assisting several of its international institutions of education,

---

69   Personal journal of Kevin, March, 2008.

including the Bolivian Evangelical University and Kenya Highlands University in 2023. The overall goal was to deepen their conscious identity in the holiness tradition and their effective integration of faith and learning. WGM staff in several nations also were being taught by Kevin the basics of Wesleyan theology.

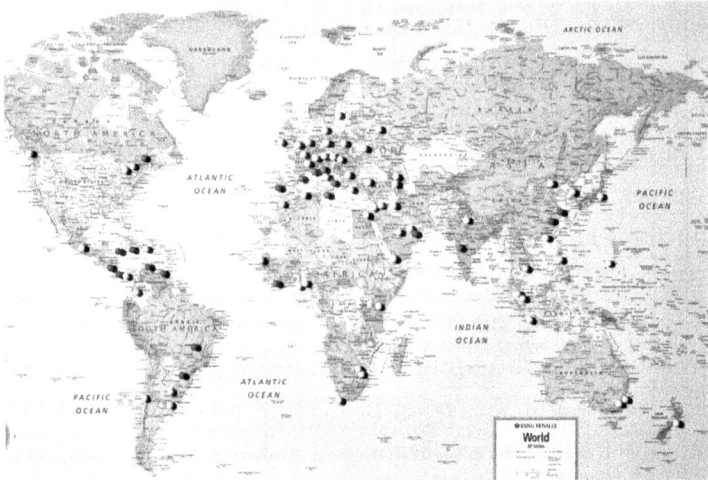

The World as Kevin's Parish. Adding Pins in the USA
and Brazil would Risk Blanketing the Countries.

After a significant conference in Albania and Kevin's productive time in Kenya, Honduras, and Bolivia with numerous personnel of WGM, its president, Dan Schafer, reported that for the first time in his thirty years of relationship with WGM he now was hearing WGM people get excited again about holiness![70] From Kevin's personal journal, here was his Bolivian schedule, quite typical.

> Four days of very fulfilling engagements. First, guiding the
> Board in thinking about integration of faith and learning,

---

70   Unfortunately, there were a few not pleased that Kevin didn't mimic their ultra-fundamentalist
commitment to the "inerrancy" theory of biblical inspiration. Kevin comments in his journal, "Why
does this fundamentalism keep nipping at my heels? By God's grace, I will keep working at loving
this part of the body of Christ."

the need to develop their faculty, as well as probing a deeper understanding of institutional identity in the Wesleyan Holiness stream. Then on campus, preaching at the church, speaking in chapel to the student body, speaking at a denominational pastor's conference, and finally to about 100 of the staff members. I will be coming back regularly to do faculty development retreats. I will begin that process in March, 2024, the first of 6 retreats with 30 faculty, top administrators, and as many board members as will come.

The map highlights the extensiveness of Kevin's global activity. Worth noting in particular are two prominent examples of Kevin's consulting with major educational institutions not associated with WGM.

Tunghai University, Taiwan. During his first trips to Asia in the 1990s as the Free Methodist superintendent in Southern California, Kevin met significant Christian leaders in the Pacific Rim nations. They began asking him to come back and teach. He did, teaching an intensive class and preaching at Holy Light, a Free Methodist school in Taiwan. When elected a bishop, with Taiwan now part of his responsibility, Kevin began making regular trips to Asia. About 2011 he was first introduced to Tunghai, founded in the 1950s as a Christian university. It had become the largest private school in Taiwan, about 15,000 students. The chaplain there, Jack Lee, reached out to Azusa Pacific University for a speaker at a conference they were hosting for about a dozen Christian schools in Taiwan and Hong Kong.

Kevin went and spoke but had to leave quickly for an engagement in Ethiopia. Lee shared with him the hope that in the future he could help Tunghai recover its Christian witness. That turned into Kevin traveling there regularly for the next few years to meet with groups of faculty about Christ-centered higher education. He preached in the chapel, a high honor in that Asian setting. Often he took with him one of the Azusa school deans to enhance their missional vision and even meet Christian leaders from mainland China. Tunghai is the first major university that Kevin invested in heavily. Many more would follow.

UniEvangelica University, Brazil. Kevin had personal roots in Brazil and, beginning about 2000 and especially after he had launched the Wesleyan Holiness Connection in the United States, he began traveling back there often, gathering church leaders and exposing Azusa students to Brazil's business community. On one trip he was introduced to leaders of UniEvangelica, a major campus about the size of Tunghai University. He told them of his work of helping schools maintain or reclaim a Christian identity and witness. Two years later this university reached out to Kevin for such assistance.

Teaching in Brazil, 2024.

The president, board members, and chaplain of UniEvangelica then visited major Christian schools in California, with logistical assistance from Kevin. They spent two days on the Azusa campus being taught by Kevin the ideals of Christian faith and higher education. They went home determined to restore the "confessionality" of their large campus, with Kevin coming occasionally to teach groups of professors about faith, life, and education. He went every four to six months, conducting six retreats with a cohort of fifty of the school's 850 full-time professors. He led a second faculty cohort in 2022 and finally insisted that select graduates of this process begin providing the leadership themselves, with his phasing out.

UniEvangelica now has emerged as the premier faith-based institution in all of Brazil. Kevin challenged it to convene a national conference of the many such institutions scattered around the country, bringing them together for the first time. They did just that, convening some three hundred educational leaders in 2023. Kevin was present to make presentations and was thrilled at the strong interest nationally and the ready acceptance of his concerns and ideas.

He proposed to leaders of this national gathering the concept of a Latin America Alliance of Christian educational institutions. It was endorsed with enthusiasm at this conference. Leaders of the United Methodist and Presbyterian churches in Brazil approached him about future assistance. This soon appeared in his personal journal: "I can't believe I volunteered to start another organization! I guess it's who I am and what I do, expanding the kingdom of God wherever I can by the free use of God's gifts in me and God's inspiration through me."[71]

In February, 2024, Kevin was teaching at the flagship of the Methodist university network in Brazil. His students included the deans, academic directors, and president of the network of five Methodist universities. One evening, about eighty professors joined for the first in a series of six faculty development sessions he would lead on the integration of faith and learning. He was redirecting the entire network in reestablishing its holiness and

---

71   Found in Kevin's personal journal, October 7, 2023.

Wesleyan foundations, reporting with excitement, "Truly history is being made in these days!"

Sampling Kevin's spirit, passion, and sense of God at work is seen in comments made to me in the process of preparing this biography (March, 2024).

> This ministry in Brazil is simply beyond belief. The impact is so very life-giving. I told Kathy it's getting more and more amazing every month!! What a powerful moment it was providing the opening MASTER CLASS and inaugurating a new seminary for the Methodist Church in Brazil. The class exploded within one day to over 2000 downloads in the denomination across the country. It marks an incredible commitment by the Council of Bishops to redirect the Methodist Church in Brazil to a more evangelical future consistent with John Wesley. Literally history in the making! We will see where God leads next. I'm living on the leading edge of the Kingdom. It's truly an E-ticket ride!

Kevin has taught often in Brazil over the years, including at what now is known as Wesley Biblical Seminary. His father had served there as president when Kevin was a little boy and brought it from almost nothing to the "gold standard" seminary in Brazil. At the time that was not quite the vision of the Brazilian Conference of the Free Methodist Church that preferred to spend money on evangelism more than higher education. Dr. Mannoia prevailed, however, supported strongly by the Japanese Free Methodists in the country who were more anxious to champion education.

This seminary has shifted leaders, facilities, and curricular emphases since and now has partnered with another Brazilian holiness body. It no longer has the accreditation it once enjoyed, lacking the high academic vision of Kevin's father. While now basically a denominational Bible school, the previous Mannoia nonetheless probably would applaud anything that meets the church's educational need. So does son Kevin who gladly serves there on occasion, anxious to honor his father's memory. He speaks Portuguese fluently and loves to be back in that setting when he can.

His teaching horizon, however, extends far beyond Brazil. In 2024, for instance, Kevin journeyed to Paraguay to teach pastors and missionaries about Christian holiness. He then agreed to return on four other occasions in the following year to teach day-long sessions on the deeper life of faith to a projected 150 pastors from multiple denominations, using one of his books now available in Spanish. The world indeed is his parish and classroom.

The Asian Theological Association and the ICHE. The International Council for Higher Education (ICHE) is one of several regional accrediting bodies for theological education worldwide. It was based in Bangalore, India, where Kevin first met its leader, Ken Gnanakan, when he was there visiting as a Free Methodist bishop. An educator/pastor also was there and Kevin ordained his wife, the first Free Methodist woman to be ordained in India. Friendships evolved that led to Kevin returning to teach in the doctoral program of the South Asia Institute for Christian Studies.

The president of the Asian Theological Association asked Kevin to help him launch the ICHE. The purpose would be accrediting schools that wish to be Christian in identity and goals but are unable to be accredited by their national or other bodies. Kevin not only helped with this launching but in 2016 became president of this accrediting body now headquartered in Zurich, Switzerland.

COVID did serious damage to this organization's functioning, its leaders being spread all over the world. Nonetheless, with Kevin as president, it continues pursuing excellence in academic programs and promoting sustainable models of higher education, particularly in countries where educational opportunities are restricted and in need of development for church and even nation building.

This is accomplished through resourcing and accreditation with a focus on integrated learning from a Christian worldview.

Underground and State Churches in China. As a superintendent and then bishop of the Free Methodist Church, Kevin Mannoia traveled often to China. He had a "handler" who set things up and followed him about. The Free Methodist Church was, after all, of little consequence in Chinese eyes and basically unnoticed. Kevin would meet groups of Chinese underground Christian leaders, the "house churches" movement, and teach them for two or three days in his hotel.

Once elected president of the National Association of Evangelicals, he learned that he would have to cut ties with the underground movement because now he was too high-profile. Also, his presidential predecessor had been on a committee formed by President Bill Clinton's administration that was to track religious persecution in China. Church contacts now would have to be coordinated through the government of China and would be closely monitored.

A board member of Azusa Pacific University was an older Free Methodist who had previous connections in China and helped get Kevin connected with high-level government officials, some of whom actually came to Azusa at his invitation. Kevin went to the China Christian Council, an extension of the government, and met the Minister of Religious Affairs who soon was invited to speak at Azusa. As dean of Azusa's seminary at the time, Kevin gave a full-ride scholarship for a doctoral program to anyone the Chinese would choose.

This appeared in Kevin's personal journal. "I am en route from Shanghai to San Francisco after a week of visiting schools and seminaries in China. This is my first visit to the state church and its leaders. I met with the Director General of the Religious Affairs Bureau who reports to the Premier. It was great to build good relationships with official church leaders in China. I trust that my old friends in the underground church will know that I have not forgotten or betrayed them."[72]

The government official who always accompanied Kevin when in China became a friend. One day he took Kevin to a huge room that housed tens of thousands of books in English that had been protected from destruction during the cultural revolution when Christian missionaries had been expelled in large numbers. Kevin arranged for Azusa librarians to come and assist with cataloging this "library" for their distribution to the network of provincial Chinese seminaries. He personally has returned often to China, once taking with him a string quartet from Azusa. He was even permitted to preach in the flagship of the state church of China in Beijing. It's a fabulous building with about 10,000 attending multiple services. He had no limitations on his sermon "as long as I didn't go political on them." This was a high honor indeed for a visiting American.

Kevin has been welcomed into prominent pulpits all over the world, and to many quite humble indeed. He recalls going to Haiti to speak at the commencement of North Haiti Christian University in Cap-Haitien. A nursing faculty member at Azusa had grown up in Haiti and was very committed to this school. She sought its accreditation by the ICHE and asked Kevin to come. Although having been in rural India many times, he can't forget the abject poverty witnessed in this area of Haiti. He indeed would work on the accreditation concern, as he continues to this day for such institutions across the globe.

Kevin's international networking has continued and likely even increased after his 2020 retirement from Azusa Pacific University. For instance, in September, 2023, he was in Kenya fulfilling a heavy schedule involving several Christian institutions. Between assignments he took a long drive on a beautiful day, plugged in his

---

72   From Kevin's personal journal, May, 2002.

Air Pods and listened to the Brooklyn Tabernacle Choir. For about an hour it was an amazing time of worship and deep reflection. He was so grateful to God for his amazing experiences and ministry growing opportunities after "retirement."

Moved deeply, Kevin reflected on his life while in the beautiful landscape of the Kenya Highlands. He was filled with thoughts of children, grandchildren, and of course his wonderful wife Kathy. He then wrote in his personal journal. "Gratitude, amazement, pride, humility, just overwhelming blessing. I love my children. I love my wife. They are very much part of my worship. Thank you, oh God!"

In the eyes of many Kevin Mannoia is a traveling Christian celebrity. In his own eyes, there is far more humility. On occasion he still will begin an address after a flowery introduction with this. "I am Kevin Mannoia, servant of God, nothing more, nothing less." And so he is.

Contextualizing the Kingdom of God

Church 2K is one of Kevin Mannoia's popular books in which he insists that anything "colonial," self-transplanting, is a perversion of the gospel of Jesus Christ. The intended effect of God's redeeming love comes only from a "contextualized" gospel. After all, the divine Word that formed the original creation became the *incarnate* Word, Jesus. That is, God assumed a human form to enable us to understand his heart and intentions *in our own setting*.

The Jesus incarnation, he understands, is the epitome of the contextualized Christian gospel. God made his love concrete, meaningful, understandable, right where we people are. The Kingdom and its Lord are now to be further contextualized by us from one people group to the next, with careful awareness of their diversity of settings. The Kingdom heart doesn't change but its face changes as it's contextualized in each culture where planted.

Each gospel planting is to become a vernacular manifestation of the Kingdom of God. We carriers of the good news should seek to try to get out of the way and let the gospel itself shine. This is the intent of Kevin Mannoia as he travels and ministers. It's why, in places like UniEvangelica University in Brazil, Kevin has taught and then backed off and encouraged locals to take over and be the examples and future teachers.

The church of today must learn to embrace such contextualism in a shrinking world. According to Kevin, a key task of any Kingdom leader is to help people discriminate between the principles of the Kingdom and the incidentals of their particular human culture. Refusing to embrace contextualism leads to preaching and teaching that results in isolation, sectarianism, and irrelevancy. It's mere church colonialism in new dress.

The Kingdom message is meant to meet people where they are and give them the hope of divine grace that comes from God into their specific setting and is activated in locally relevant ways. An important caution always is appropriate, however, in Kevin's view. The Kingdom message must not be so obsessed with contextualizing and relevancy that it loses sight of its own identity and becomes nothing more than relativism, a cultural religion easily acceptable locally. That's the Christian message having lost its divine identity.

My wife and I recently were visiting live stage performances in Branson, Missouri. One thing is made clear in each theater. Patriotism should be the grateful business of all Americans. The red-white-and blue flies everywhere and all performances begin by recognizing with applause all military veterans in the hall. They, after all, have paid a high price for our continuing freedom. The premier performance in town when we were there was "Queen Esther."

This powerful presentation brings to life dramatically the Old Testament story of two Jews who stood against a man in power who was insisting that they bow to him with total allegiance. "Death to them all!" was the response when the man refused and the Jewish queen dared support him. The outcome makes clear that faith in God comes at a cost and yet eventually is rewarded by the Lord of all kingdoms. Human arrogance is short-lived indeed. Faith in God must be lived out in very real places and find ways to survive and communicate while remaining true to itself.

Kevin explains that to sit at the Communion Table with Christ is to declare one's ultimate allegiance to Christ. It's joining the spiritual force working in this world to undermine and renew it, communicating with it relevantly while not caving in to it and losing the redemption message. To be "holy" is to hold membership in a higher order than any human arrangement. It's to pledge allegiance to the King who is above all kings. We are caught between contrasting biblical views of human governments. They are deserving of our obedience (Rom. 13) and yet sometimes revolting in God's eyes (Rev. 13). What we must never do is equate loyalty to any nation or empire with loyalty to God! Contextualize, yes; cave, no.

The presidency of the ICHE was accepted by Kevin Mannoia with the concern that it not become just another American organization. He now reports that "I am the only American on my board. We have only had one conference on U. S. soil." He resists ICHE schools wanting to replicate western patterns in their quite different cultures. That's why he says, "Our accreditation manual is NOT a list of standards. Our accreditation is principle-based. We urge each school to show how it lives those principles *within its distinctive culture.*"

The ICHE seeks to be Kingdom oriented *and* culturally contextualized. That's largely because President Mannoia insists, "If there is any note I want to play on the global piano, it would be that God's Kingdom transcends any culture. We are citizens of the Kingdom FIRST, and then we are Americans, Brazilians, Chinese, etc."

Kevin has come to consider himself a world Christian. "Of course, my growing up years set that DNA in me, and the fact that my ministry is significantly global shapes that too. I don't spend a lot of time in the developed nations. The biggest issue for a Kingdom mindset over a colonial mindset is the internal disposition of the heart. I feel quite comfortable virtually anywhere in the world. The leveling ground is the Kingdom."[73] When traveling, which is often, Kevin seeks to be less an American from California and more a servant of Christ from the heart of God.

The consummate teacher/preacher, and the cut-up character.

This global worldview affirms with appreciation the scores of missionaries from the West who had gone "to the field" in years past. Some of their methods may have been uninformed and less than perfect, more colonial than they intended. Still, Kevin honors their missionary efforts, insisting graciously that "by and large the intent of the heart was pure. So, let's not throw the baby out with the bath water." We must honor the past while we reach to the future. One means of doing this is Kevin's current *Anchored and Reaching* weekly podcast series.

---

73   See Kevin's *Church 2K: Leading Forward* in the chapter "The Boy and the Man with No Shoes."

This series is designed for curious Christians who hope to impact the world while remaining deeply rooted in their faith. Co-hosted by Kevin Mannoia and Susanna Fleming, each episode features engaging conversations, practical insights, and diverse perspectives from Christian leaders who embody the dual values of being anchored in Christ and actively reaching out to the world. Encouraged always is living a dynamic Christian life grounded in biblical truth and fueled by a passion for positive change individually and in society.

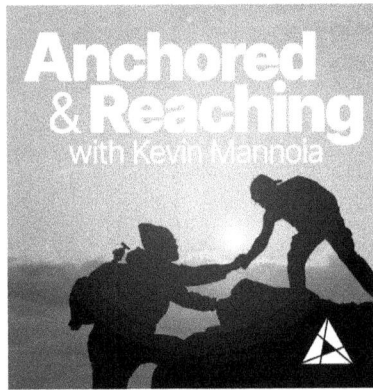

Logo for Kevin's popular blog, and an image of his ministry in general.

One podcast focuses on personal identity. Who are we Christians in rapidly changing times? How can we be grounded in a changeless identity when all around is in flux? Kevin has an excellent radio/video voice and appearance. He introduces the "Identity" podcast this way. "This eight-part mini-series may be the most important thing we can talk about. We are moving into a pluralistic environment globally. How can we be secure in who we are amidst all the change? Hang on while we press deeply into the crevices of leadership formation."

CHAPTER TWELVE

A VIA-MEDIA MAN

Simple formulas are rarely enough. Required is a crucial balancing, an embracing of paradox. A faithful following of Jesus Christ requires both passionate commitment and considerable humility, both available only with intentional and disciplined effort to meet and trust the Person who himself is the Truth. *Via media* is a Latin phrase meaning "way between extremes." John Wesley was an English Anglican priest whose thought was "conjunctive." Kevin Mannoia serves in this continuing tradition. Like Wesley before him, sometimes his thinking and ministry practices become too expansive to fit within establishment structures.

Kevin Mannoia is a *via media* man in the best of the Wesleyan tradition. He often has found himself in the awkward middle of difficult issues where it hurts but where the fuller truth and needed ministry lay. Such a multi-dimensional ministry doesn't mean being compromised by some muddled accommodation. It means dealing with differences in a manner that champions "trust in and relationship with the Person who himself is the fuller Truth."

In the past when religious cults over-emphasized their dominant leaders and distinctive doctrines, vigorous public debates were common. "A minister once told me that as soon as his converts were baptized, they came out of the water 'ready for dispute.' This spirit of controversy must disappear and God-fearing believers everywhere must rise above their petty differences and seek common ground where all can work together in evangelizing the world."[74]

Such "rising above" is part of the Wesleyan Holiness tradition of Christian faith at its best. It seeks personal *and* social holiness, affirming God's sovereignty *and* human choice, the crisis *and* process of salvation, being set apart to God while being effectively in touch with the practical needs of humanity. Kevin has championed such combinations, liking the phrase "Anchored *and* Reaching." He's sought common ground in the middle for the sake of the church's world mission.[75] This *via media* middle way is risky, costly, delicate, the right way to go.

To a doctrinal purist, paradoxes and twin commitments suggest dangerous drift toward heresy. Nonetheless, Wesleyan-Holiness people like Kevin Mannoia are *both* profoundly conservative in a biblically anchored faith and passionately active in missional engagement to the least of God's children. For Kevin, such *via media* is a personality trait, an evangelistic tool, a leadership style, an essential means of activating divine grace for a lost and needy world. It's to be embraced with passion and humility.

Kevin's son-in-law Daniel sometimes rolls his eyes when the family is in a crowd where they know nobody and Kevin is somewhere in the hall chatting vigorously with someone he acts like he's known forever. Comments Daniel, "Is there any crowd where someone doesn't know Dad?" At least in Christian crowds, there appear to be relatively few. Kevin connects, shares divine grace, and rarely is forgotten when the event is over. His father Jim was

---

74   H. M. Riggle, *Pioneer Evangelism.* Riggle, one of the more forceful early evangelists of the Church of God movement (Anderson), saw no compromise involved in open cooperation with other Christians who differed with him on a range of doctrinal incidentals.

75   Kevin's brother Jim Mannoia emphasizes *via media* in his book *Christian Liberal Arts* (pp. 190-194). Diversity and community are both essential to an authentically Christian liberal arts education. Diversity stimulates the moral and cognitive development of students. Without its dissonance comes the danger of degeneration into mere indoctrination. Christian liberal arts education requires "a reconciliation of community and diversity."

much the same way, as was Jesus long before either of them. Finding his way around the differences people have in their faith journeys, Kevin connects with the core of the faith and finds ways to connect with the core of others for the sake of a lost world.

Maybe Carla Sunberg has said it best. "One of Kevin's great strengths is his ability to get people together around a table. He has incredible relational power, coupled with no fear of walking into places of power and conflict knowing who he is and what he believes. This networking ability is a gift to the contemporary Christian world, along with his unusual ability to articulate the nature and importance of the Wesleyan Holiness tradition of the Christian faith.[76]

Nurturing Tomorrow's Leaders

Networking, being active in the middle, relational, *via-media*, is Kevin Mannoia's style of leadership formation in the church. This is "education," a leading from the present toward a desired destiny. It's activating and linking today with the needs of tomorrow. It's recognizing and developing potential in people who often are unaware of it in themselves. It's being God's agent in bringing the Kingdom of God into being just ahead.

Kevin Mannoia has been blessed with a parade of Christian giants who passed his way and helping ignite his own potential. He would include Dennis Kinlaw of Asbury University and Seminary who "attracted me greatly." Beyond a superb biblical scholar, Dennis was a holiness leader who could cross barriers and engage with impact and appreciation in many circles. He was well accepted widely when most holiness leaders seemed more sheltered in isolated denominational cloisters. Kevin has a clear church home,

---

76   Rev. Carla Sunberg was encouraged by Kevin Mannoia to become a leader in the Wesleyan Holiness Connection he founded. She now is a General Superintendent of the Church of the Nazarene.

the Free Methodist Church, but he's hardly allowed this beloved home base to be an isolated shelter. He reaches, links, moves on without uprooting his past.

Clyde Van Valin was the area Free Methodist bishop when Kevin began his full-time ministry in Texas. He helped Kevin focus on the inner formation of pastoral life and warned him of the political nature of the church. "Kevin, be careful of the church. It will hurt you." The hurt comes especially when the church shelters itself defensively like a fortress rather than connects openly with the whole of God's people and the mission of Christ in the world. Kevin is an anti-fortress brother. He goes, reaches, teaches, connects, and nurtures new leaders. Clyde ordained Kevin an Elder and "imprinted me with healthy patterns and priorities of character and a mystical journeying into the heart of God." Clyde died in 2000, but his wisdom has never left Kevin.

Ted Engstrom was a huge encourager who helped Kevin see the importance of expressing his distinctive identity and leveraging the influence of his roles globally. Sam Kamaleson helped Kevin focus on the deep inner working of personal formation that often gets overlooked in church "success." Says Kevin, "He encouraged reflection, deep pondering, and thoughtful conversation that is more profound than merely doing stuff."

Jack Hayford was especially important in dealing with some critical cases of ministerial moral failure that Kevin had to handle as a young church leader. There also have been George Barna and Bob Schuller who both invested time and wisdom in Kevin, and Ken Medema whose ministry of music exposed Kevin to "the hidden side of deep personal formation." These are only a few of the long parade of giants who have crossed the life and ministry paths of Kevin. He's in their debt and quick to admit it.

It takes a village and the wise listen and learn to the wide range of voices available. Many spoke into Kevin and increasingly he became a mentoring giant for many others. "I'm convinced that my path forward will have to do with helping people, ministerial candidates, universities, boards, and faculty with a deeper understanding of our Holiness mind and living."[77] Kevin continues to connect, converse, and counsel widely. Many have and will be blessed.

The Consummate Connector

In 1987 the officers of the General Assembly of the Church of God (Anderson) invited Bishop Clyde Van Valin of the Free Methodist Church to function as an observer-evaluator in its annual sessions. Clyde told the Assembly near its conclusion that its focus on Christian unity "is a message that we all need to hear expounded and demonstrated." For the June, 2000, General Assembly, a similar note was sounded by a former Free Methodist leader, Dr. Kevin Mannoia, who then was president of the National Association of Evangelicals.

He referred to the Assembly's inspiring new leader, Robert Pearson, commending his fresh vision and cautioning about the sacrifices his leadership would require. How sad that many such leaders often pay a personal price for moving ahead aggressively. Such a price would be just ahead for Bob and Kevin.

Currently appearing on the website of the Free Methodist Church are ten defining values of this denomination. One is: "Connectional: We are a church which recognizes and values its nature as a connectional church united with others in the ministry of Jesus Christ, and not possessing an independent mind set." That's Kevin Mannoia, a loyal son of this denomination. He has sought to champion this very connectional vision, especially through his launching of the Wesleyan Holiness Connection soon after his departure from the National Association of Evangelicals.

---

77   Found in Kevin's personal journal, 2022.

Kevin has a restless spirit spurred on by a connecting and uniting message and leadership style.

Many of his early international activities involved programs of Azusa Pacific University. He was Professor of Ministry on campus, although often he was away from the home campus. When in the United States, he served at various times local churches and parishes as a board member or advisor. In California these would include The Rock Church, San Diego, a Catholic parish in Alta Loma, Upland Christian Academy, the Salvation Army's School for Officers Training at Crestmont, and America's Christian Credit Union. This isn't an exhaustive list.

Kevin has ministered closely with Presidents Mendell Thompson (ACCU), Shirley Hoogstra (CCCU), and Jon Wallace (APU).

Elsewhere in the United States, Kevin would serve as a member of the Board of Trustees of his undergraduate alma mater, Roberts Wesleyan University and Northeastern Seminary, and Seattle Pacific University. He became the close advisor of several presidents of different universities and worked closely with diverse Christian leaders like Daniel O. Aleshire, longtime executive director of the Association of Theological Schools, Ann Riggs (Quaker), Associate General Secretary of the National Council of Churches USA for Faith and Order, Ted W. Engstrom, President Emeritus of World

Vision, Clark H. Pinnock, prominent evangelical theologian from Canada, and Stanley Hauerwas, American theologian and ethicist of Duke University Divinity School. Two or three pages could be filled with the listing of such prominent names.

Kevin certainly has been an active connector wherever he's been. He would establish the Wesleyan Holiness Connection and under its umbrella gather "Affinity Groups" like the Presidents Network, the Chief Academic Officers Network, the Women Clergy, and the Freedom Network. His global teaching and consulting would extend to universities and churches that sought the input of his emphases on identity in the Wesleyan tradition, Christian holiness, and effective servant leadership. Typical would be Simpson University that reached out asking for help in re-establishing a clear Wesleyan-Holiness understanding of its university and seminary, A. W. Tozer Seminary. Kevin has been more than glad to help when such calls came, and many did and still are.

President Bob Brower of Point Loma Nazarene University knew Jim Mannoia, Kevin's older brother, through a range of higher education meetings. This was before he ever encountered younger brother Kevin. Bob says that Jim is certainly well-spoken and generally more formal and traditionally academic than his brother. Then Bob met Kevin and "almost from the beginning it's like I have known him forever."

Says Bob, "Kevin was so open and frank about anything we were dealing with. He listens so well and provides an on-target sense of needed insight. He has a profound capacity to relate to people. He sees hope and promise in anyone he meets. I think he knows at least half of everybody! Recently Point Loma went through a large transition, replacing its veteran faculty and staff persons with a younger generation. The University needed to refresh its sense of institutional identity and Kevin does that very thing so well."

Kevin has mentored new Christian leaders by the dozens, probably the scores. Deana Porterfield and Kevin first met when he was

Azusa Pacific's seminary dean. He asked her to play the piano at faculty/staff chapels and sometimes met with her to discuss knotty issues. He heard about her Pentecostal and Nazarene roots and encouraged her to get back into the Wesleyan Holiness Christian stream. "Deana was clearly an upcoming leader. When she decided to consider the presidency at Roberts Wesleyan University, my undergraduate alma mater, she called me and we walked together through that process."

Kevin, left, guiding a graduate class in Brazil.

The year after she went to Roberts, she asked Kevin to rejoin the Board of Trustees there which he had left in 2004. Why did he rejoin? It was particularly to help secure the school's institutional identity in its Wesleyan Holiness stream.[78] Deana also wanted his help with internationalization. Kevin soon was assisting the Roberts honors program director, Amy Kovach, in taking students to Brazil each year. In 2023 Deana became president of Seattle Pacific University, another Free Methodist school, and Amy was Vice President of Academic Affairs at Mount Vernon Nazarene

---

78   From Kevin's personal journal, January, 2015: "I am looking forward to Board service at Roberts again. I want to help Deana but mostly want to live out what I am increasingly understanding my calling to be. I am not called to institutions, but to Kingdom identity in people, leaders, and groups. I want to offer all I can to help Roberts Wesleyan recapture a deep sense of identity in the Wesleyan-Holiness stream of the church. It certainly has those roots."

University. The shadow of Kevin's personal influence extends to all of this. Deana observes: "Kevin has drive, is futuristic, and projects command. He's full of ideas and energy. Some find all this intimidating, and he has tried hard to get the negatives of this under control."

Courtney Young may say it best. She texted Kevin in 2022 with these words that really moved him. "Happy Father's Day to a man who is a father to many who are lacking a father figure in their lives. You see the best in others and have a gift of investing in people and developing them so they can flourish. You act as a safe space." Courtney worked with Kevin at the Rock Church in San Diego from 2015-2022. At one point she was questioning her ability to facilitate a key meeting with its managers and directors. "He patiently encouraged and prepared me, and afterward gave feedback and celebrated with me. He sees potential and helps one rise!"

"I was in tears as I read Courtney's Father's Day greeting," recalls Kevin. "It means so much, especially coming from a cancer survivor, one year away from losing her father, just finding her voice as a leader, a brave, courageous woman." Many others might have written similar notes, people like Susanna Fleming, A. J. Zimmermann, Lisa Penberthy, and Jason Mayer. Kevin was central in each one's personal and leadership growth. He led to the Christian commitment of Kassa Teklebrhan, former freedom fighter and Chair of the Congress in Ethiopia. There are many more.

Says Jason Mayer, "Kevin has been a guiding light in my journey as a follower of Jesus and a pastor. His passion for encouraging profound thinking and expansive love has shaped my perspective on faith and ministry. His emphasis on finding one's unique voice and contribution to the world has been transformative. His positive influence continues to resonate in my spiritual and pastoral journey, reminding me of the power of thoughtful reflection, boundless love, and the strength that comes from a supportive community."

Carla Sunberg currently is a General Superintendent of the Church of the Nazarene and former Chair of the Board of Directors of the Kevin's Wesleyan Holiness Connection. She concludes this about him: "He is the consummate connector. He makes you feel good about yourself. He's an encourager, a mentor, a champion of women in ministry. He evaluates situations well and tells you the truth as he sees it, and he's usually right. He did all that for me!"

Printed Pages and Pivotal Images

In the midst all this personal and institutional connecting, Kevin Mannoia realized that much of his influence would have to come through the printed page. He began to write relatively short books that, as he likes to say, can be read "in one plane ride" and understood by any interested reader. Appearing over time were his influential *The Integrity Factor, Church Planting, 15 Characteristics of Effective Pastors, The Holiness Manifesto* with Don Thorsen*, Masterful Living,* and *Expressing Life* (see the bibliography for details). All these books have strong relational aspects in their subject matter and even in how they came about. A prime example is the fifteen characteristics book co-authored by Kevin and his good friend Larry Walkemeyer.

This book was researched collaboratively with nine "panelists," highly successful pastors including Maxie Dunnam and Jack Hayford. Larry began his Doctor of Ministry program at Azusa Pacific and asked Kevin to be his project mentor. He agreed. "We set out together to make a difference!" James Earl Massey, himself a highly successful African-American pastor, comments on the published result. "This is a crash course on ministry. The work of pastoring can be a many-splendored experience when there is an openness to God, an understood calling, a love for people, and a commitment to serve." Kevin and Larry had them all and were anxious to share.

The actions of the highly successful minister were found in this research to flow naturally from an identity that is Christ-like and integrated into all that's done. A minister is to approach every relationship with a mind-set of servanthood, demonstrating what living like Christ looks like in today's world. This requires belief in the power of the Holy Spirit and the presence of close friends quick to challenge or affirm the pastor toward more godly character and personal excellence.

Kevin notes that most of the fifteen identified characteristics of highly successful ministers do not relate in any significant way to professional *performance*. The bigger truth points to matters of *character* and the inner *spiritual condition* of the minister. Success flows from many things, but especially from "the godliness of character more than the brilliance of a person's leadership skills, more than the statistical outcomes of the local church." This key insight would be expressed in a series of Kevin's coming books, articles, podcasts, lectures, and sermons. Aspects of it would be graphically conveyed in a series of Kevin's favorite images. Following are eight quick examples.

First, one leader recalls a moving image of Kevin himself. He was seen alone in a humble posture during an historic meeting in London, England. It was in a hotel dining hall very early before anyone else had arrived. He was having breakfast, sipping coffee, and obviously pondering the Word of God—Kevin's ministry comes out of personal discipline and a deep spirituality. Whatever else he is, he is a Christian contemplative always in search of greater truth, a more expansive vision, and their intended personal and social impact.[79]

Jesus preferred to teach through parables, images, and stories, never through long narratives of systematic theology. Kevin has a similar literary mind and communication style, including a fertile

---

79   Recollection of Dr. David Han, shared October 9, 2023.

imagination. He prefers short books, crisp stories, vivid images of core Christian truths. Such he believes communicate best in contemporary culture. Here are the eight images that often have surfaced in his public communications and writings.

1. The Holy River of God (God's universal work of redemptive love flowing through all the world). As with any river, the holy river of God has a source. It does not begin with councils, doctrine, or studies, not in ecclesiastical structures or actions of the institutional church, divine though they may be at times. It's not set in motion by the fiat of a bishop or pastor and does not automatically spring up spontaneously just because two or three Christians gather together. Rather, this grand river begins in the very heart of God and is shaped by the nature of God and the present actions of God's Spirit. Its flow is the most accurate reflection of the character and passion of God being active in the desert of our world.[80]

Various streams of Christian tradition now feed into this one river. Whatever their differences, all are valuable when focused on the person of Jesus Christ, our common Lord. We disciples should be humble and cease judging each other and instead focus on enriching each other with our diverse divine gifts. Diversity can either be an obstacle to or an enrichment of Christian unity. This is the very purpose for which Kevin Mannoia founded the Wesleyan Holiness Connection, championing the enrichment potential.[81] "There is a river whose streams make glad the city of God. God is within her; she will not fall. God will help her at break of day" (Ps. 46:4-5).

2. The Brutal Man and Field of Death (social justice must be sought now). The scene is a traffic jam in the heart of India, with

---

80   Kevin Mannoia, in Barry Callen, ed., *The Holy River of God*.

81   See the panel presentation by Barry L. Callen presented to the Steering Committee of the Wesleyan Holiness Connection, October, 2023, Wilmore, Kentucky.

Kevin stuck in a cab. The heat and stench are awful but what he saw was worse. A man with no shoes was kicking without mercy a little boy on the street. It was brutal and unrelenting and Kevin was horrified. That awful sight soon was joined by another image, "Over the Wall." Small girls, even mere babies, are undervalued and sometimes thrown over a wall into a field of death that slopes down to a swamp. Why were Kevin's own children safe and healthy in California, loved and seemingly assured of a bright future? A twist of fate? Can anything be done to stop this awful injustice? The church is called to bring the Kingdom of God near—somehow and *now*![82]

3. The Star Gate Effect (escape the narrowness of our own limited cultures). The Kevin Mannoia family enjoyed watching on television the adventures of the *Stargate SG-1* team dealing with distant planets on the other side of the galaxy. How is the church team to successfully target its mission to a distant goal by passing through the star gate? A series of codes are required for success, with the center always being "Jesus is Lord." Failure to see the richness of the Kingdom will result in missing the wave of God in the world.

The Kingdom of God does not change although its face does as it is contextualized in the various cultures where planted. The task of church leaders is to help people learn to discriminate between divine Kingdom principles and the prevailing cultural standards of us limited humans. The star gate effect forces such discriminating thinking. The Kingdom of God is too rich, full, mysterious, and awesome to allow any limited perspective to claim for itself the whole. Frequent trips through the star gate are required. We must open our minds and imaginations.[83]

---

82   Kevin Mannoia, *Church 2K*, 27-36.

83   Kevin Mannoia, *Church 2K*, 39-50.

4. The Cloverleaf Lesson (look to the center and the edges will care for themselves). Learning to drive a car is a good way to learn this lesson. Stare at the curb on your right and the car unintentionally will drift that way. When Kevin was teaching his daughter to drive and they were first on a clover leaf leading to the freeway, she became especially nervous, focusing on that ever-moving curb on her right. Her father helped by telling her that we tend to go where we look. Therefore, focus on the center and somehow the edges will take care of themselves. The set of the mind influences behavior.

Christian disciplines are behaviors intended to assist the mind in focusing on Christ, the divine kingdom, the center. "We must be so committed to the transcendence of God, the centrality of Jesus Christ, the power of the Holy Spirit, and the full authority of biblical revelation that anything contrary to them, by default, is excluded."[84] The center of Christian faith never can be described merely by a set of propositions about the cultural particulars of how we should think or act. We must stop judging by the incidental edges of our lives and thoughts. All believers must be encouraged to be *center-seeking*. When that's our preoccupation, all else somehow falls into place.

5. The Stick Figure with Bent Knees (*minister* to people on God's behalf, but *serve* only God). Advertising signs are everywhere. Once one in an airport directed Kevin Mannoia to a chapel. Arriving there changed his life and ministry. His early ministry in Texas had become overloaded with discouragement and questions. He couldn't manage to please everyone. Spiritual power was largely absent and his ministry passion diffused. It was only a small sign, a stick figure with bent knees. It wasn't the sign so much as where it led Kevin and the big lesson God taught him there.

---

84   Kevin Mannoia, *Church 2K*, 61.

"How easy it is to fall prey to the temptation to reduce one's very identity as a Christian leader to a set of vocational activities designed to please people."[85] This question now came to Kevin. "Who was Jesus serving when he emptied and humbled himself?" It was his Father and *not* his disciples! He loved and faithfully taught them, yes, but in obedience to his Father. The disciples often were not pleased by what he said. Pleasing them wasn't the point. We who believe are no longer to be our own, but God's. One result of this is not always to be trying hard to please people. Be careful to whom your knees are bent.

6. The Puzzle of One Piece (unity within diversity is the beauty of God's church). "In the extreme effort of some Christians to expect that all other believers should think and behave just like them, they project intolerance of the diversity in the church. How narrow, how myopic, how ignorant of the deep mysteries of God! How awful it would be if we all thought, acted, and worshiped the same ways, held the same ideas on politics, social issues, theology, or mission. Only when we begin to find connection among the diverse parts will we start to see the picture God has crafted. Unity in the Kingdom is a deep oneness that derives from common identity in Christ.

God is three, yet God is one."[86] God's people are many and yet they are to be and can be one. The many-ness should add to the beauty of the one-ness, not detract from it. This, unfortunately, escapes many believers who persist in seeing the puzzle of God's people made up of only one piece, their piece.

7. The Picket Fence (lower the organizational divides among Christians and church partnerships for increased mission

---

85 Kevin Mannoia, *Church 2K*, 72.

86 Kevin Mannoia, *Church 2K*, 82-87.

effectiveness). Soon into his leadership of the National Association of Evangelicals, Kevin told this to *Christianity Today*. "We have perhaps drawn the circle too closely. We don't need to be looking for litmus tests. We should be replacing block walls with picket fences." Kevin intended the NAE to stop defining itself as those truly "conservative" believers opposed to the faulty beliefs of "all the other guys."[87] Let's make it easier to see each other, touch each other, love each other.

Our Lord prayed for the unity of his disciples for the sake of his mission. Christian holiness is the one spiritual dynamic, the "catholic spirit" (John Wesley) that can enable real oneness, regardless of diversity. It can enable disciples to become a coordinated spiritual force preparing for a common addressing of the issues of our time. Picket fences better allow us to see and champion the precious truths held by neighboring Christian traditions. They answer so much better than walls the question of John Wesley. "Although a difference in opinions or modes of worship may prevent an entire external union, yet need it prevent our *union in affection*? Though we can't think alike, may we not *love alike*?"

8. The Bottom of the Iceberg (the integrity of behavior on life's surface depends on the depth and stability of the foundation that sits deep out of sight). Identity gives rise to behavior. It's like an iceberg. About one tenth of the mass is found above the waterline. Nine-tenths lie unseen below. There is one iceberg with two dimensions. The top represents the activities while the bottom the identity. The bottom answers the critical question "Who am I?" while the top answers the resulting question, "Why am I here and what will I do?"

---

87   It would be productive to explore the parallels between Kevin in the Christian world and Aziz Abu Sarah in the travel world, each seeking to bring together communities polarized by seemingly intractable conflicts. A Palestinian raised in Jerusalem, Sarah's journey is from a radical seeking revenge to a peacemaker seeking reconciliation. See his *Crossing Boundaries: A Traveler's Guide to World Peace.*

The top speaks to activity, performance, achievement, and competence. The bottom deals with nature, formation, person-hood, and character. The top is able to keep balanced and stable only to the extent that the bottom is well formed and deep. This speaks to the nature of Christian leadership. Servant leadership is not about pleasing others. Trying to fulfill the differing agendas and expectations of people in any organization is a formula for overload and eventual collapse. While we gladly perform service *for* people, we are not their *servants*. A Christian servant leader belongs to *One alone*.

To learn these eight graphic lessons is to glimpse who Kevin Mannoia really is and what he's been trying to teach and be across the years.

Political Centrism

Being a via-media man has brought Kevin into the political arena, but cautiously. There's a fine line that he's attempted to walk. He's engaged certain public issues of the day from a Christian stand-point, but without intentionally taking political sides on hot topics and contested elections. He's a centrist, a connector, a King-dom advocate without being a biased politician on crusade for a personal agenda.

For instance, Kevin's standard position in the U. S. presi-dential campaign of 2016 was to instruct pastors how to engage their people in the election—not which candidate to support. He would point beyond the candidate to the platform and its perceived relation to the values of the Kingdom of God. Who and what is best aligned with one's personal convictions as bibli-cally informed? He does admit that in that 2016 election neither of the two presidential candidates was very palatable to him for different reasons.

Kevin recalls some "pretty intense conversations" he had with business and church leaders in Singapore during that 2016 time. Again, he was careful to walk the line described above. As campus Chaplain at Azusa Pacific, he had Rev. John Cager of the AME church speak at the faculty/staff chapel on the Thursday just after that general election. "John did a masterful job of navigating the minefield in a very lighthearted way."

If not openly declaring for Hillary Clinton or Donald Trump, Kevin more recently has admitted to one strong international bias. He had just returned from a most successful trip consulting with a Christian institution in the central Asian nation of Kyrgyzstan. Russia had launched an ugly war against its neighbor, Ukraine, causing Kevin to unleash some uncharacteristically harsh and politically biased words. "Russian president Putin has become what many consider a global monster, now moving brutally to take over and annex Ukraine. It's nothing short of global bullying. It makes me angry. Frankly, I hope God will somehow intervene even if it means taking his life. Suddenly the imprecatory psalms make a lot of sense to me."[88]

Political centrism, *via media* for Kevin? Yes, generally, except when the will of God and the well-being of humanity are so obviously being violated in a dramatic and disgusting manner. His normal stance is much like that of Eugene Peterson: "I live in company with Pentecostals and Presbyterians, Republicans and Democrats, evangelicals and schismatics. I am their pastor, not their policeman."[89]

Anchoring *and* Reaching: Gender Identity

Kevin Mannoia is well aware that seeking connections and common ground can be personally costly when attempted in relation to

---

88   Found in Kevin's personal journal, October, 2022.

89   Reported in Peterson's biography *A Burning in My Bones* by Winn Collier.

today's most difficult moral issues. No matter. He is a connector *with conviction*, and sometimes this conviction pushes him toward personally costly action. A stimulus for this may have been formed early in life.

Kevin had a really good friend when they were students together in Warsaw High School in Indiana. His friend was a very popular senior dating one of the prettiest girls. The two young men occasionally talked about spiritual things. One day Kevin was handed a letter in which his friend described his "coming out." Kevin didn't fully understand what that meant as a young kid.

Sadly, years later, Kevin learned that this man had committed suicide. "I was heartbroken that maybe he had been trying to ask me for help and I was too dense to get it. I do believe he loved the Lord and I will see him in heaven." The issue apparently was one of sexual identity and the great pain of its associated public rejection. As an adult, Kevin would choose to help such persons who were being unfairly discriminated against, while also holding to biblical standards as he understands them. It's a difficult but, he judges, sometimes necessary road to walk.

Deana Porterfield worked with Kevin at Azusa Pacific University on some difficult public matters. She now observes, "Being in the Wesleyan tradition, with people like B. T. Roberts proudly in the background, puts one in an awkward (ideal?) position. It anchors one in the best of the Christian/Biblical tradition and also propels one outward to engage with courage some of the most difficult and controversial of public issues." Such engaging can be "messy," she admits, "appearing too Christian for some and not Christian enough for others. Nonetheless, it's where our Master calls and often where Kevin has gone, sometimes at considerable personal cost."

Here are examples of Kevin's engagements and their personal costs. They rest on this. "Can people who self-identify as lesbian, gay, bisexual, or transgender live as growing disciples of Christ? *Yes,* judges Kevin. Should the church deploy into leadership one who is humbly appropriating God's grace in not living out the practices of that broken condition? Again, *Yes.* Should the church raise to leadership one who is practicing those behaviors as an expression of that condition? *No.*"[90] Respect and love, absolutely. Approval, no.

1. Christian Declaration of Marriage. While President of the National Association of Evangelicals, Kevin convened a task force that developed the "Christian Declaration of Marriage." It was signed by Bishop Anthony O'Connell of the National Conference of Catholic Bishops, Richard Land of the Southern Baptist Convention, Bishop Kevin Mannoia, president of the National Association of Evangelicals, and Robert Edgar, General Secretary of the National Council of Churches. It defines marriage as "a holy union of one man and one woman" and calls for "a stronger commitment to this holy union" and a reversing of the contrary course of contemporary culture.

Soon after, Edgar withdrew his signature and thus the NCC's identification with the Declaration, saying, "I support loving relationships between people. We don't condemn traditional marriages, but we also don't condemn unconventional relationships between loving, caring people." Kevin expressed disappointment at this withdrawal. A little-known fact is that, following this withdrawal, the Standing Committee of Orthodox Bishops of America expressed disappointment that the NCC had withdrawn support and subsequently expressed its own unanimous support for the Declaration.

2. "Gracefully Engaging the LGBT Conversation." In the late summer of 2015 Kevin was wrapping up his ten-month process of developing a statement on "Gracefully Engaging the

---

90 This viewpoint is found in the document "Gracefully Engaging the LGBT Conversation," a document of the Wesleyan Holiness Connection authored largely by Kevin Mannoia.

LGBT Conversation." He hoped it would be a helpful tool representing the Wesleyan Holiness Connection that he had founded to serve its various constituencies. His initial draft had been sent to numerous people for comment and had been presented at the Southern California Holiness Pastors' Day, at *One Table* (LGBTQ group at Fuller seminary), and at various regional and national WHC gatherings—university presidents, athletic directors, and academic and student life officers.

Kevin says, "I feel strongly that Christians should lean forward in proactive engagement rather than wait to be put on the defensive in a reactionary way." Such a public position statement was thought to be truly biblical. Being biblical for Kevin, however, is not any simple quoting of a text or two. "My hermeneutic recognizes that Scripture itself was a human undertaking. I certainly believe it to be infallible and authoritative in what it intends to teach, but not inerrant in its full textual presentation. It was, after all, compiled in great strife and argument. I do not equate Scripture with God."[91]

Even so, the Bible is believed to be the primary medium of the revelation of God in Jesus Christ. In a modest way, the resulting statement, "Gracefully Engaging. . ." (Sept. 2015), was hoped would convey the divine insight badly needed. Primarily Kevin's work after considerable collaboration (*via media*), it attempts a constructive and compassionate Christian viewpoint that seeks to be *anchored* in biblical revelation and *reaching* in love and understanding. Here is the anchored part:

> People with a gender identity that is not the same as their physicality, whether by personal choice or the result of physical or psychological factors, reflect a condition of a dis-integrated wholeness of God. Those with a physical attraction to

---

91   Found in the personal journal of Kevin Mannoia, February, 2017.

same-sex persons as an expression of their own sexuality also reflect the condition of the human family being out of sync as a result of our not reflecting the integrated wholeness of God.

And the reaching part?

As Christian leaders who walk with our own limp, we reach out with acceptance and grace, embrace with inclusive mercy, and act with motivating love, offering the hopeful call of God to wholeness and restored intimacy through Jesus Christ.

Kevin explains further. "Homosexuality is inconsistent with what I believe is God's vision for us humans. We are created in God's image, male and female. Variations on that intention need not impede fellowship in the Kingdom. The grace of God exists for all our variations as we seek fullness in spite of the human predicament. Living in Christ is living humbly under the grace that helps us in our weakness."

In 2017 Shirley Hoogstra and Shapri LoMaglio (president and counsel of the Council for Christian Colleges & Universities) asked Kevin to write a document that supports the idea of federal legislation that collaborates with the LGBTQ community in ensuring its civil rights and protecting religious freedom. Some of the more conservative elements of the church resist any such accommodation while others sense its urgent need. Kevin accepted the request and wrote a one-page document to explain why graceful engagement is acceptable spiritually and theologically. The CCCU loved and used this document. In addition, in prominent instances Kevin chose to initiate direct action in relation to public policy and state law.

3. Common Ground. Kevin was invited into the national arena of Christians and the LGBTQ community engaging for the common good. The concerns of this marginalized community were being studied by "Common Ground," an effort to reduce bias and increase participation of young athletes regardless of gender identity. The effort became sponsored by the NCAA and initiated primarily by Pat Griffin of the University of Massachusetts, leader of the NCAA's program of "Social Justice Education."

This effort is where Bob Brower, longtime president of Point Loma Nazarene University, first interacted with Kevin Mannoia, and where both first met Pat. She had built friendships with some leaders of faith-based institutions and begun with them to seek common ground on behalf of students in athletics. This was despite the large gap in belief between Christians and the LGBTQ community. Pat soon met Gary Pine, Athletic Director at Azusa Pacific University, "a white, heterosexual, conservative Christian man" says Pat, "a white, lesbian, politically very liberal-leaning atheist woman." They developed an unlikely relationship and Gary invited her to visit his California campus, speaking to various persons but not yet meeting Kevin Mannoia.

Gary would become a member of the leadership team of Common Ground and later visited with Pat on the East Coast, now with Kevin along. Pat was impressed that Kevin seemed "genuinely interested and helped me understand something of the range of beliefs and institutions of Christians." He did more, following up by enabling Pat and a few of her colleagues to spend considerable time with a group of presidents of faith-based institutions. They met first at Roberts Wesleyan University where Kevin was a Board member and then on the West Coast with Kevin personally leading the conversations.

Pat saw these as "incredible opportunities for significant exploration not only around athletics but for the whole of higher educational institutions." She now speaks of Kevin as "a major enabler of real conversation." He's willing to risk judgment from his own community while, says Pat, "leading with love. He doesn't only say the right things, he acts upon them."

4. California Legislative Initiatives. Legislation was pending in California that would eliminate state grants to students in Christian institutions of higher education in the state because they were "biased" against LGBTQ persons. President Jon Wallace of Azusa Pacific University offered to have Kevin Mannoia assist with somehow blocking this legislation. Kevin agreed to help mobilize pastors. In three regional centers in California, he gathered nearly 1,000 pastors, Protestant and Catholic, in this emergency effort. It was successful even though the sponsor, Evan Low, had all necessary approvals from both houses to send it to Governor Brown for signature into law.

Kevin reports that it was "a God Moment when Evan called me the night before. I cried and told him I would pray hard for him, knowing the firestorm he would incur from the LGBTQ community. The bill was reduced to a "disclosure" bill requiring only that schools tell the public who they are on such matters as faith-based institutions. This was no problem for these schools.

Although Kevin had been key to this victory, he insists that "my preferred MO is not being reactionary, fighting against somebody." In two other instances, he would have opportunity to be more proactive. He states his motivation. "I am honestly trying to seek ways for us to walk in grace and fellowship with those in the LGBTQ community without compromising our orthodoxy or basic understanding of God's vision. It's in that space that the tension exists. I am currently on a pursuit to talk to people and listen while at the same time representing the Christian understanding that we have inherited."[92]

Kevin was being a *via media* man trying to navigate the awkward relationships of seeming opposites. He was insisting that Christians and LGBTQ people have common ground on which they can stand together, at least mutual respect. A pluralistic

---

92   In Kevin's personal journal, August, 2016.

society that thrives depends on trust and relational respect among the groups within it, diverse or not. Seeking such ground on the issues of gender identity would be a treacherous enterprise and yet a worthy one to pursue.

Another bill emerged in the California legislature and again Kevin was asked for help. It also was authored by Evan Low and was designed to outlaw "conversion therapy" and fraudulent Christian advertising that guaranteed the success of such therapy when forced if necessary on LGBTQ persons. Kevin agreed with Low, LGBTQ state leader, that any forceful attempt to alter one's perceived gender identity is dehumanizing and thus unacceptable.

Even so, Kevin was very concerned that the language used in the new proposal was rather broad and potentially could be used to keep Christian pastors and churches from doing routine ministry for people in crisis. It also might be used to restrict pastors from working in the office or at the altar with persons struggling with homosexual inclinations, and to stop Christian bookstores from selling certain books.

Kevin actively supported Mr. Low's opposition to practices that harm people with unwanted and forceful "therapy." Still, he insisted that the church should be able to help such people through grace-filled ministries short of undesired harmful practices. He pressed for wording refinement and that this proposed law be reduced to a "resolution" that would state a general position while lacking the force of law. This was a middle-road position, clearly an improvement from the Christian point of view, while admittedly still carrying the possibility of misperceptions of all parties involved.

Kevin took the risk, believing three things. First, the evidence of the success of "reparative" therapy to alter gender orientation is questionable at best. Second, its forceful employment is "inconsistent with Christian living." Third, it is important for Christians to engage constructively in such critical social issues regardless of the associated risks of misunderstanding.

The bill did not become law. Kevin appeared with Low in a televised hearing of the Judicial Committee in the California capitol on behalf of a moral call for compassionate treatment of all people, particularly LGBTQ people being targeted for "therapy and conversion" by some religious groups. There followed joint participation in the drafting of a substitute resolution far more acceptable. Insists Kevin, "It was a clear example of honest dialogue between people with very different views of sexuality" (Mannoia and Low), men who actually had become friends.

As expected, Low was criticized by his LGBTQ caucus for seeming to back down. Likewise, the effort of Kevin at first was misreported harshly in the conservative Christian press. One said Kevin's father surely would roll over in his grave if knowing what his son had done. Kevin's sister Sharla was incensed by this low blow. She is proud of Kevin for doing the Christ-like thing. "Rather than condemning, being unkind, he reaches out a hand. He knows that what he's done is right and he's strong enough to handle the abuse that's come. He knows how to be a Christian in the post-modern world. You don't run and hide or circle the wagons to fight, but engage, listen, try to understand."

One admiring friend offered admiration for Kevin couched in what might be mild criticism. He imagined Kevin saying, "I'll be the point guy, even the fall guy if necessary to protect the Christian colleges and Wesleyan Holiness Connection as we look for a compromise." So he "stepped forward like a bull in a china shop, wouldn't stay in his lane, took the heat, did what good there was to do." The extremely conservative Christians apparently preferred to criticize from a distance. Why not allow the proposed law to be enacted and then insist that it be thrown out summarily by the Supreme Court? Combative and reactionary, not Kevin-like. He prefers positive and honest engagement up-front. This he judges the more Jesus-like approach, reason together, build mutual trust and find middle ground as possible.

Instead, the conservative Christian press initially assumed that Kevin was supporting gay rights, maybe even the gay position. Kevin's assessment? "It was a typical right-wing effort to raise money and smear anyone not actively defending the traditional biblical stance on gender identity." He goes on to report with some pride of accomplishment, "Today there is no law in California restricting the church or faith-based schools from conversion therapy."

More fair and thoughtful conservative press retractions did soon appear, reporting this essentially. There has been a positive step in Christian engagement. Kevin Mannoia and a group of California pastors he gathered gave limited support to a non-binding resolution submitted by LGBTQ Assembly member Evan Low to the California legislature. This effort replaced a bill originally introduced that would have restricted the rights of Christian pastors. While not fully endorsing Mr. Low's resolution, they did agree with the call to equitable treatment of and compassion toward all people. They at least elevated the tone of discussion among people with deep differences on human gender identity. They did stand uncompromised in their belief in biblical truth and have helped avoid a new law undermining the autonomy of Christian people seeking to minister to persons in crisis.

Kevin, a sensitive father of three young adults who were aware of these press releases, wrote to them. It was a father's effort to help them understand what he had done and why. He concluded with some bluntness: "There are good people who have eyes to see. Unfortunately, the evangelical extremists live on controversy and love to be militant. I don't think I have ever been sent to hell more times than in the last few weeks, and that by Christians. All I tried to do was protect organizations from the scathing and unspiritual stance of the conservative fundamentalists. I sought to bring God's holiness to bear in gracious engagement. I'm glad to say that I remain a friend of Evan Low and I'm honored to have represented my Christ in all of this."

Kevin's children did understand and speak proudly of what their father had done. Says one: "He just did what Jesus would have done. Is that wrong?" He stood in the "messy middle" of a tough issue and did so without fear and at considerable personal cost. Some good was done, not all but some. Some actual friendships were made with persons holding very different opinions. Says one, Pat Griffin, about Kevin: "He's different. He listens. He at least cared about me when most of his Christian colleagues just throw rocks!" He's a *via media* man, dare we say a Jesus man with love in his heart as well as convictions in his mind.

CHAPTER THIRTEEN

THE RICH WESLEYAN STREAM

Christian holiness is about transforming individuals and communities into reflections of the Spirit of Christ active in today's world.[93] Kevin Mannoia has been committed to refreshing an understanding of the current relevance of holiness, particularly expressed through the Wesleyan stream of the Christian faith which always has been his home. He has done so for denominations and institutions of higher education worldwide.[94]

The people of our Lord exist in various wisdom streams of Christian history, streams of differing polities and theologies. These each have the potential of enriching the one river of divine presence flowing through today's very dry world. There is good in all streams when fully committed to Jesus as Lord. They are not to be *judging* each other so much as *enriching* each other for the well-being of the whole. While diversity can be an obstacle to Christian unity, it should be a rich resource for enhancing the entire body of Christ.[95] Herein is where Kevin has invested much of his ministry passion.

---

93 Kenneth L. Waters, Sr., in Barry L. Callen, ed., *The Holy River of God* (2016). For an extensive exploration of Christian holiness in the contemporary setting, the Wesleyan Holiness Connection commissioned the 2023 book *Christian Holiness* by Barry Callen.

94 See especially the Kevin Mannoia books *The Holiness Manifesto* (with Don Thorsen, eds., Eerdmans, 2008) and *Expressing Life* (Emeth Press and Aldersgate Press, 2023).

95 Excerpt from the plenary address of Barry Callen to the Wesleyan Holiness Connection's annual Steering Committee meeting, October, 2023.

The Wesleyan stream of Christian faith roots in the outstanding ministries of the Wesley brothers, John and Charles, in eighteenth century-England. Their revival, vision, theology, and hymns soon had great impact in North America and elsewhere. The Christian Holiness Association has its roots in the 1860s when ministers began holding camp meetings to promote revival in the churches primarily by the doctrine and experience of Christian holiness.

The Wesleyan Theological Society was a CHA commission beginning in 1970. The WTS's overriding concern, especially through its *Wesleyan Theological Journal*, is scholarship in the Wesleyan Holiness tradition, while the CHA was stimulating increased unity and mission among the several holiness denominations.

The beginning of the twenty-first century found the world full of urgent needs. Unfortunately, the Christian community remained seriously divided. One Christian tradition, the Wesleyan-Holiness, carries the potential for increased Christian authenticity and unification, and yet it had its own internal divisions and lingered in the shadows of modernity. A "Catholic Spirit," according to John Wesley, should pervade the communities of Christians. When there is conflict and competition, the mission of the church is thereby polluted and weakened. Wesley asks, "Although a difference in opinions or modes of worship may prevent an entire external union, yet need it prevent our *union in affection*? Though we can't think alike, may we not *love alike*?"

Encouraged by such potential of holiness and unity in the contemporary church, a small group of friends determined to be catalysts for spawning fresh Christian relationships in North America and then beyond. Eventually there would arise the Wesleyan Holiness Connection founded by Kevin Mannoia. It would be a new vehicle for "following the nudges of the Holy Spirit, empowering pastors and leaders to more authentically embody their denominational heritages, and boldly lead in relevant engagement with the modern world as God's holy people."[96]

As Kevin often said to his children, don't forget that you are a *Mannoia*. Now he began saying to a whole segment of contemporary Christianity that it must not forget that they are *Wesleyan and Holiness*. That segment, he was quick to point out, includes the tradition's significant African-American and Pentecostal wings scattered across the United States and the globe. He was anxious to foster mutual awareness of each other and thus growing unity of spirit and action.

A Breakfast Beginning

The story of the Wesleyan Holiness Connection begins simply. Three friends had a breakfast conversation in November, 2002, in Pasadena, California. Drs. Don Dayton, David Bundy, and Kevin Mannoia had common concerns and we're looking for some way forward. Kevin later recalled his "eureka" moment. It was frustration that the Holiness Movement seems always relegated to the margins of history. That was history's loss and it must be changed!

The idea of launching a holiness "Study Project" emerged at the table that morning. This need was in David's mind because he knew that the Christian Holiness Association (later Partnership) was going "defunct." Such a fresh unity concept had deep roots in the childhood of Kevin although he was unaware of the CHA's current circumstance or of David's thoughts about a future path for reviving this tradition.

Kevin's family had served as Free Methodist missionaries in Brazil and there young Kevin had encountered several streams of Christianity. He had observed that each in its distinctive way seemed to enrich the larger life of Christ's whole people. Diversity

---

96   Christopher D. O'Brien, in Barry L. Callen, ed., *The Holy River of God* (2016).

had its downsides but also its richness if the whole can somehow be focused toward a unified cause, that of Christ and not the agendas of isolated groups of his followers.

For Kevin, the diverse expressions of the Christian gospel seen in Brazil eventually came to highlight for him the differing and yet potentially constructive contributions to the contemporary life and mission of the one, holy, apostolic church. This seed was nurtured in Kevin by the time the Mannoia family returned to the United States in 1970. He was in high school and it was only a little seed then, but it would grow.

He soon attended a theological conference in which one speaker expressed a negative view of the Wesleyan-Holiness tradition of Christianity. Announced the speaker, this tradition apparently lacks the ability "to renew itself" in the face of its divided expressions. It has become "merely a repository of historical information." This depressive observation irritated Kevin. After all, he had seen at work in a global context the vibrancy and relevancy of this very tradition. He decided that the message of Christian holiness was being unfairly devalued and wrongly viewed as archaic, not sophisticated enough for the needs of modern Christianity.

Things weren't good, to be sure. The Holiness Movement, so strong a Christian expression in the late nineteenth century, had become in the twentieth little more than a loosely connected group of denominations with differing emphases and minimal internal acquaintance. The holiness bodies were suffering from lack of cohesion, draining them of the ability to accomplish their classic goal of "spreading scriptural holiness across the land."

Therefore, something began to burn in Kevin's heart and was formalized by a decision made during that 2002 breakfast meeting. There would be created a multi-year academic event designed to address the failures and yet the considerable potential of the Wesleyan Holiness tradition and its needed impact on the contemporary problems of the church and modern culture.

A Study Project was set in motion by Kevin, the activist. He would provide the inspiration, leadership, and administrative ability necessary to get something new and uniting done. Don Dayton, David Bundy, Bill Kostlevy, and Don Thorsen were to be included in any of the coming gatherings, Kevin thinking of them as the "brain-trust" of holiness history that would give credibility to the proposed work. He was anxious, however, that the Study Project not be a mere academic exercise eventually completed and stuck on a library shelf.

Therefore, Kevin called denominational heads to seek funding, blessing, and the naming of their best leaders to work on a "fresh articulation of holiness in the 21st century." Positive responses came quickly. Ironically, this fresh step forward coincided with the termination of Dr. Dayton from the Azusa Pacific faculty, the very campus where initial sessions of the Project would convene. Amid the excitement of future exploration, this ending for friend and colleague Don was exceedingly painful for Kevin. Life is a mixture of joy and agony. Kevin certainly has known plenty of both.

That little 2002 breakfast gathering in Southern California was just a moment in time among friends, and yet it was destined to become far more. Paul Rader, highly respected holiness leader, reached out to Kevin and encouraged him to push forward. At first Kevin was opposed to creating another "organization" that quickly might fall prey to the typical organizational cycles and patterns. He wanted more of a spontaneous networking of individuals and denominations guided as the Holy Spirit would see fit.

A new century had begun and already Kevin had on his resume a pastorate, bishopric, the presidency of the National Association of Evangelicals, a seminary deanship, and numerous contacts and ministry activities around the world. His vision, however, was larger even than all that. He wanted to know what could be done to involve Christian church leaders of many denominations in reshaping the modern body of Christ so that it could better impact more deeply for the Master the culture of a new century.

Soon the new "Study Project" was in motion, initially consisting of about forty scholars and church leaders representing thirteen historically Wesleyan-Holiness denominations. Even a representative of the Roman Catholic Church participated—holiness, after all, is more than a modern Protestant reality and potential. The objective was to "commit to a fresh articulation of holiness in the 21st century." Yours truly came on the scene at this point as the scholar named to represent the Church of God movement (Anderson). The initiative and connecting gift of Kevin Mannoia was making it all possible.

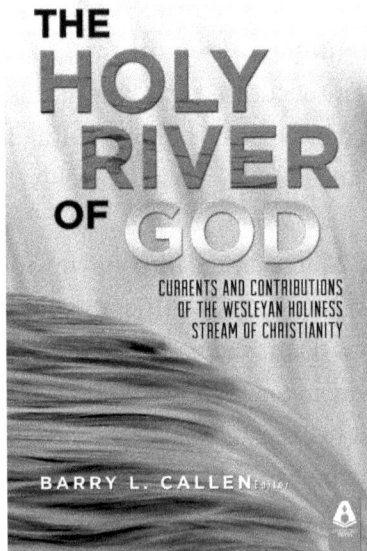

THE
HOLY
RIVER
OF GOD

CURRENTS AND CONTRIBUTIONS
OF THE WESLEYAN HOLINESS
STREAM OF CHRISTIANITY

BARRY L. CALLEN, Editor

Highlighting and enriching the stream.

The inaugural meeting of the Study Project was in May, 2004. It convened on the campus of Azusa Pacific University near Los Angeles where Kevin was a prominent religious and educational leader. The denominations represented committed three years of support to the effort. In addition, America's Christian Credit

Union, where Kevin also was a leader, made a significant financial commitment and would continue to do so in all the years ahead. Mendell L. Thompson and Fawn Imboden became great supporting friends of the emerging Wesleyan Holiness Connection, he as the ACCU President, CEO, and Treasurer, and she as Vice President and Chief Development Officer and a willing hands-on assistant for many WHC events.[97] Kevin served the ACCU as a member of its Board of Directors from 2006 to 2022, and as Board Chair from 2019 to 2022. Mendell's successor, Vicki VannBerstein, continues this great partnership.

Kevin hosted the gatherings of the Study Project, setting the agendas and coordinating connections of the effort with the supporting denominations. Soon produced in this ongoing study process were the documents "The Holiness Manifesto" (2006) and "Fresh Eyes on Holiness" (2007). The first detailed the crisis being faced and the vibrant Christian message available to address it, while the second focused on ways to live out the Manifesto in today's setting.

Soon these would be published, along with supporting essays, in the 2008 book *The Holiness Manifesto* co-edited by Kevin Mannoia and his Azusa Pacific University colleague Don Thorsen. While William Eerdmans Publishing isn't normally associated with the Wesleyan Holiness wing of the faith, it respected Kevin and the quality of the effort and agreed to publish this early summary volume.

Since the initial Study Project and the three-year commitments to it by the cooperating denominations were coming to an end, Kevin couldn't imagine an end of his vision and took further action. He convened a meeting of the denominational heads in Dallas, Texas, and reviewed with them the significant work already

---

97   See this story of the ACCU as told by Mendell Thompson and Fawn Imboden in Barry Callen, ed., *The Holy River of God* (2016).

accomplished. What now? It was agreed that ending this ecumenical effort on behalf of Christian holiness and its relation to current culture was unthinkable.

Therefore, launched as a follow-up to the Study Project was the Wesleyan Holiness Connection. The hope was that such an ongoing togetherness eventually could bring into more unity the racial divide within holiness ranks, even its split into "pentecostal" and non-pentecostal wings of the tradition, and enhance the cultural relevance and impact of the denominations. The WHC was conceived as an evolving relational network of churches and leaders.

It soon was incorporated in California, quickly attracted several para-church groups as affiliates, and spawned a series of Regional Networks and even a new publishing work, Aldersgate Press established in 2011. Kevin Mannoia was in the lead from the beginning, articulating and motivating the venture. Recognized with appreciation as the "Founder," he was named Executive Director by the Board of Directors, and soon also as Publisher when Aldersgate Press was formed. He named Dr. Barry L. Callen as the Editor to carry the load of seeking, selecting, and preparing manuscripts for publication. Thirteen were released in the next eight years, impressive works on the several dimensions of Christian holiness and its relevance to the contemporary scene.

Steering Committee of the Wesleyan Holiness Connection. Founder, Kevin Mannoia upper left; his successor, John Mark Richardson front center.

Eventually Kevin asked Dr. David Han to replace him as Publisher. Meanwhile, Kevin was busy forming Regional Networks of the WHC and the President's Network that he convened and encouraged to revive the significance of Christian holiness in the curricular and extra-curricular functions of their colleges, universities, and seminaries. Considerable expansion was in the wind.

Expansion on Multiple Fronts

Given his family's missionary background, world view, and international contacts, it was natural for Kevin Mannoia to begin moving the Wesleyan Holiness Connection into the international arena. His previous roles as superintendent and bishop of the Free Methodist Church, and then head of the National Association of Evangelicals and Azusa's seminary dean, had brought him numerous personal relationships with church leaders abroad, especially in Asia and Latin America. He was anxious to expand the WHC family worldwide.

In 2010 Kevin encouraged the convening in São Paulo and Rio, Brazil, leaders of the United Methodist, Free Methodist, Wesleyan Methodist, Nazarene, and Salvation Army churches. His speaking to these gatherings among scenes of his boyhood brought enthusiastic response and the formation of the *Conexao Wesleyana de Santidade* (WHC) in Brazil. Kevin made additional visits in 2011, inspiring in this nation the development of strong relational church bonds. These bodies began learning each other's stories and understanding better the nature and potential of a more Wesleyan Holiness tradition in this time and in their places.

Soon branches of the WHC were appearing in Kenya, the Philippines, and the United Kingdom, with Kevin always personally involved. By then the World Gospel Mission had become affiliated with the WHC in the United States. Its president, Hubert Harriman, was featured speaker at a gathering of a Midwestern regional network of the WHC meeting in Indianapolis. He and Aldersgate Press Editor Barry Callen became acquainted and soon a new book co-authored by them, *Color Me Holy*, was off the press of the WHC's publishing arm. In cooperation with World Gospel Mission and the African Gospel Church, this book then was translated into Swahili, reprinted in Nairobi, and gifted to every pastor of that African body in Kenya.

Word of the new WHC gathering of God's people around the transforming dynamic of Christian holiness was beginning to circle the globe. The intent was not to build new institutions to compete with failed existing ones. It was to bring new spiritual life and fresh uniting vision to existing bodies. While clearly it was God making all this possible, it was Kevin Mannoia who was the one primarily providing the energy, making the contacts, and spreading the word. Someone with a charismatic personality and a heart full of passion for this cause had to be up front. God had called Kevin to this and he willingly, even excitedly was stepping forward.

The WHC expansion, however, involved more than the international arena. Because of Kevin's personal commitment, he felt the need to address the problematic arena of women clergy. So many evangelical Christians were taking the view that the Bible insists that women be kept out of church leadership. Kevin's Wesleyan tradition told him that this was very wrong and needed to be challenged. That's when Carla Sunberg appeared on Kevin's personal radar. She met Kevin around 2007 through her leadership of the Wesleyan Holiness Women Clergy organization. Since the early 1990s that body had been linking the holiness denominations together after the folding of the old Christian Holiness Association.[98]

Kevin began talking to Carla about how the WHWC and his Wesleyan Holiness Connection could best be related. He

---

98 Carla, with a twinkle in her eye, enjoys reminding Kevin that the WHWC was busy at the task of linking leaders of the holiness denominations before his WHC was born. Women can, should, and have led the church. Kevin smiles back and certainly agrees.

recognized that the WHC was too male-dominated. Would it be good, he inquired, for the Board members of the WHWC to all become members of the WHC's Steering Committee, without the WHWC necessarily coming under the umbrella of the WHC? The answer was affirmative and eventually Carla herself would become chair of the WHC's Board of Directors.[99] She is anxious to recall one historic event that, while not a specific program of the WHC, came about largely because of Kevin Mannoia and his strong commitment to the legitimacy of women clergy.

Kevin had invited Carla and Kimberly Dirmann[100] to be part of a major event at the Rock Church in San Diego where he was a prominent pastoral consultant and vice-chair of its Board. He had been working with lead pastor Miles McPherson to open pathways for women in ministry. The launch event at the church was planned and turned out to be an incredible night with some 1,600 women present!

Carla speaks of it as "historic, a holy moment, Spirit-filled." Pastor Miles McPherson, a former NFL football player, framed the evening by saying, "I don't know exactly how you feel, but I remember growing up as a black child in Brooklyn in an atmosphere of prejudice. I think that's the way it is with you ladies." Immediately the place erupted in applause. Carla then taught from Scripture on the subject of women in ministry and Kimberly preached an inspired sermon. Kevin was so pleased.

On another front, the WHC faced a possible organizational expansion that finally didn't happen. The Global Wesleyan Alliance had evolved about 2010 parallel to the Wesleyan Holiness Connection. The two groups shared some members but were different in

---

99   Kevin also was a governing leader of America's Christian Credit Union, strong financial supporter of the WHC. When its longtime president retired, he was instrumental in bringing to its presidency a gifted woman, Vicki VannBerstein.

100 Kimberly was the supervisor of about 180 churches in the Foursquare denomination in Southern California, obviously an especially gifted clergy leader. Kevin soon thought of her as one of several possible persons who might replace him as WHC Executive Director when that time came.

focus. The GWA is an annual gathering of denominational leaders in the Wesleyan Holiness tradition who enjoy being together and at times find it helpful to discuss practical matters of their denominational relatedness.

It is at least rumored that some in this group were not comfortable with Kevin's actively bringing into the WHC's fold the Pentecostal wing of the Wesleyan tradition. This caused a quiet hesitancy about GWA people being "all in" with the WHC. By 2013 Kevin had become concerned that the GWA's continuing existence might be creating some organizational confusion.[101] In recent years there was active consideration of the GWA coming under the umbrella of the WHC but that didn't develop. Sensitivities and missions aren't exactly the same.

Kevin's vision and energy could not be contained inside the WHC, significant and diverse as it was becoming. "I dream of a worldwide network of apostolic leaders ushering the church into a new day of missional transformation in the world. It will be built around truth understood primarily as a person, Jesus Christ, reflecting the Kingdom in community, driven by apostolic energy to take light into darkness, and guided by relational connections, not institutional mindsets."[102] A dream of that breadth eventually would see Kevin active on fronts other than the WHC.

Time to Move On

Kevin Mannoia's intent from the beginning was for the WHC to be organic, more a spontaneous movement than a new organization. He came to realize over time that with all the expansion

---

101 From Kevin's personal journal, March, 2013: "I have been concerned over reports of the denominational leaders starting what they call the Global Wesleyan Alliance. I thought it would just go away, but it seems to be creating confusion with the WHC so I figure it's time for me to get into it and try to clear things up." He did, but with no change resulting in their separate existences and functions.

102 This is from Kevin's personal journal, July, 2004. He sought to fulfill this dream in part through the WHC, and later well beyond it.

it must be stabilized for longer impact. While not thrilled with this necessity, at least he understood that it had to happen, even with "a movement." This would include his own eventual backing away and allowing others to assume leadership beyond the founder.

The transition process began to be urged by Kevin, resulting in the 2022 emerging of new leader, Bishop John Mark Richardson of the Church of God in Christ denomination. The "founder syndrome" can be real and had to be gotten past. Kevin had realized as early as 2015 that he wanted most "to live out what I am increasingly understanding my calling to be. I am not called to institutions, but to ideology, to Kingdom identity in people, leaders, and groups. A sweet spot of my calling is to affirm, uplift, and invest in pastors a big vision."[103] He urged forward key WHC individuals like Carla Sunberg, Dan Schafer, John Richardson, and Kimberly Dirmann. The decision of the Board of Directors finally came down to John.

Kevin was thrilled with the 2019 WHC Steering Committee meeting hosted by the Salvation Army in London, England. It was time for leadership transition and the process needed was a strong look back at foundational roots and a daring look forward at new possibilities. A wonderful sense of unity and cohesion prevailed as the group toured together the historic sites of the ministries of John and Charles Wesley and William and Catherine Booth. The Wesleyan Holiness tradition runs deep and all present in London were freshly aware that it remains very much alive in these troubled times.

Kevin was aware that his public involvements in other Christian organizations and issues occasionally spawned negative press coverage, especially his LGBTQ legislative involvements in California. He was anxious to avoid such negatives being transferred

---

103   From Kevin's personal journal, January, 2015.

to the WHC. This sensitivity likely played at least a small role in hastening his desire to see new leadership emerge and he move on from this much-loved ministry.

Carla Sunberg was chair of the WHC Board at the time of Kevin's final departure from executive leadership. Member Dan Schafer was particularly helpful from his role as president of World Gospel Mission, even acting as temporary CEO of the WHC for a short period. A Salvation Army leader emerged as an outstanding CEO candidate but chose another role. The WHC administrative operations, now without the highly valuable support of Fawn Imboden, were moved temporarily to Indiana, assisted by World Gospel Mission located there. Then John Richardson said he was interested in assuming leadership. Kevin, a mentor of John over many years, was most pleased indeed.

Kevin couldn't be clearer. The WHC "is a reflection of who I am throughout my life, a representation of my DNA. I long for it to be a healthy and dynamic representation of God's holiness unified and active in the world."[104] Bishop Richardson made his admiration of Kevin equally clear. "He's an incredible voice, the premier one in the holiness world of our generation. No one parallels him in going into a room, commanding respect, and articulating the holiness message and relevance for our time." Dan Schafer adds this: "Kevin is a visionary, seeing things others don't see." Kevin says, "I am thrilled that the WHC is into its next chapter. I love John Richardson and that God has called him here."

There would be many new chapters ahead for Kevin. For instance, shortly after leaving WHC leadership Kevin would begin traveling the world assisting the work of World Gospel Mission. His numerous international contacts are giving WGM access where unknown before. Also, many WGM staff fall below

---

104   From Kevin's personal journal, October, 2019.

expectations when it comes to in-depth theological understanding, especially about Christian holiness. Kevin is leading training sessions on such topics around the WGM world. To use one of Kevin's favorite images, this WGM involvement is only the tip of the iceberg.

CHAPTER FOURTEEN

STRUGGLING TOWARD THE CENTER

"Pilgrim" is an apt word for the Christian's faith journey. It began with Abraham launching by faith into the dark unknown. Later Israel wandered in the wilderness in search of the promised land. The people tried to believe and kept moving. Paul continues this image by praying for endurance and patience as believers in Jesus walk and grow and move on in their knowledge of and faithfulness to God (Col. 1:10). Taking the lordship of Jesus Christ seriously involves a life journey of yielding to divine control and focusing on divine mission. Christian holiness is such yielding and focusing.[105]

Kevin Mannoia reported in 2023: "As my life has unfolded, my institutional and personal relationships did become numerous and worldwide. The platforms from which I operated, however, were always secondary to my principal ministry focus. Clarifying that focus didn't happen all at once or without pain." When it did get clarified, he often would begin a public address with: "I'm Kevin, servant of God, nothing more, nothing less." The center had been discovered.

Finishing his college work six months early, Kevin stayed around western New York before beginning his seminary studies in Illinois. In this free time he learned to fly. One day his instructor

---

105   The dimensions and dynamics of the Christian believer's life journey of faith are detailed in Barry Callen's *The Jagged Journey* (Cascade Books, 2018).

had him do "turns about a point," locating a barn or cow on the ground and flying a perfect circle around it. This process symbolizes a life preoccupation of this novice pilot. Life motivations and ministries have had to find their way around a carefully located center. For a long time it wouldn't be a perfect circle.

A core theme of Kevin Mannoia's life and ministry has been a deliberate double. The dual focus has been "*KNOW GOD, MAKE GOD KNOWN.*" Another form of the same focus is the name of his popular podcast series, "*ANCHORED AND REACHING.*" He's been focused on the absolute truth of the biblical revelation while also being determined to represent such truth humbly in a modern world that's focused otherwise.

The words "determined" and "humbly" appearing in the same sentence surfaces a tension of opposites that necessarily follows a difficult line. We see this line at numerous points in Kevin's journey. Sometimes it shines with the joy of success and sometimes flares with the pain of misunderstanding and rejection. By definition, it's always full of warm relationalism. The goal in integration, uniting people and structures now awkwardly and unnecessarily separated. Straddling this delicate line is at the center of Kevin's Christian calling. It's his passion, his agony and glory.

Sometimes this centering passion brings praise and sometimes pain. It's rarely ignored because Kevin often has been found standing in "the messy middle" of some troubling issue or relationship and being closely observed by both sides. This was seen in his NAE presidency and APU seminary deanship. He had insisted that seminaries must maintain high accountability to the guilds *and* high commitment to the church and its mission. Ivory tower isolation from practical church life? No! Does the practical life of the church have any real need for the academy? Yes! Finding that middle ground was a goal of the new Haggard dean when Kevin's tenure there began.

Kevin insists that churches in our modern setting must not keep defining themselves defensively by what they are *not*, not liberals or fundamentalists or Pentecostals or whatever. Instead, they must be *center-seeking*, focused on the person and gospel of Jesus Christ. Commitment must be to the transcendence of God, the centrality of Jesus Christ, the power of his Holy Spirit, and the full authority of biblical revelation. "The center is not a holy grail of the perfect combination of theological nuances."[106]

Narrowing the Focus

James Mannoia, Kevin's older brother, reported this to the students of Greenville University while serving as its president. "My training is in physics and philosophy. In physics I specialized in optics, spending a lot of time in a very dark lab thinking a lot about light. As a philosopher I specialized in metaphysics, which means I spent a lot of time wrestling in the dark with a lot of definitions, wishing I had some light!"[107]

Younger brother Kevin Mannoia did not specialize in physics or philosophy, but did focus considerably on matters of vision and light. His life and ministry had their times in the dark before his calling became relatively clear by the end of his college days. This clarity expanded by increments over the years, with things finally becoming quite clear at least by his sixties. Here are six turning points of the growth in clarity that sharpened Kevin's vision focus across a lifetime. The Christian life is a journey that requires faith and growth and often time.

1. Claiming the Call. An early focusing time was Kevin's decision during his college years to change his academic major. He was a student at Roberts Wesleyan University. Since 1972 his father had been Lead Pastor of the neighboring and historic Pearce

---

106   Kevin Mannoia, *Church 2K.*

107   V. James Mannoia, Jr., *Paradox and Virtue: Talks to My Students.*

Memorial Free Methodist Church. Kevin well remembers being in his bedroom talking with his father about the future and his thoughts about changing his major. It had been sociology and now maybe should be changed to religion and general ministerial preparation.

They discussed Kevin's new sense of call from God. The young man even had admitted wanting one day to be a bishop in the ministry of the Free Methodist Church, or maybe the president of one of that church's colleges, like Roberts Wesleyan. Was this desire wrongful human ambition? He doesn't remember his father's exact response, but at least it was cautiously affirming and the major was changed. Kevin trusted the understanding and judgment of his beloved father.

2. Which Master to Serve? Kevin increasingly discovered essentially this. The key to successful Christian discipleship is complete surrender of personal will and ambition. Integrity of discipleship would come to mean that the source of Kevin's very identity had to be that of a *servant of God*. His personal ambitions had to be fully surrendered to the will of God. This process is demanding and would take time for a strong-willed and ambitious young man. Kevin recounts the process in his book *The Integrity Factor*. He certainly took a large step during his final year of seminary three years later. It would be his expanded understanding and experience of "sanctification."

A significant step on this path came during Kevin's pastoral assignment in Dallas, Texas. Difficult circumstances brought him to the centering point that his life was to focus on a simple theme: *"Know God and Make God Known."* It was a crisis time in his early ministry. Kevin was bright, active, engaged, pastoring, working on a doctorate at the University of North Texas, Chaplain of the large Dallas Lions Club, and soon simultaneously pastoring the Kimball congregation and serving as superintendent of the twenty-three congregations of the Texas Conference of the Free Methodist Church. His sister Sharla was in his congregation and knew about some of the trouble brewing.

A group of Pastor Mannoia's own people, even one staff person, were quietly undermining his local ministry, a few calling his integrity into question with accusations of selfish manipulation. One congregation he was supervising was in financial distress and had to be forced to lose its beloved property. Kevin acted responsibly in his role as superintendent, not making friends in the process, however. "I probably moved too fast in this situation and may have been unnecessarily unkind." If "sanctified" at the time, it surely was being tested to the maximum.

Administrative decisions usually can be second-guessed. Kevin and his family once took a five-day driving tour of several Texas churches, in part "to lick my wounds" while attempting to spread a vision of forward ministry. There were problems in the conference that demanded the highest forms of diplomacy. The young superintendent moved actively, maybe too quickly, judging later that he may have intensified some of the problems by not being patient and generous enough.

In the midst of this complex of tensions, Kevin received a call from Spring Arbor College inviting him to come as a top administrator, with the intent of his assuming the presidency eventually. He once had been a small boy in that little town living on Harmony Road. It would have been a comfortable option, but maybe a running away from trouble. Eventually he turned down the offer, choosing to keep on the Texas road with its lack of harmony. He somehow would work through the issues with God's help.

Divine help finally came to Kevin in the interfaith chapel of the Houston airport. It was an important turning point in his life. "It was as if God had downloaded an insight into my brain. Put most simply, I was called to *serve* God and *minister* to people." There can be only one master. There always will be people who cannot be satisfied with leadership. Wisdom and patience with people is a must, but ultimately the service is at God's direction and not always to people's preferences.

Kevin, buoyed with this critical insight, flew on to Greenville University where he was to speak at spiritual emphasis week. A revival broke out. God was directing. His servant Kevin was learning to be humble and obey God, not pander to people.[108] This is easier to say than sometimes to do.

3. It's Not Position or Accomplishment. The year 2004 may have been the worst in Kevin's entire professional life. He was the Dean of Haggard School of Theology at Azusa Pacific University. Several personnel situations were bringing tension between him and the two top administrators of the university, to say nothing of a few of his faculty. One situation was the prime catalyst for his eventually having to leave this deanship. The painful irony was that this circumstance was bringing dissension at the very time that Kevin had launched the Holiness Study Project (later WHC) aimed at unifying the separated elements of this tradition for the sake of maximum cultural impact. How much was Kevin's very identity wrapped up in his position as seminary dean?

The prime catalyst for Kevin's departure was a prominent faculty member whom he had brought to Azusa (the detail above). This prominently published professor had the potential of exceptional value to the accreditation and reputation of the university. Unfortunately, he also had some personal habits that could be troublesome indeed, and Kevin had known this from the beginning of his coming. However, Kevin's experience and pride told him that he could handle this problem arena. In fact, the problems got beyond the dean's ability to contain and handle. Finally this faculty member was forced from the campus, leaving the dean to struggle

---

108   See more detail in chapter seven. Also see Kevin's *The Integrity Factor,* pages 67-70.

with his failed role of handling the situation. Worse than that, his own relationships with top administrators were strained and his leadership now in question.

What's the big lesson Kevin learned? "I'm so amazed that God took this awful mess, caused in part because of my own pride, and in coming years turned it into the most formative in my whole life! I learned that my vocation is *not tied to a position or accomplishment.* I now wake up every day thankful for God's amazing grace!" This learning came slowly and hard. Kevin's personal pride would pop back up occasionally to his private shame. He had to keep learning that it's not position or accomplishment that establishes one's identity before God.

When a Board member at Roberts Wesleyan University, with Deana Porterfield the president, Kevin privately called her attention to the presidential opening back at Azusa Pacific and encouraged her to consider it. To her he seemed to be suggesting that APU is bigger, more prestigious, maybe her next step up the leadership ladder. Her response wasn't positive. She heard him demeaning Roberts by subtle comparison with the bigger Azusa.

President William Crothers of Roberts Wesleyan University presents the 1997 Alumnus of the Year Award to Kevin, and Kevin with Steve Hoskins when Receiving the Wesleyan Theological Society's Pastor-Preacher-Scholar Award.

Roberts was the "mother ship" of the Free Methodist denomination and Kevin's alma mater. He would be loath to demean this school. Still, Deana saw in him "some male ego that thinks bigger is better." She observes very kindly, "We all have some rough edges to work on, and for Kevin it's what on occasion appears to be aggressive personal ambition. His heart is right, but not always his first suggestion."[109]

Here is a key life lesson that Kevin and colleagues urged on the student body of Azusa Pacific University in the winter of 2013, basing their thoughts on Ephesians 4. It's a lesson that Kevin himself increasingly has sought to learn over the decades of his own life and ministry. "Often we place value on our vocation based on the *outcome*—how well we perform, how much we give, how impactful we are. But when Paul anchors life in Christ, the value of what we do is no longer based on the outcome but *the Caller*. What you do is valuable because of the One who called you to do it."

4. Championing "Integration." A prominent Canadian theologian, Clark Pinnock, had been teaching at Trinity just before Kevin studied there as a seminarian. What happened during this theologian's Trinity tenure was a significant shift of his theological focus. It led to a much more "open" style of thinking and a new tradition of such thinkers. The dynamic of this shift was Pinnock's realization of the "profound mutuality" that exists between God and the creation, especially with humans. This dynamic sent him more toward the Wesleyan Holiness tradition of Christianity, Kevin's personal homebase.[110]

---

109 This appears in Kevin's personal journal, July, 2011: "High administrative position makes you think you are powerful, influential, important. Soon you begin to want it and strive for it. Yet it is such an empty role, here today and gone tomorrow. Once gone you are left with the empty feeling of being valueless. 'Oh God deliver me!' I pray for the quiet inner peace of Christ. That is what I long for more than anything. I ask God that He only remind me that He loves me."

110 For the full story, see my biography of Clark H. Pinnock, *Journey Toward Renewal* (2000). Also see *The Openness of God* by Pinnock and others (1994).

Clark had left Trinity just before Kevin arrived as a student, but this shifting of theological thinking was still in the air and bringing the kind of tension Kevin would encounter, especially during his coming years as president of the National Association of Evangelicals. Increasingly, Kevin himself would embrace such an "open" approach to theology. Beginning during his early ministry years in Texas, Kevin began to exhibit various dimensions of this profound mutuality.

This more open and flexible thinking about the Christian faith would lead to an increasingly "messy" even if stable life and ministry. It would be well centered in standard orthodoxy while also being active at the edges, places normally avoided by "classic" theology. These edges have been called "integration" activities. Deana Porterfield sees this reflected in the origins of Free Methodism.

B. T. Roberts was "both a solid fundamentalist and an active social reformer." He began the publication *The Earnest Christian* as early as 1860 without knowing that by that title he one day would be describing Kevin Mannoia. The publication was "devoted to the promotion of experimental and practical piety."[111] Such piety would be based in a humble holiness openly expressed in daring experimental engagement with the troubles of the world on behalf of the wonderful reforming grace of God in Jesus Christ. One day that would be Kevin Mannoia.

Deana recalls working closely with Kevin at Azusa Pacific on campus-related LGBTQ issues, seeking how best to handle the tough questions that come when anything is done other than insist on something's clear wrongness. "He has a passion for living in the *middle space* that opposes the severe polarization so troubling our world today." She and others view Kevin as a unique mixture. He seeks middle ground without giving up his core beliefs. He can be

---

111　Now available from First Fruits Press of Asbury Theological Seminary are volumes of this the publication's issues of long ago, still so relevant in many ways.

gentle and listen well. And yet, he is strong in what some personality assessments call "command." The potential for good is high indeed, as is the potential for the perception that he's much too ego-driven.

Deana has more to say. "He's the man you want on the plane if it's going down. He'll stand quickly, organize critical activities, get people to listen, and save lives with strong leadership. Some will bristle at that strength, and he works hard at managing those negative side effects of the command strength. What Kevin always needs are a few wise friends close to him who can and will speak truth to him and pull him back when his futuristic command gets a little out of whack."

Kevin is who God made him to be. So much good would never have happened without him. Even so, God also created others to keep a needed balance for Kevin. There have been times when they were not present and Kevin got too far ahead and in trouble. If one is a subordinate of his, it's hard to push back against the strength of charismatic command, especially when its intent is all good. Kevin's driving intent is to spread the good news of Jesus Christ, heal a divided church, and have a Kingdom-of-God impact on the sickness of today's society. It's hard to argue with any of that.

Kevin's bringing into being the Wesleyan Holiness Connection was a visionary command move. He saw the problem, denominations in the same theological tradition not knowing each other or working well together for the same grand cause. He created a framework in which they could come together, have fellowship, and catch a common vision. This took strength of decisive initiative and considerable patience. Kevin repeatedly has pictured a series of streams finally being enabled to flow together into "the holy river of God."[112] Wisely, he brought together the best minds and leaders available and sought a dialogical environment in which

---

112   See *The Holy River of God*, Barry Callen, ed.

he would not be the dominant voice even if he were the originating guiding light.

One sees in Kevin much the same integrationist goal when considering the curriculum of Christian higher education. His brother Jim shares many of his insights and commitments here. Jim's book *Christian Liberal Arts* enumerates the outstanding values of the "liberal arts" and how they should forcefully shape the goals of a Christian educational institution. Jim insists that Christian universities should strive to help their students go beyond the extremes of dogmatism and skepticism to achieve a balanced critical commitment.[113]

They also must aid their students in adjusting to real world problems, but without sacrificing academic quality. This will involve the integration of multiple disciplines, values accompanying informational learning, theory joining practice, a process from which both faculty and graduates will acquire the capacity to resolve the thorniest dilemmas facing society and the Christian community. Jim attempted to share this vision with faculty and students in a series of chapel addresses when he was president of Greenville University. He had done previously as academic vice president and dean of Houghton University.[114]

Kevin's educational worldview radiates this same integrative challenge. He recently has sought to popularize his brother's work with his own *Expressing Life.*[115] Over his many years at Azusa Pacific University, and now dealing with Christian schools worldwide, in part through his presidency of the ICHE, Kevin calls for an integrative view of the curriculum, and even of the meaning of Christian "salvation." Note this summary statement shared with Azusa Pacific University in 2010:

---

113   V. James Mannoia, Jr., *Christian Liberal Arts.*

114   V. James Mannoia, Jr., *Paradox and Virtue: Talks to My Students.*

115   Kevin Mannoia, *Expressing Life.*

> "Salvation" is the integration of orthodoxy, Christian action, and the development of Christian character. God seeks to transform all those who choose to be followers of Jesus in every aspect of life. Without an active expression of faith in action and in the transformation of our dispositions, orthodoxy becomes divisive and exclusive. In the absence of the historic beliefs of the Christian faith and a renewed character, action becomes rudderless and cold. Apart from a grounding in the affirmations and activities of faith, inner transformation becomes subjective and sedentary. Salvation calls us to confess truth, practice truth, and embody truth.

This is a grand vision of integration, a core component of Kevin's evolving sense of personal identity and mission as a called Christian leader.

Across 2023 and 2024 Kevin Mannoia joined his special friends Barry Callen and Don Thorsen in a publishing venture. It was conceived and styled in a very Kevin-like way, integrative and relational, center-seeking, theology in direct service of the church. We were attempting to bring to a new generation of believers not a "fixed and timeless orthodoxy" but to a collection of enduring "golden nuggets" of Christian truth. Again Kevin-like, we were gathering these nuggets of truth *in community* with a host of our friends. We weren't attempting to write and hand to others a finished "systematic" theology. Our common style was more mentoring, trying to stimulate and resource the creativity and callings of others.

We, Kevin, Barry, and Don, were suggesting only that our collection had gathered some sturdy elements to be used in the structural framework of tomorrow's Christian faith house. We had identified for the inside of that house a few essential fixtures and pieces of belief furniture that seem to serve best for lighting and powering and even decorating tomorrow's Christian theology. We trusted that the Spirit of God will help others turn this collection of building materials into a vibrant faith witness to the Person of Jesus, who is the Truth. May their diversity bring enrichment and viewpoints that are global and not narrow. May many hear them with care and find their ways home to God.

5. Approach Relationally and with Love. Wesleyan Holiness Connection leader and World Gospel Mission president Dan Schafer responded this way to the question, "What should be emphasized in a biography of Kevin Mannoia?"

> His unusual ability to network. He knows how to move things forward because of the people he knows. He's a visionary, seeing where to go and even how to get there. Some visions never get off the ground, of course, but some of them do and fly really high. Kevin has no fear in tackling hard topics, even to his own detriment if he thinks the church's well-being is in peril. He believes in engaging culture, not just throwing rocks at it, and doing so without surrendering his biblical beliefs.[116]

That is, approach relationally and with love, but do approach with courage as necessary. The late James Earl Massey, beloved in the Wesleyan world and beyond, said this:

The topic of reconciliation is strategic and timely because everywhere one looks conflicts between persons and groups are playing themselves out, with publicized, prolonged, and uncivil struggling over differences. All of them are deepened by the drama of power and its abuse. Voices of wisdom addressed to those involved in the fray are all too few. Kevin Mannoia is one of the rare persons of goodwill.[117]

---

116 One of Kevin's podcasts is titled "Generous Engagement." See the 2015 statement of the Wesleyan Holiness Connection, primarily Kevin's work, titled "Gracefully Engaging the LGBT Conversation."

117 In the *Wesleyan Theological Journal,* 2002.

In the 1990s Bill Clinton sat in the high seat of power, the presidency of the United States. Kevin's *The Integrity Factor* had been released about two weeks before White House intern Monica Lewinsky broke the news of her long sexual relationship with the president, he forty-nine, she twenty-two. Kevin wasn't one to try gaining political advantage out of a sordid situation. He, however, did send Bill a copy of his new book which is something of a journal of his own private journey of maintaining integrity when facing the perils of being an active leader. When the two men met later, Bill didn't mention the book. Regardless, Kevin makes efforts, takes initiatives, intervenes with healing oils when others hesitate to do anything or hurry to act in their own self-interest.

At least six university presidencies in North America have been suggested to Kevin by recruiters over the years. That top seat of campus power requires wisdom, diplomacy, and decisiveness. Kevin has been perceived as having all these and has counseled various persons into and through their own presidencies. Always his native ego has been flattered at receiving invitations to seats of power. His loyalty to his home denomination has inclined him to take any invitation seriously when from one of the Free Methodist schools. Even so, his general distaste for the distractions of institutional administration has prevailed.

His forays into one presidency, that of the NAE, and one academic deanship at Azusa Pacific University have left some deep scars as well as the fruit of special privileges, relationships, and lessons. They also have tended to temper any remaining ambition he may have for sitting in a seat of power. His current presidency of the International Council for Higher Education seems dynamic, international, and pioneering enough to release rather than restrict his energies and passions. Not so with the possibility that came his way in 2016 to consider being the new Executive Director of the Association of Theological Schools in North America. This invitation was flattering indeed but not long considered.

When difficult issues are being faced, Kevin finally has learned to approach gently and with love rather than reaching for the clout of any positional power. He's learned that he wishes to be no "bird in a cage," a man forced into a maze of institutional responsibilities in restrictive managerial environments. He has become more of a comforter, counselor, connector, and Christ-like encourager. He now wants the freedom to respond to "the Spirit's nudges." He privately admits some grief at the death of his presidential dream that goes clear back to his college days. "It was a dream that drove me early on. Now I truly believe I can release this to the Lord."

It's not easy being a mystic among controlling managers, a religious romantic surrounded by cogs in a highly institutionalized church and world. Kevin is a mystic and romantic, now with a deep spiritual identity that's both his personal glory and at times his private agony. Reading his journal yields three strong and persistent desires of Kevin:

1. I want to be an entrepreneurial leader not an academic manager.

2. I long to be free, to dream, to go, to lunge, to run.

3. I know God can use me if only I will stay out of the way.

Kevin now shares this privately. "My calling seems to be really clear: to invest in leaders; to bring the Kingdom near; to make connections and help people see the church as a united movement that transcends the rituals and structures of the institutions. I see clearly the distinction between the institutional church and the organic church."

Where does he see the real loyalty of all Christians belonging? "Are we principally loyal to the church's structures and methods or to our citizenship in heaven? We are to be Kingdom-centered people, appreciating our nations and cultures, of course, but not deferring primarily to them as our life or faith references."[118] Kevin has struggled over a lifetime to find the center around which his own identity and calling should fix themselves securely.

---

118   In Kevin's private journal, August, 2015.

CHAPTER FIFTEEN

THE JOURNEY CONTINUES

The life and ministry journey of Kevin Mannoia is hardly over. He's always looking ahead to discover what most needs to be created, or at least fixed, and who needs connected to whom and for what grand cause. Sometimes he acts like his Grandpa Gilroy, just sitting on the porch, gazing at the sky and thinking.

Kevin loves science fiction, including *Star Trek, Star Wars, Star Gate*, etc. He may be the only Free Methodist bishop to have had a "ready room" connected to his office and spaceships on the shelves. He loves the classic order, "ENGAGE!" "What's next?" "Let's go and do it!" Maybe God's call to realize the divine Kingdom on earth should obey the directive of Captain James T. Kirk, "To boldly go where no man has gone before!"

"When people ask me about my future plans, I tell them I have none other than what God makes clear to me. I wait, listen, and then act."[119] Is Kevin moving on to something new? He says no, "I'm taking the next natural step. I want to get out of me everything that God has put in, whether by books, podcasts, a new alliance in Latin America for faith and learning, or whatever." He's motivated by *vocation* rather than *deployment*. "God's truth is a whole. Holiness is its many expressions. All of it is what I have been and will be about."

God is amazing, mysterious, and unending. There are deep quadrants of outer space not yet explored. Real spaceships haven't

---

119   In Kevin's personal journal, November, 2022.

been owned by Kevin, but cars certainly have. Cars matter to him. He sometimes would drive up in a crazy old car that he wanted to tinker with, or in one case do a total rebuild to like-new condition. That Cougar became something special indeed for the family, with the Mannoia kids and now grandkids loving to get special rides or then drive it themselves. Kevin can be counted as one of the kids.

It's not that the cars have to be expensive. Careful steward-ship does matter to Kevin as a result of Free Methodist tradition of "frugality." There is to be a simplicity to life that allows one to represent the humble Jesus who gladly served the poor. When traveling to Brazil, Kevin has several really nice places he stays, and yet he can stay in the most sparse of circumstances where others would fear to go. He grew up in Brazil as a boy and has an understanding of and love for the poor of that land. Jesus told his disciples to go, not take all that much with them, and roll with the punches as they come (Matt. 10).

If Kevin can find a good deal to get what's needed in the cheap-est way possible, or there's a way to get someone else to cover the cost of his travel, he'll find it and do it. He and his wife Kathy have come to have many nice things in life, but never have these been the goal of life. The couple have known how to live on relatively little. Kathy has known how to make quite nice the simplest of things.

Kathy and Kevin now have lovely homes, one in the nearby mountains of California. They also are generous people and tend to maximize the impact for good of everything they have or do. They are less settlers and more journey people. If Kevin is the family pilot, Kathy is the fully-qualified co-pilot. While so much of life's ground has been covered, the journey and ministry continue.

Outside Church Structures

Kevin Mannoia does his best work outside the heavy burdens of complex and rigid organizational structures. He insisted from its beginning that the Wesleyan Holiness Connection be a spontaneous networking of denominational leaders and church scholars and not just another Christian organization. He had struggled with the organizational life of the National Association of Evangelicals, frustrated with its differing mission understandings, staffing intrigues, member competition, and computer software breakdowns. He has stayed away from university presidencies, in part knowing that the complex academic and business structures would burden his deep desire to function freely and creatively as the Spirit leads. He doesn't function at his best in a cage with tightly defined boundaries.

Here's what tends to make Kevin's ministry journey continue and expand. He inspires and nurtures people and organizations toward bigger and better tomorrows, sometimes in spite of themselves. "When you catch his vision and feel his energy," judges Deana Porterfield, "things just take flight." Amy Kovach is a perfect example. A faculty member at Roberts Wesleyan University, she caught his vision of an honors program in Brazil and became motivated to be the detail person who could come alongside Kevin and put feet to the vision. Kevin brought the idea, provided the contacts, and then Amy happily brought the operational mechanics.

In similar ways, there are Jon Wallace at Azusa Pacific University, Vicki VannBerstein at America's Christian Credit Union, John Mark Richardson now at the Wesleyan Holiness Connection, Deana Porterfield at Seattle Pacific University, and numerous others. They all have been mentored and motivated as leaders by Kevin, especially shaped as mature carriers of the Wesleyan Holiness tradition of Christian faith into their differing institutional settings and roles.

Get on a plane or be in a meeting with Kevin and he will introduce you to nearly every person you need to know. He just knows people and is the consummate connector. And there's more than just knowing people. Kevin really cares about the well-being of people, the institutions they serve, and above all the cause of Christ being served through them. He thrives when being within a flourishing Christian structure where he has access to top leadership and opportunity to do influential mentoring and motivating on behalf of his vision of God's present action in the world.

When in a rare case access is no longer there or not appreciated, or he becomes the top leadership himself but the structure functions as an obstacle to the vision, Kevin finds his way to the door, painful as that might be. The NAE and The Rock Church are prominent examples. That's not to imply that he is shallow in commitment wherever he is. Things went somewhat south for him at Azusa Pacific, for example, and yet he remained there for years, finding alternate avenues of productivity within the institution— or creating them if they weren't yet there.

The developing legacy of Kevin Mannoia has come to center in demonstrating and communicating what it means to live in the Wesleyan-Holiness stream of Christian faith. He sought to do this at Azusa Pacific University, was very influential in this task at Roberts Wesleyan University, and has pursued this goal for institutions around the world, especially through his current presidency of the ICHE. By 2024 he was giving serious thought to where and how his many materials could be housed and made available for years and even generations to come. There are hundreds of videos, podcasts, articles, interviews, etc.

Lifelong friend and ministerial colleague Dr. David McKenna observes this. "Without a doubt, Kevin is a far-sighted leader for Christian ministries, ranging from the Texas and Southern California Conferences, through the bishopric and NAE presidency, to his current thrust on behalf of the Christian holiness movement, primarily through the Wesleyan Holiness Connection which he birthed. History suggests that his visions may at times be too advanced, too far ahead of some organizations he has led. Still, there is no doubt about his articulate voice and personal integrity. The outcomes may be limited on occasion because of his need to read more carefully the context. If he had better adjusted his vision to some contexts, he would be universally remembered as a vibrant, articulate, and also effective Christian leader."

That's a very mild criticism from an admiring and life-long colleague and friend. Kevin hears and understands it, responding: "I tend to move rather fast as an aggressive leader and generally I will create chaos wherever I go. But it's out of chaos that God created all things. As long as we think we have things in good order, God's creativity is imprisoned. So, wherever I go things tend to change. I'm not satisfied with the status quo. I encourage disequilibrium within which the Lord can shape new things. I used to tell pastors that I look forward to the day when the church is out of control. When it's in our control the Holy Spirit has no place to work."

While bringing fluidity and change into organizations, Kevin's own theological mind also has changed over the years. "Theology is the story of God walking with us and seeking to restore the image of God in us. I have become much more relational, maybe Wesleyan, in my theology—less prescriptive and propositional and much more relational, experience-oriented, and descriptive. I don't anymore like to talk about 'systematic' theology. I have a high view of Scripture but realize the considerable level of humanity that went into constructing and canonizing the Bible's text, and now our wide variety of manners of interpreting it."

Kevin is clear about the problem of biblical interpretation. "You can be 'biblical' in your own mind and still believe just about whatever you want to believe—always calling it biblical. You can say you believe whatever the Bible says, that is, *whatever you understand the Bible to say*. You and I can use the Bible to support a wide range of things, and usually their opposites as well." He has come to a different understanding of the nature of truth than he knew when young.

Much like the big shift that happened for Clark Pinnock back at Trinity just before Kevin's seminary years there, this picture has emerged for him. "Propositional truth becomes cold, hard, judgmental, and exclusive. It becomes an objective set of precepts which becomes the measure of whether someone is "in" or "out." However, Christian truth for Kevin has become much more relational, centering in knowing and relating to a particular *person*, Jesus. The result allows some unsystematic theology, some ambiguity admittedly. More importantly, the result is increased mutuality of Christian community where vulnerability, humility, and the true nature of life in Christ become real. Unity becomes possible regardless of diversity. Mission mushrooms.

Thinking beyond the institutional involvements of Kevin's impressive ministry, most of his high goals may not be fully accomplished until after his personal lifetime. The eventual accomplishments will come more through those many gifted persons whom he has skillfully mentored. He's invested generously in numerous younger people who in turn are likely to shape tomorrow, motivated by Kevin's continuing vision. Meanwhile, this very personal reflection of Kevin is worthy of note.

> I know there are people whom I have hurt unintentionally, people who think differently and are critical of me. I wish there were a way to wipe away the resulting pain that I and they carry. *Heaven is the answer!* This causes me to think about leadership. Is it possible to lead, act, develop, or catalyze change without institutional and personal friction? Movement always creates waves of disruption. I mourn that part of my participation in the human condition.

Beyond his sorrow for causing any past hurt is his continuing dream of the future.

> I dream of a worldwide network of apostolic leaders ushering the church into a new day of missional transformation in the

world. It's built around truth as a *Person*—Jesus Christ, reflecting the Kingdom *in community*, driven by apostolic energy to take light into darkness, guided by relational connections rather than institutional mindsets. It's a revolutionary brokering of the new ecclesiology.

Here's another personal reflection of Kevin's. "I am hopeful that my whole life can be a testimony to the power of God to work through one committed to the Kingdom and the call to reflect God's holiness in relevant and transforming ways." There are many people, like Barbara Rose, who judge that Kevin indeed is just such a testimony. When she lived in Spring Arbor, Michigan, as a teenager, she cared for Kevin who lived two doors down Harmony Road. Now she smiles with pride and a little embarrassment when recalling that once she changed his diapers!

More seriously, reports Barbara, "I didn't really know Kevin well until in 2016 when I became a Board member with him at Roberts Wesleyan University and Northeastern Seminary. I have come to deeply respect Kevin. He is knowledgeable and insightful, yet humble. He cares deeply about people and justice. A global Christian, he sees the big picture and is passionate about the Wesleyan tradition and the future of Christian higher education. He's the kind of leader and role model the world really needs."

The Prayer of Jabez

Kevin Mannoia once confessed this. "I seek to live in the Kingdom of God more than anything else. It seems this desire makes me hypersensitive to everything not in the Kingdom's sweet spot, not made of Kingdom DNA. Administrative stuff feels claustrophobic; institutional imposition is heavy and burdensome. I'm daily confronted with the lure of my human longing to be recognized by position, to be known. My insecurity rises. Am I doing something that's meaningful? Will it become increasingly irrelevant? I pray that my duties will be significant as an expression of my passion to live wholly in the Kingdom and definitely not for myself."[120]

This discipleship journey of Kevin goes on. He's striving for Christian maturity is reflective of the biblical prayer of Jabez (1 Chron. 4:9-10). This believer of long ago sought the rich blessing of God on his life so that his opportunities for extending God's reign in this world could be increased. A prayer for the expansion of influence and relevance can easily become selfish, human ambition readily recognized and resisted by others. Kevin fears that he's been down that side path, at least a short way and especially early in his ministry. He's repeatedly sought forgiveness and the cleansing of God's Spirit for any such diversion. Recall his practice of addressing crowds with, "I'm Kevin, a servant of Jesus Christ, *no more, no less.*" He admits to really be talking to himself when he says this in front of a crowd. "I need to remind myself of my servant place."

The mother of Jabez had given her boy that name because "I bore him in pain." The Jabez prayer includes "keep me from evil so that I may not cause pain." Kevin has been a leader in the church and leaders sometimes cause discomfort when introducing change. The fact is that sometimes Kevin has not been all that careful, moving quickly, causing some pain maybe not needed, and receiving his share in return. Was the excessive speed primarily personal ambition? Hardly, at least never intentionally, and certainly less so in recent years.

Bruce Wilkinson's commentary on the ancient prayer of Jabez reveals how Kevin often has prayed. "The farther along in a life of supernatural serving you get, the more you'll need the final plea of Jabez's prayer." It's, "Oh, that you would keep me from evil!" Kevin once put it this way:

---

120   In Kevin's personal journal, April, 2009.

I was thinking about all my experiences in Asia, South America, across the country, in so many denominations, with so many leaders. I have written, spoken, consulted, yet to what end? How does God want to use all of that for some divine purpose? I really don't know. What's important to God is that I am humble, walk with a limp, and hold things loosely. It's a hard lesson easy to teach but difficult to live. The strong attachments to self-importance are hard to let go of at the deepest level.[121]

Kevin addressed the General Assembly of the Church of God (Anderson) in June, 2000. The session began with small groups holding hands and praying sincerely for their expanding ministry. Kevin called this sound in Reardon Auditorium a "holy murmur." God's people were humbling themselves before God in prayer. Like Jabez of old, the murmur was a wave of holy request. "Oh God, expand our vision, enlarge our circle." Kevin later commented to that Assembly that such a sacrifice of prayer is pleasing to God "when joined by obedience and flavored with spontaneous joy."

Even with such joy, certain questions have troubled Kevin at times. As he was first assuming his seminary deanship at Azusa Pacific University, hardly three years from being a bishop, he wondered this privately. "I see the Free Methodist bishops again entrenched in the old paradigm that is institutional and management focused. Same for the NAE. Why is it that the places I go to instill the new often revert to the old when I'm gone? Is it something I'm doing wrong? Is my whole outlook on leadership in the church incorrect? Why does God keep putting me in those places if they do not persevere?"[122] Apparently Christian faithfulness comes with blessing but not necessarily guarantees.

---

121 In Kevin's personal journal, July, 2005.

122 In Kevin's personal journal, August, 2001.

Death and Dreaming

In January, 2012, Kevin's sister Sharla called to tell him that their dear mother Florence had passed away. Kevin says that "immediately my thought was of her stepping into heaven." Often this question had come from his brother Jim and sister Sharla. Why had Mother had to suffer the loss of memory prior to death? There was no purpose apparent. Kevin's response was this.

"For me, the answer was somewhat selfish. Even though she was unaware of things (so we assume), her very presence helped me face and think about death and how to approach it. Now with her transition, it is a sad time yet full of underlying joy. The wall between heaven and earth is permeable. In mourning there is a true embrace of the fullness of life, including death."

It was a great privilege for Kevin to officiate at the marriages of his daughter and one son, Kristyn and Christopher, thereby bringing into the family such special people as Daniel and Victoria. Even at the rehearsals Kevin found his emotions welling up, and later found himself reflecting as he often has. Kevin was so grateful. Yes, he was uncomfortable with how empty the home now seemed, but there still was Kathy—what a blessing! And there also was this.

> This is life, the inevitable changing of the generations. May my children and grandchildren rise to become servants of God in ways that will surpass my ability and my dreams!

Kevin admits to having lived with this haunting thought. "I wonder when people will discover that I don't know what I'm doing!" There's been a certain sense of insecurity that's troubled him on occasion, confident as he has typically seemed to others. He now says, "I think I'm ready to hand things off whenever I know I'm at my limit."

Kevin's dreams often have been about the church in a new time, the church that God desires. "It's a healthy and holy church whose members experience close relationships to the Truth, the person of Jesus, not to a doctrine, and are servants of God, not slaves to people. This church will welcome diversity of both worship styles and personal backgrounds as demonstrations of God's rich unity." What question will dominate in God's ideal church? The question will not be "Who has the biggest church?" but "Where is there real Kingdom effectiveness happening?"[123] May it be so, and soon!

As for Kevin personally, I doubt that anyone has ever accused him of lacking personality or a sense of humor. He recently teased his wife that eventually he'll be getting a dramatic tattoo. It will be an artistic continuance of his life's theme. On his left arm will be "KNOW GOD" with an upward arrow, and on his right "MAKE GOD KNOWN" with a downward arrow. I suppose he and Kathy will have to settle in a tropical climate so that his wonderful message can be on regular display. On the other hand, likely he won't follow through.

More extensive than body-art witnessing for the Lord, Kevin plans to go all the way one day. He once was granted access to a morgue where his daughter Kristyn had been assigned a cadaver for medical training purposes. He was deeply impressed by the importance of this gift of a body on behalf of the future well-being of humanity, deciding then to give his own body to a future medical student. This Christian man will serve as he can for as long as he can with whatever he has, alive or dead.

When reaching age fifty, Kevin did some life analyzing, knowing that he tends to over-analyze sometimes. "I am reminded that it's not so much the positions I hold that make any difference. Rather, it's the legacy of Christian character I will leave. I'm concluding that I'm not as special as I thought a mere seven or eight years ago. I'm an ordinary person with an ordinary life trying to serve God

---

123 This is drawn from Carole Lambert's review of Kevin's 2007 book *Church 2K: Leading Forward* published in Azusa Pacific University's *Research Reporter*.

and leave footprints for others to follow. Perhaps I have had an over-inflated sense of destiny, and that's been my greatest obstacle and the greatest cause for hurt when reality came."[124]

Here's another private reflection when Kevin had reached sixty years of age. "As I think about my college years, I realize how much they formed me. How different I am now, how naïve I was then. But it was the path to where I am now and I am so very grateful. When my life on earth is over, I will be gone and in a few years only a fading memory, and after that nothing. So, what's important now is *living intimately with Christ.*"[125] These are lines from Kevin's favorite song, *Your Grace Still Amazes Me.*

> "My faithful Father . . .
>   Your tender mercy's like a river with no end."
>
> What happens each time I come into God's presence?
>   "I stand in wonder once again."
>
> Why? Because . . .
>   "Your grace still amazes me, Your love is still a mystery."[126]

"Every day," says Kevin, "I indeed am amazed at the grace of God. I think about what God has allowed me to do and has blessed my family with." This amazement reflects the much earlier words of Frenchman Blaise Pascal:

> When I consider the short duration of my life, swallowed up
> in the eternity before and after, the little space which I fill and
> can even see, engulfed in the immensity of spaces of which I

---

124   From Kevin's personal journal, July, 2005.

125   From Kevin's personal journal, May, 2015.

126   *Your Grace Still Amazes Me,* by Phillips, Craig, and Dean.

am ignorant and which know me not, I am frightened and astonished at being here rather than there; for there is no reason why here rather than there, why now rather than then. Who has put me here? By whose order and direction have this place and time been allotted to me?[127]

Kevin's answer to these questions is a simple, "God as graciously present with us in Jesus Christ!"

Kathy once gave her husband a birthday card and wrote this on it: "I love you with all my heart!" This caused Kevin to write this in his personal journal.

I am simply slain in emotion and wonder. She does, really! God does, really! I don't understand it, but I receive it. May I also give it. Isn't that the mystery of Kingdom? Not the theological implications of vicarious atonement; not the recreation of Christ in us; not the reversal of disintegrated brokenness into integrated wholeness. BUT the simple mystery that God LOVES me, really. Why then do we trivialize and dirty such a sacred reflection of God's own loving nature with divisive, bitter, territorial, limited, intellectual, adversarial polemics? God forgive us for making such a mockery of the beauty of your mystery so freely available to us in an all-consuming participation in your pure, complete, perfect love. Help me, God, to be available for your use; to be a reflection, albeit inadequate, of your nature of holy love and life-giving wholeness that never ceases and is not contained by any stream of doctrine or boundary of limitation.[128]

As the year 2024 dawned, this appeared in Kevin's personal journal. "*Masterful Living* is the epitome of living the holy life.

---

127 As found in number 205 of Pascal's *Pensees*.
128 In Kevin's personal journal, October 8, 2023.

It's to this about which I am passionate and to which I have given my ministry life." Full of the Master, yes, but Kevin never has attempted to live such a life alone. With reference to honored friend David L. McKenna but also applying to many others, Kevin added this:

> Thank you, Lord, for others, people who think big thoughts and actually know my name. They are manifestations of your very presence in my life. You see me, you know me, you love me. When I am uncertain, these godly others are YOU to me!

We conclude this life story with words that Kevin chose to use in the front of an early book. They are a deep reflection on his own life. It's been a long journey. He's been on divine duty, faced much, grown much, struggled much, and been graced richly by the Lord God, his beloved King. Here are the words:

In a hidden valley, just over the hill,
   a young shepherd boy surrenders his will;
As he lifts his voice in praise to his King,
   only the lambs will hear and follow as he sings.

In a hidden valley a leader is born,
   he has faced the fierce and weathered the storm;
So with humble heart and love for his God,
   he becomes royalty with a staff and rod.[129]

---

129 Song by Steve Green, words by Kelly Willard, appearing inside the front cover of the 2006 edition of Kevin Mannoia's *The Integrity Factor,* a book dedicated to "Kathleen, My Partner on the Journey."

Published Works of Kevin Mannoia

Existing are scores of Kevin Mannoia's public communications in articles, lectures, sermons, podcasts, teaching outlines, elements in the books of others, etc. Appearing here are only his published books to date.

1. *Century 21 Church Planting Manual* (Light & Life Press, 1995).

2. *Church Planting: The Next Generation* (Clements, 1994, 2005).

3. *The Integrity Factor: A Journey in Leadership Formation* (Regent College Publishing, 1996, 2006); Mundo Cristao (Portuguese edition, 2009).

4. *Church 2K—Leading Forward* (Precedent Press; 2007).

5. *15 Characteristics of Effective Pastors,* with Larry Walkemeyer (Regal Books, 2007; Spanish edition, 2009; Baker Books, 2014).

6. *The Holiness Manifesto,* with Don Thorsen, eds. (Wm. Eerdmans, 2008).

7. *Masterful Living: Fresh Vocabulary for the Holy Life* (Aldersgate Press, 2011, 2015; Portuguese and Spanish editions (2012, 2021).

8. *Expressing Life: A Primer on Integrating Faith and Learning* (Emeth Press and Aldersgate Press, 2023).

9. *Golden Nuggets: Christian Wisdom for Church Life and Mission,* with Barry Callen and Don Thorsen (Emeth Press and Aldersgate Press, 2024).

Bibliography

Some of the published works referred to in the main text of this biography—other than those of Kevin Mannoia himself.

Burtchaell, James, *The Dying of the Light* (Wm. B. Eerdmans, 1998).

Callen, Barry L., *Journey Toward Renewal, Intellectual Biography of Clark H. Pinnock* (Evangel Publishing House, 2000).

_____, *Aspects of My Pilgrimage: James Earl Massey* (Anderson University Press, 2002).

_____, ed., *The Holy River of God* (Aldersgate Press, 2016).

_____, *The Living Dead* (Cascade Books, Wipf & Stock, 2022).

_____, *Christian Holiness* (Emeth Press and Aldersgate Press, 2023).

Holmes, Arthur, *The Idea of a Christian College* (Wm. B. Eerdmans Publishing, 1987).

Jones, E. Stanley, *Song of Ascents* (Abingdon Press, 1968).

McKenna, David L., *The Triumphs of His Grace* (Resource Publications, 2023).

Mannoia, Kevin W., *Century 21: Church Planting, The Next Generation* (Clements Publishing, 1994, 2005).

_____ *The Integrity Factor: A Journey in Leadership Formation* (rev. ed., Regent College Publishing, 1996, 2006, Portuguese, 2009).

_____, *Church 2K: Leading Forward* (Precedent Press, 2007).

_____, with Larry Walkemeyer, *15 Characteristics of Effective Pastors* (Regal Books, 2007, Spanish, 2009, Baker Books, 2014).

_____, with Don Thorsen, eds., *The Holiness Manifesto* (Wm. B. Eerdmans, 2008).

_____, *Masterful Living: Fresh Vocabulary for the Holy Life* (Aldersgate Press, 2011, 2015, Portuguese, 2012, Spanish, 2021).

_____, *Expressing Life* (Emeth Press and Aldersgate Press, 2023).

Mannoia, Jr., V. James, *Christian Liberal Arts: An Education that Goes Beyond* (Rowman & Littlefield, 2000).

_____, *Paradox and Virtue: Talks to My Students* (Westbow Press, 2021).

Pinnock, Clark, and Barry Callen, *The Scripture Principle* (Baker Academic, 2006; third edition, Emeth Press, 2009).

Richardson, Arleta, *Maria* (Light and Life Communications, 1998).

Peale, Norman Vincent, *The Power of Positive Thinking* (Touchstone, 2003).

Raymond, Jonathan S., *Higher Higher Education* (Aldersgate Press, 2015).

Riggle, H. M., *Pioneer Evangelism* (Gospel Trumpet Publishing Company, 1924).

Snyder, Howard A., *Populist Saints: B. T. and Ellen Roberts* (Wm. B. Eerdmans, 2006).

_____, *Concept & Commitment: A History of Spring Arbor University* (Spring Arbor University Press, 2008).

www.ingramcontent.com/pod-product-compliance
Lightning Source LLC
Chambersburg PA
CBHW071409090426